Survival Guns

Survival Guns

A guide to the selection, modification
and use of firearms and related devices for defense,
food gathering, predator and pest control, under conditions
of long term survival.

Mel Tappan

the JANUS PRESS

To Nancy, Mother and Dad – who make survival a bright prospect

Table of Contents

Acknowledgments

Although I am solely responsible for any errors or omissions, I am grateful to many others for their contributions to this volume. In particular, I am indebted to Jeff Cooper, Burt Miller and Brad Angier who graciously listed the items which they would each include in their personal survival batteries. I also wish to express my sincere thanks to Arnold "Al" Capone, master gunsmith and proprietor of King's Gun Works for his many useful comments on modifications, general gunsmithing and the hidden weaknesses in some modern gun designs. Mr. Capone and his knowledgeable staff, including his son Bill Capone and his associate Bill Ward, have also been very helpful in providing many hard-to-find items for examination and illustration. My appreciation for many courtesies goes to Mr. Jerry Knight of Kerr's Sport Shop, Beverly Hills, as well.

I cannot possibly list all of the manufacturers and suppliers of guns and accessories who have contributed sample products for testing, but I am extremely grateful to them all. Without their help, this book could not have been nearly so comprehensive.

More than anyone else, however, my wife Nancy is responsible for the existence of this book. Not only did she perform the usual, loving functions of a writer's wife, such as providing gentle daily encouragement and insulation from the hundred homely distractions which any writer worth his salt seizes upon to keep from writing, she also served efficiently as typist, photographer, messenger, proofreader, editor, critic and best friend. She has even steadfastly refused to question my sanity during the months when guns covered every horizontal surface in the house, and she has probably signed for enough firearms and ammunition to keep her on the ATFD and FBI surveillance list for the next hundred years. I cannot imagine a more perfect collaborator. I salute her with my whole heart.

Mel Tappan
Los Angeles, California

"Make preparation in advance . . . you
never have trouble if you are prepared for
it."

THEODORE ROOSEVELT

Introduction

Why, in this age of the urban, industrial, interdependent society, would anyone write a book on guns for survival use — or, perhaps more to the point, why would anyone want to read it?

For those who are interested in camping or backpacking there are already dozens of excellent books available, some of which suggest including a small, lightweight firearm in your kit in case you become lost and have to live off the land for a few days. There are even a scant handful of books which share the premise that a defensive firearm in the home is a good idea even in urban areas, since it is patently impossible for the police to be everywhere at once; and even if those books were not at hand to guide the prudent householder, it doesn't take much specialized knowledge to choose a home defense gun for city dwellings, since almost any reliable 12 guage repeating shotgun will effectively serve to discourage intruders until help arrives, without endangering the neighbors' health or property.

But this is not a book about short-term emergencies nor the guns which might be used to cope with them, although much of the information in it could prove useful under such circumstances. Even though *Survival Guns* is a relatively simple title and most people know, at least in a general way, what it means,

I intend it to convey a very specific meaning in the context of this book and perhaps that requires some comment.

The use of the word "Guns" may seem a trifle lax to strict lexicographers and artillery officers; but since I intend to discuss a broad range of shooting implements, some of which are not firearms — such as air rifles, crossbows and even slingshots — I have chosen "guns" as the most inclusive generic term available to indicate any sort of device from which a projectile is discharged.

"Survival" is a somewhat more elusive term, however. Despite its limited literal meaning of "continuing to live" and some of its more dramatic connotations which lead to visions of plane crashes in the Amazon jungle, there is, I think, a more perceptive way in which to understand it. Adrift at sea, lost in the wilderness, living in the aftermath of a disaster — all of the usual images which the word "survival" evokes have one thing in common: the attempt to stay alive in situations where outside help is, even temporarily, unavailable.

If it seems curious that a human experience so fundamental as merely staying alive without the support of others requires a term so dramatic as "survival" to describe it, consider the fact that almost 90% of the American people live in cities. Their food and clothing come from the labor of others, various forms of energy are processed and delivered to their homes by others; the shelter they live in was probably built by others, it is protected from fire by others and from intrusion — more or less successfully — by others. Because this common interdependence, which is the quoin of a complex civilization, so completely pervades urban life, we tend to lose sight of how vulnerable we are — how unable we are, through our own direct efforts, to provide the core necessities which we require to support our own lives.

Without really being aware of it, most of us have subcontracted almost all of our life support activities to other people, corporations, governmental bodies and machines. Not only does this circumstance contribute to the sense of frustration which is symptomatic of modern man, it is life-threatening should there be an interruption of these vital services. We need only project ourselves into a natural disaster, a shipwreck or a riot to realize just how dependent we have become on the uninterrupted functioning of the social order merely to stay alive.

What would *you* do if, for example, a week from next Wednesday there was no gasoline at the pumps, no food in the supermarkets, no electric power or city water, the banks were all closed and a surly mob had formed in the center of town, looting and burning out of frustration and fear? Could you and your family survive even for a few weeks where you are without additional food or water and, perhaps, with little or no police or fire protection?

Probably not; but one might well ask why any rational person living in the greatest country in the world during the waning years of the 20th century would be concerned about the risks of continuing to rely upon others for his survival. Outside the realm of speculative fantasy, what could possibly — seriously — disrupt this delicate, symbiotic social ecology which sustains us? There are a number of conspicuous possibilities.

It is becoming increasingly less fashionable and more injudicious to dismiss completely the concerns of that smugly disparaged group which used to be called the "bomb shelter crowd." In an era when the United States can fight interminable wars with the intent of not winning them, purely for reasons of political expediency, when every sovereign nation large enough to have its own map color in Rand McNally has thermonuclear potential, when the detailed plans for a working atom bomb are published in a $4.00 paperback for the use of any terrorist organization or isolated sociopath who can lay hands on some fissionable material — then, perhaps, we ought to reconsider whether the bomb worriers are the irrational psychotics which the press so consistently assures us they are.

Legitimate as their concerns may be, those who are seriously concerned about the likelihood of thermonuclear war are by no means the largest or most zealous segment of our society who recognize the need to prepare for self-sufficiency. A far larger and more politically heterogeneous group is comprised of modern homesteaders — growing thousands of people of all ages who feel that intense urbanization has taken away more from the quality of life than it has given in return. These people are leaving school, quitting high-pressure — often meaningless — jobs or taking early retirement in order to secure a secluded piece of land and enjoy the peaceful satisfaction of living directly from their own efforts. Their point of view might be summarized in a statement by the late Arnold Toynbee: "What mankind needs is a restoration of the quality of life that the industrialized countries have forfeited." While it is true that a great many of these people are completely alienated by "the system" and are often denounced as "drop-outs" who can't cope with reality, I submit that the kind of hard, natural style of life which they have chosen as an alternative is the very matrix which produced the men who made this country great. Perhaps living where you please, *as* you please, joined closely with the natural order of things has more to do with reality than our urban preoccupation with school bonds, busing, freeway construction, smog control and efficient garbage disposal. My only significant point of disagreement with these modern-day homesteaders is that their vision and, consequently, their plans often do not go far enough. Simply moving out of the cities, simplifying one's needs and beginning to produce one's own "necessaries," desirable as that can be, may not be sufficient to ensure safety from widespread social disorder, if the "system" collapses. Isolated farms make prime targets for looters fleeing from strife-ridden cities.

Yet another group ardently concerned with preparing to live self-sufficiently includes those who believe that we are on the verge of a major economic crisis in this country. If the hundreds of thousands of Americans who entertain this point of view are not now the largest single classification of self-sufficiency adherents, they soon will be, since the probability of a total economic collapse is daily becoming less hypothetical and more apparent. In fact, if we continue to finance the growth of government through inflation — by deficit spending and the creation of fiat money — such a collapse is certain. The only questions which require speculation concern timing, degree of severity and social consequences.

The possibility of New York City's impending bankruptcy is

in the headlines as I write this chapter and it takes little imagination to project what would happen in such a city if there were suddenly no money to pay firemen, police, power and water employees. If you believe that New York is the only major U.S. city which may face insolvency during the coming months or if you believe that the Federal Government itself is not subject to the same kind of economic problems for essentially the same reasons, you are misinformed.

Since I do not intend this book to become a forum for lecturing on economics, I suggest that if you are unmoved by the conclusions I have just stated, or if you find them shocking, outrageous or interesting, you would be well rewarded by reading Harry Browne's two books, *How You Can Profit from the Coming Devaluation* and *You Can Profit from a Monetary Crisis*. Even more succinct and dramatic are the first 66 pages of Alvin Toffler's new book, *The Eco-Spasm Report*. Although his proposed solutions seem more horrible than the problem, Toffler's analysis of our current economic plight and its probable consequences is brilliant; and his scenario on the Eco-Spasm should cause anyone with a vestige of sense to formulate immediate plans for the survival of himself and those he cares for. It should suffice, for our purposes here, to recognize that if our money becomes worthless, there will be no continuation of those vital products and services upon which we rely to stay alive; specifically, no food will come into the cities if there is no means of paying for it, and "social disorder" is a mild way of describing the holocaust that is almost certain to follow the threat of mass starvation.

While we are on the subject of possible food shortages, it is worth noting that an increasing number of very credible scientists are predicting world famines, based on factors having nothing to do with economic crises. The July, 1975 issue of *National Geographic* contains two chilling feature articles that provide an excellent summary of the evidence. Paul Ehrlich, the eminent Stanford biologist, is quoted on page 29 as saying, "The race between population growth and food production has already been lost. . . . Before 1985 the world will undergo vast famines — hundreds of millions of people are going to starve to death

. . . unless plague, thermonuclear war, or some other agent kills them first."

Even some of those who dismiss all of the previous concerns that I have listed are beginning to take seriously a phenomenon which is relatively new in this country, although it has toppled numerous governments abroad: terrorism. The July 21 issue of *U.S. News and World Report* contains a worthwhile article entitled, "Threat for Bicentennial Year — Terrorists Getting Ready." It points out the affinity of these hard-core radical groups for dates with historical significance — such as 1776-1976 — and outlines some of the preparations which the Weather Underground, the S.L.A. and other violence prone organizations are making in honor of the 200th birthday of this great nation: weapons stealing, practice bombings, practice kidnappings and other forms of extortion.

If you believe that these people are "just a bunch of misguided kids" playing at being revolutionaries, I suggest that you read the manifesto of the Weather Underground, *Prairie Fire*, and some of the "guides" to terrorism such as *The Anarchist Cookbook*. These egotistical little murderers intend to destroy our country by means of outrageous, wanton acts of widespread violence, and they mean to do it in the 1970's. There have been suggestions that they may attempt to hold entire cities as hostage under the threat of nuclear explosions, and there is little doubt that they possess the technology to make those threats plausible.

Whether the terrorists succeed in their nefarious plans or not it seems prudent to be prepared — as individuals — for their attempts.

By now, I expect that a number of readers who were not already familiar with some of the more ominous viewpoints which I have chronicled are prepared to conclude that I am unpatriotic, an unrealistic sensationalist or a harbinger of doom. There is not enough space in this book to persuade the pervicacious to a revised opinion, if that were my intent, but even those who would acknowledge the possibility that one or more of these potential catastrophes might befall us could raise at least two legitimate questions:

Q. *Can't we do something to prevent these calamities from happening, instead of merely preparing ourselves to live through them?*

A. *Frankly, I doubt that there is a workable answer that could be understood and agreed upon by enough people to be implemented. To cite but one example, I have been professionally involved in economics for 20 years, but neither I nor a roomful of economists could put forth a working plan to correct enough of what is wrong with our economy, at this point, much less cause it to be adopted, assuming that we could all agree in a general way about what needs fixing – and even that is a remote possibility.*

Q. *Isn't it cowardly, or a "cop-out" not to try to make the system work, even if you don't know what to do? Making preparations for a major disaster seems unpatriotic.*

A. *It depends on what you mean by "trying to make the system work." I think it is foolish to expend all of your energy trying to bail out an obviously sinking ship before you have taken the precaution of putting on your life-jacket – regardless of how much you love the ship. If you want to try to reform the government and make it responsive to the will of the people, I sincerely hope that you succeed, but I also hope that you will first be prudent enough to make some preparations for your personal safety, in case you don't succeed. Then you can work for whatever cause you believe in with full energy and no apprehensions.*

I have written at length about the attitudes of various groups of people who are concerned with making survival preparations, because a great many individuals who have such private concerns themselves are afraid to voice them; and, consequently, they feel alone and apprehensive — perhaps they even think that they may be a little crazy for entertaining such apparently unpopular thoughts. I would like to reassure such people that they are not alone in their anxieties. Subscriptions to the *Mother Earth News* and the *Personal Survival Letter* will quickly confirm that their condition is not uncommon.

People who take reasonable precautions to protect themselves against potential dangers instead of merely hoping that, ultimately, the government will not allow anything terrible to happen are not necessarily mental cases, regardless of how many "group-think" experts dismiss their concerns and offer Greek and Latin names for what ails them. I might add in passing that the overwhelming majority of my personal survival consultation clients are psychiatrists, psychologists and physicians.

If you are still reading at this point, I shall assume that you are more or less seriously entertaining one or more of the concerns I have outlined, even though nothing more may be involved than the kind of logic which causes us to buy fire insurance despite the fact that we don't really expect our homes to burn. The awareness of contingent danger should be enough to make earnest survival preparations worthwhile.

Let us assume that, for whatever reason, you have decided to begin making reasonable and prudent arrangements so that if you choose to, or if circumstances make it necessary, you can live self-sufficiently, relying completely for your survival upon yourself, whatever inner strength you are in touch with, your natural environment and your skills. Your first consideration will probably be finding a safe place — a personal haven.

Obviously, the location you choose should afford an environment which is not hostile to life; the climate should provide a reasonably long growing season and not be excessively demanding on you physically. Look for an area with sparse population and determine that you will be far enough away from major metropolitan centers so that you will be less likely to be intruded upon if civil disorders should occur. Conspicuous farms in well-known food producing areas should be avoided since they would be target areas for looters during a crisis, but make certain that your safe place has abundant water, plant and animal food, fuel and raw materials for constructing shelter.

Depending upon how seriously you are concerned and how safe you want to be, you may want to build and stock hidden storage facilities for food and supplies, and, possibly, a dwelling, as soon as you can after you acquire the property. At the least, you should consider buying a mobile shelter which you can set up at your retreat on short notice. Some are even planning to forego a fixed retreat site in favor of keeping a van, camper, mobile home or boat stocked and ready at all times.

Once you have determined your retreat plan, selecting tools should be your next consideration. If you do not acquire them in advance, you will have to make them from whatever is at hand, since there are many things which you cannot do without them, and the skill and energy required to fabricate everything you might need would be enormous. You cannot, for example, make fire with your bare hands. If you have the knowledge, you can find rocks in most areas which can be struck together to make sparks, or you can fashion a fire drill, but it is much easier if you have matches, a butane lighter or a burning glass. Although neither is a perfect replacement for the other, the right tools compensate to some degree for lack of skill, and skill may partially substitute for the lack of tools; and while it is obviously better to have plenty of both, tools can be acquired more quickly, in greater abundance and with less effort than skill. Further, having the right tools often helps you to develop certain skills better than improvising does. If you want to become a marksman, for example, it is easier to learn with a finely tuned target pistol than a zip-gun.

Two characteristics distinguish humankind from the rest of the animals: self-awareness and the ability to accumulate tools in anticipation of circumstances which have not yet occurred. The former is at the core of all that is worthwhile in human experience, and the latter allows us to stay alive long enough to seek some meaning from the condition in which we find ourselves. Even though some other creatures, such as the apes, are toolmakers and users to a degree, they only respond to immediate problems. When bananas are hung out of their grasp, they can fit two sticks together in order to reach them, but only man acquires tools in preparation for solving problems which are not yet in evidence, but which are conceived of only as future possibilities.

Recognizing the importance of proper tools in survival planning and being deeply concerned about the ripening probability of a total socio-economic collapse, I began, more than a year ago, to write a book called *Tools for Survival and Self-Sufficient Living*. As my research progressed, I became aware that, of all the tools necessary for self-sufficiency, guns are the most important and least understood in that context by the majority of those who are making serious survival preparations. This conclusion is also supported by my experience as a survival consultant. Fully 90% of the people who come to me for professional help with their planning require extensive counseling in the area of firearms and related devices. And not all of these people are novices. Several are law enforcement officers and many — perhaps a majority of them — use guns for recreation, a few own guns for home defense, and some are even lifelong firearms enthusiasts. All of them realize, however, that the considerations involved in selecting and using guns as tools for long term self-sufficiency are quite different from those which relate to target shooting, defending an urban dwelling, law enforcement operations or even casual hunting. Quite a few competitive target shooters have never even fired a shotgun, and many champion skeet shots who have their guns serviced regularly before each tournament are amazed to discover the reliability factor of their pet smokepoles away from the loving hands of their favorite gunsmiths. And I know of more than one highly ranked pistol marksman unable even to qualify for a starting position in a practical combat match. So it matters little whether you are a gun buff or a beginner; there is much specialized information to consider in selecting, modifying and using guns as practical tools for a practical — and possibly necessary — way of life.

I can think of no better way to close these opening remarks than by quoting a particle of wisdom from Theodore Roosevelt: "Make preparations in advance . . . you never have trouble if you are prepared for it."

1 Guns as Tools for Survival

I am asked one question so often that it has virtually etched a groove in my brain: "What is the best survival gun?" And always I have to answer that question with a question: "What do you want to survive and how do you expect a gun to help you?"

A gun is simply a tool and, like most other tools, the more specialized it is, the more efficiently it does its job. You wouldn't expect to saw a board with a screwdriver or to drive a screw with a saw, nor would you find it particularly easy to drive different sizes of screws with one screwdriver or to cut logs and dowels with the same saw. Similarly, you should not expect one gun, or even one example of each type of gun to do everything that these tools are capable of doing for you. Some guns do one thing well and others, another; so your choices are: 1) to own several, 2) to restrict your options or 3) to try to do a variety of things poorly.

In the light of those alternatives, I am going to recommend that you consider acquiring a number of different, highly specialized arms, perhaps quite a few more than you now think are necessary. For the most part, these recommendations will not be inexpensive, and many of them will be hard to find; but before you decide that you can't afford to do what is necessary to achieve a versatile battery, let me urge you to suspend your decision at least until you have examined my reasons for these seemingly extravagant suggestions.

First, let us try to determine what you may be up against if you choose, or are forced, to live self-sufficiently. Specific tactical problems posed by the location and design of each individual retreat can only be dealt with in consultation, of course, but, in a general way, I think we can develop some guidelines which will be useful for almost anyone who is considering self-sufficient living.

Whether you anticipate a calamity of some sort or whether you merely want to enjoy the satisfactions of a simple, rural life, you will almost certainly have to deal with the realities of seclusion. To those of us who have spent most of our lives in the hectic environment of cities braving rush hour traffic, overcrowded restaurants, and frequent rude encounters with our fellow city dwellers, the thought of moving to an isolated spot in the countryside seems an unmixed blessing. But there are problems. Depending upon how isolated your retreat is and whether mass social disorders become a reality, trips to the supermarket will fall somewhere between inconvenient and impossible. You will have to provide at least a substantial portion of your own food. Again, depending upon your location and the prevailing social conditions, you may be threatened by intruders and the nearest help may be miles away — if it is there at all.

There are other considerations of course, such as communications, energy and psychological factors, but the primary concerns involved in living apart from population centers, assuming that you have made advance provision for shelter, are securing food and insuring your personal safety. And as I write these words, mentally I see two hands go up in the back of the room: one wanting to know why guns are necessary in providing food when you can grow crops and raise domestic animals, and the other, denying that personal defense is a necessary factor in retreat living, and objecting to my implication that deadly force might be required if it were.

It is true that one can grow a great variety of plant food, and the wise will also stockpile a substantial supply of storable food, but there are problems involved with relying entirely on either or both of these plans exclusively over a long period of time. In addition to the fact that crop failures are not unknown, particularly among novice tillers of the soil, a proper human diet is difficult to achieve with plant food alone. Although not impossible, it is not easy to obtain complete and sufficient protein from plants, not to mention adequate B-12, the most common dietary deficiency among vegetarians. Proteins, in order to be assimilable at all by the human digestive system, must be balanced. Read *Diet for a Small Planet,* and you will realize just how complicated your eating pattern would have to become in order to satisfy only the protein requirement.

Then there is the matter of quantity. Animal protein not only contains complete protein, it contains it in much more concentrated form than any other food. Even if you could balance your vegetarian diet so that all of the necessary amino acids, in the proper proportions, were present in your stomach at the same time, the quantities of food you would have to consume in order to get *enough* protein would be enormous, even assuming a greatly increased appetite resulting from a vigorous outdoor life.

Essential fats are even more of a problem because they cannot be stored successfully for any appreciable period of time. Regardless of the preservation technique employed, fats become rancid in no more than six months to one year, and since you will die without them, you must have a continuing fresh source of supply. In time, perhaps, you could devise methods for extracting proper oils from vegetables and grains, but large animals (most small game is too lean) offer an immediate and, for most, a satisfactory solution to the problem.

In addition to hunting large and small game for the pot, there is another important use for firearms in food production: pest and predator control. If you are completely dependent for your survival upon the food you produce yourself, a rabbit in the garden, a fox in the hen house or a hawk diving on your lambs is not merely an annoyance, it is a life or death matter.

Discouraging predators and pests is not the only non-hunting use for a gun in the country. Livestock often — and for no apparent reason — turns mean and unpredictable. And I am not just talking about bulls; cows and even sheep frequently turn feral and kill human beings. Also, packs of starving, feral dogs are not an uncommon sight to farmers in most areas and their attacks can be particularly vicious. Snakes can be killed with sticks or rocks, of course, if such weapons happen to be handy; or, if you see the snake soon enough, you can avoid it, but if you spend much time in snake country, a gun is comforting. Few successful working farms are without guns.

So far as raising domestic animals instead of hunting is concerned, there are several factors to be considered. The amount of work necessary is probably less with hunting, but the degree of certainty attendant to raising your own animals probably offsets that consideration. You will have to provide food for domestic animals, of course, and that might pose a problem under some conditions. Most important, however, regardless of the advisability of doing it now, keeping livestock could pose a threat to your security in the event of social disorder. Farm animals make noise, and a cock crowing may sound like the dinner gong to hungry looters in the next valley. Raising domestic animals now, hunting during a crisis, and trapping to acquire breeding stock later on is one possible solution.

Whether the reason that you are considering retreat living is concern about a thermonuclear holocaust, an economic collapse, overpopulation and famine, terrorism by radicals or simply living a more satisfying life away from the cities, you should give priority to arranging your personal security. Even now, in both small towns and metropolitan areas, the police cannot protect you at the instant when you need protection. As Los Angeles Police Chief Edward M. Davis put it in his strong speech before the NRA Convention earlier this year, "I can tell you that today's law enforcement cannot protect you. When you call, do the police immediately appear . . . if the law enforcement agencies can't insure your protection and the protection of your family from hoodlums, it becomes your responsibility." Obviously, if you are living in a remote area, and if social disorders do occur, this element assumes even more importance. Self-sufficient living, regardless of its motivation, involves protecting oneself and one's family from intruders instead of relying upon the state, or someone else to do it.

Now some readers, especially some of those who are leaving the cities only to pursue simpler, more serene lives, may feel that the portions of this book which deal with weapons for personal defense are unnecessary and even distasteful to them — and that is certainly their prerogative. I do not wish to set myself against any man's conscience. I would point out, however, that nowhere in

5

this country is there a place sufficiently remote for one to be certain that a motorcycle gang, or a similar group of simian sportsmen may not intrude and turn a sylvan paradise into hell on earth. As more and more people move to secluded areas, these places become less secluded and less secure. Not everyone who leaves the city has a peaceful intent, for the troublemakers tend to follow any significant flow of the population. The dramatically rising violent crime rate in rural areas and small towns should confirm that farmhouse defense is a factor which any rational retreat dweller must consider seriously.

Months ago, when I first outlined this chapter, I planned to soften my remarks about personal defense in order not to offend the many idealistic people who so abhor violence that they would be unwilling to consider defending themselves, even if they were convinced that the risks of not doing so were ultimate; but something happened to change my plans. A gentle family, friends of mine, who had been living for two years on a seven acre homestead, were attacked by a gang of motorcycle riders on a peaceful Sunday afternoon in the spring. The 23 year old husband had just returned home from helping to raise a neighbor's barn, and his 21 year old wife — the mother of two year old twins — had just said goodbye to the parents and children from nearby farms who had come to help celebrate the twins' birthday, when the gang appeared.

Both the young father and his wife were immediately apprehensive and they took shelter with the children inside their house, barricading the doors with furniture. They did not own a gun on moral grounds; they believed that there were better ways of solving any problem than through the use of force. We had discussed the matter many times and although I admired them for their kindness and the fierce sincerity with which they held to their principles, I disagreed with their point of view and told them so on many occasions. It is no longer possible to debate the matter with them, or to analyze how their non-violent beliefs might have been better employed on this occasion. They are dead; and so are their twin daughters. We only know what happened that day from two hunters who happened by, attracted by the screams of the victims and the insane merriment of their tormentors.

Since they were armed, the hunters had little trouble capturing two of the murderers and driving the others away. But several of them escaped and are at large now. And who can say how many more like them will surface in the face of coming hard times?

Whether or not you believe that we are approaching a catastrophic crisis, surely you can see the pervasive effects in our society of fragmentation — the inglorious tendency we have to enlarge our simple differences. As we become increasingly fragmented into special interest groups — racial minorities, women's rights advocates, organized labor, student activists, environmentalists, governmental apologists and all the rest — this passionate devotion to partisan causes diminishes our tolerance for other points of view; and friction, often leading to violence, increases. Even if no more specific disaster overtakes us first, civilization is, for this reason, on a short fuse. As unresponsive governments and unrestrained impatience for change on the part of the aggrieved minorities kindle the hostility which is potential in all of us, it is daily less tenable to rely on someone else to protect your life and property.

I have included the protection of property, as well as life, because in a survival situation the two are inextricably associated. Horse thieves were hung in the days of the Old West, not because men were more vicious then than they are now, but because leaving a man without means of transportation on the prairie was tantamount to imposing

7

a death sentence. Similarly, property loss — particularly the theft of your food and supplies — under survival conditions may place your life and that of your family in jeopardy. If it makes you squeamish to think of shooting at a band of looters who are stealing your seed corn and wheat, consider that someone who deprives you of the means of existence by force is condemning you to death. Can you think of a good reason why you should prefer your death to his?

If we can agree that defense is worth considering, both now and in an uncertain future, let us examine some of the special problems which retreat living involves, in contrast to urban home protection.

Home

Members of the household who might need to use a weapon may not be motivated to become proficient in its use, or to practice often enough to retain their skill; therefore, the simplest, not necessarily the most effective weapon is indicated.

Usually, there are no more than one, two or three intruders to deal with. Sustained rapid fire is not called for.

Time of attack is usually brief. Shots would attract neighbors or police.

Retreat

All members of a retreat group could reasonably be expected to spend the necessary time to learn how to use a number of weapons well, so the most efficient, rather than the simplest should be chosen.

You will probably encounter bands of looters. Sustained rapid fire will be a probable necessity.

You may very well be "under siege" for an extended period of time, and there will be no one to help except yourself and your immediate group.

Ranges are short, since, normally, you may only shoot after an intruder has entered your home.

You may encounter both short and long ranges and you can expect your assailants to make use of barriers and available cover.

A burglar in the home *may* not be armed or may not be armed with a firearm.

Almost certainly, your attackers will be armed — perhaps very well armed, if they have robbed a military installation (a good reason for not having your retreat near one).

An intruder in the home is not likely to be skillful in the use of firearms. Sociopaths do not usually possess the self-discipline to become marksmen, and unless crazed or in need of a drug fix, the intruder may not be sufficiently determined to stay after meeting even the threat of resistance.

Looters at your retreat are likely to be well organized and extremely determined; and, probably, at least some of them will be skillful with weapons — otherwise they would not have lasted long enough to attack you! Threats will not be enough. You must be prepared to repel an attack forcefully.

You should be concerned that any shots you fire not leave the room they are fired in, because of dangers to others in your household or neighbors, particularly if you live in an apartment house.

In a properly planned retreat, the range and penetration ability of the shots you fire should only concern your attackers.

From these comparisons, it should be apparent even to a novice that while choosing a gun for urban home defense is relatively simple, the retreat situation requires much more extensive planning in order to encompass both a greater variety of situations and the likelihood of more frequent attacks by greater forces of attackers. In essence, the home defense criteria suggest the need for only a single weapon, the primary characteristics of which are, in addition to adequate power, simplicity and safety to the user. It need have only short range capability and should have limited penetration potential. Since very little actual shooting can be expected, it does not need a large magazine capacity or the ability to be quickly reloaded. A short, double-barreled shotgun in 12 or 20 gauge with outside, rebounding hammers should satisfy all of these requirements. A little more skill on the part of the user would make a handier weapon feasible: something like a .44 Special double action revolver.

Neither of these weapons, however, would be likely to enhance the possibility of your attaining graceful old age under crisis conditions at your retreat, if you had nothing else in your battery. The circumstances outlined call for the capability of accurate, rapid and sustained fire at close, moderate and long range, utter reliability under heavy use, instant availability and one shot stopping power. That is a lot to ask of any gun, and in fact, as we begin to discuss the capabilities and limitations of various types of weapons, it will be apparent that you need several to be adequately prepared for the eventualities which might be anticipated.

Now, although we will examine the subject at greater length elsewhere in this book, it seems appropriate to make some mention here of stopping power, since that is a central issue in choosing defensive weapons. Any gun will kill if the bullet is placed properly, but in defense shooting, we are not necessarily concerned with killing. Our purpose is to cause a dangerous opponent to cease his attack *instantly*, before he can do harm, and merely inflicting a wound which may ultimately prove fatal does not suffice unless it also disables the attacker at once.

If it weren't for this consideration of instant stopping

power, the .22 long rifle hollow point would be the perfect defense cartridge. It is cheap, accurate, has little recoil to disturb the aim and it is capable of inflicting an extremely dangerous wound, producing considerable hemmorhage and a high probability of infection. In fact, however, the .22 is inadequate for defense because it lacks the ability to stop an opponent reliably with a single hit on the torso. There is a documented case on record of a 50 year old man who absorbed 18 rounds of .22 long rifle hollow points, killed the shooter and two other people, then walked more than three miles to seek medical aid. The fact that he died several days later was cold comfort to his victims.

The criteria for selecting working guns — those which you use for hunting, protection from animals, predator and pest control — are somewhat different from those relating to defense weapons, and perhaps a comparison of the two categories would be helpful.

Defense	Working
PURPOSE:	PURPOSE:
Protection against attack by armed or otherwise dangerous human beings.	Hunting, protection from large or otherwise dangerous animals; predator and pest control.
CRITERIA:	CRITERIA:
Absolute reliability with minimum maintenance.	Should be free from chronic breakage, but greater precision requires more careful use and maintenance.
Instant stopping power — high degree of shock.	Great penetration needed to kill large animals. More important than shock.

11

Capable of sustained rapid fire.

Rapid fire unnecessary. Can be built for long wear with finer tolerances.

Reasonable combat accuracy — capability of hitting human torso as follows:
pistol to 75 yds.
rifle to 500 yds.
shotgun (shot) 50 yds.
(slug) 80 yds.

High degree of accuracy necessary to place bullet in small area, often at long range, for sure kill and minimum meat destruction. Predators and pests are comparatively small and are usually shot at long range.

Weight:
Heavy enough so that recoil from sustained fire does not interfere with useful accuracy.

Weight:
Lighter and less cumbersome, since they are intended to be carried over long distances and are seldom fired more than once or twice on a given occasion.

Strength of action:
Capable of handling moderately powerful ammunition.

Strength of action:
Capable of handling highest pressure, most powerful loads for large game, and high intensity, flat shooting rounds for pests.

Versatility of ammunition use:
Need only fire one type.

Versatility of ammunition use:
Need to fire loads of different power as well as different bullet weights and shapes.

What emerges from an examination of this comparison is that we are faced with the necessity of owning two distinctly different batteries of guns, if we are to be reasonably prepared for living self-sufficiently. Now, I have no doubt that a few extremely skillful people could — and may — survive with inadequate tools. There are also people who walk away from high speed blow-outs in automobiles, incredibly high leaps from burning buildings, train wrecks and plane crashes, but it hardly seems prudent to rely on being a statistical exception, particularly when all it takes to be properly prepared is the expenditure of some outrageously inflated dollars.

You *can* kill a deer with a .22 — under perfect conditions. You can also carve a canoe from a tree with a penknife; but neither is easy nor particularly practical. If you learn nothing else from this book, remember this: don't plan to improvise. While you still can, get enough guns and get the best. Regardless of how carefully you plan your retreat, there will almost certainly be unanticipated circumstances which will force you to improvise and, perhaps, make great demands upon both your emotional and physical strength, but they can be confined to non-critical areas. If you lose your matches, you can make a fire by at least a dozen other means, given time; but if you are attacked by a band of looters or set upon by feral dogs and you are inadequately armed, it could cost you your life.

Under such circumstances, doesn't it make sense to provide yourself with the most suitable weapons you can possibly afford — now?

2 Handguns

The key to the selection of any tool is its intended use; and in the case of the pistol, that primary utility is convenience: constant and immediate availability. There would be no need for handguns if it were not for the inconvenience of carrying shotguns and rifles. Depending upon the range involved, a shotgun or a rifle can do everything a handgun can do, and it will usually do it better — everything, that is, except *be there* when you need it, instantly available to protect you from unanticipated danger or to put food on your table when you need it most and expect least to find it.

If you were anticipating an attack upon your retreat, or if you were setting out on a hunting trip, desperate for food, the handgun probably would not be your weapon of choice; because it is harder to shoot accurately than a rifle, it hasn't the spreading pattern of a shotgun, and at its best, it is less powerful than either rival can be. But, sooner or later, you will be tempted to leave your retreat without your rifle or shotgun — perhaps to bring in a load of firewood, work in the garden, forage for wild edibles, feed your livestock or drag up a freshly killed buck for butchering. At such times, your pistol becomes the most important weapon in your battery. It is a tool which should be chosen carefully, learned well and carried always; for when it is needed, it is apt to be needed emphatically.

If you agree with the idea that social disorders may be in the offing, or even if you only respond prudently to the current statistics on violent crime, the need for a combat pistol with which you can be armed at all times should be obvious. But if you haven't spent a good deal of time away from the city pavements, either on a working farm or in the true wilderness (not a supervised, overcrowded campsite), you might not be aware of how many instances there are in the field when one needs an effective weapon; and, unless you have carried an eight or nine pound rifle for a few long days while climbing, logging or packing out meat after a successful hunt, you may have no idea of how cumbersome a long gun can be as a constant companion.

Perhaps the frequency of attacks by wild game on humans is exaggerated by adventure writers — still, such attacks do occur, especially in the springtime in bear country if one should inadvertently intrude between a sow and her cub. And game has a way of appearing while you are gathering firewood or boiling the noon kettle — your rifle safely propped in the crotch of a tree, out of reach.

Elmer Keith recounts two incidents in his entertaining book, *Sixguns*, which underline the outdoorsman's need for a pistol. On one occasion, Keith was thrown by a wounded bull elk which he had approached too closely before making certain that it was dead. His rifle was lost in the snow during the fall and young Keith was able to save his life only because he was wearing a snugly holstered heavy handgun. Later, during his career as a "bronc stomper," he was thrown by an outlaw horse and dragged for a considerable distance before he could draw his .45 Colt to dispatch the horse. Only a handgun would have served in either instance.

Poisonous snakes are an ever present danger in most parts of the country, and while it is true, as I have been told — condescendingly — by my betters, that most snakes can be avoided if you are alert, and they can be driven off with sticks and rocks if you are so disposed, the facts remain that snakebites can and do kill, sticks and rocks are not always handy and you may not find it convenient to select one under every possible circumstance. I can personally attest to that latter observation, based on an experience which I had while I was a graduate student. One spring afternoon, desperately trying to make the cut in the Ph.D. program, I decided that I needed a pleasant, interruption-free place to study and I settled for a sunny meadow in the hills behind Stanford. Although I am not particularly "snake-shy," being an outdoorsman of sorts, I am aware that they exist, and on that distant occasion I took what seemed to be reasonable precautions before settling down in the newly mown grass to read. Snakes avoid heat and I was sitting in the sun away from any rocks or logs that might provide shade. Snakes are supposed to be sluggish and lay up in the heat of the day; it was mid-afternoon. Nevertheless, while I was reading, I became aware of a rustle in the grass — not a warning rattle, mind you — just a slight noise. Before I was fully conscious of what was happening, a bullet from the pocket pistol which I habitually carried in those days caught a 5 1/2 foot rattler in mid-strike about 8 inches from my right knee. When more knowledgeable woodsmen tell me about snakes and rocks and sticks, I try not to smile.

Another circumstance, which we observed in the last chapter, is that livestock frequently make unprovoked attacks on humans as do rabid animals and packs of stray dogs. Further, if you are living off the land, it is wise to be equipped to take game for meat whenever the opportunity presents itself. To this growing list, add the occasional shot at a coyote or marauding mountain lion, the now or never chance to end the tunneling career of a chuck who has decimated 30% of your garden, and you will have a pretty good idea of the practical uses for a handgun around your retreat — or anywhere in the out-of-doors, for that matter.

Assuming that you are now convinced of the fact that you will probably need one or more of these convenience tools, you face the matter of selection. For gun-buffs, this is a rather easy task; you simply buy everything which looks promising that you can afford and swap with your friends until you are satisfied that you have exactly the right combination. I have been doing just that for about 30 years now and I expect to have almost everything I really want in a while — or a bit longer. A more practical approach to the problem involves us in that bromidic controversy which every book on firearms seems at some point to embrace: the revolver vs. the autopistol.[1]

In reality, the argument is a specious one for our purposes, whichever side you take, for you can only say that one mechanical device — particularly a tool — is better than another in terms of purpose and function. Could you declare, in an absolute sense, that a hammer is better than a drill? It really depends on whether you want to drive nails or make holes, doesn't it? The question of whether you should choose a revolver or an auto involves the same logic; yet hardly a day passes that a letter doesn't arrive

[1]There are really three types of handguns: the revolver, the auto and the single-shot pistol, but because of its limited uses, we will discuss the single-shot in the chapter on special purpose weapons. Technically, the automatic pistol, as it is commonly called, or the auto, autoloader or autopistol is not automatic at all. You must press the trigger once for each shot fired in contrast to a true automatic or fully automatic weapon which continues to fire so long as the trigger is depressed. The autopistol, as I prefer to call it, is semi-automatic, self-loading or autoloading and you will find it often referred to in the firearms magazines as anything from a self-feeder to an automatic to a self-shucker or merely an auto.

18

asking me which the sender should choose — and, alas, the sender almost never tells me what use he has in mind for his about-to-be-acquired tool.

In the abstract, both autos and revolvers apparently have some serious drawbacks; however, in the context of use, each is quite satisfactory — but for a different job. In fact, some of their seeming disadvantages become virtues if only you will seek the proper use for each weapon. For example, the fact that the auto pistol[2] tends to launch its empty brass into the most inaccessible spot in the immediate vicinity may seem a flaw to the handloader and the woods buff, but in a combat situation, the fact that you don't have to take time out to dispose of your empties before reloading could save your life. The slow, relatively awkward, one-at-a-time loading arrangement of the revolver, which unsuits it for the sustained rapid fire often needed in a defensive situation, proves to be one of its major advantages as a working gun: you can load an assortment of rounds — from bird shot to light small game cartridges, to bear killers — right alongside each other in the cylinder, and your revolver will function flawlessly. This ability to employ the technique of progressive loading is one of the things which makes the revolver such a versatile tool in the field. With it, you can be ready for almost any non-combat shooting situation that might arise. A look at the respective characteristics of each type should make it clear why the autopistol is a superior choice for

[2]The typical auto pistol carries its ammunition supply in a detachable magazine. It is made ready for firing by fully retracting its movable slide and then releasing it sharply, thereby stripping off a round from the magazine and inserting it in the chamber, which is cut into the rear portion of the barrel. The auto is fired by pressing the trigger once for each shot, until the magazine is empty. When the gun fires, the force released causes the slide to retract, compressing a heavy spring, and ejecting the empty cartridge case. The spring drives the slide forward again, stripping a fresh cartridge from the magazine and inserting it in the chamber. The recoiling slide also cocks the firing mechanism and readies it for the next shot.

combat use and the revolver is a more suitable working gun.

Revolvers

Although there are some significant differences between them, I think it will be useful to consider the double action and single action revolvers together. Both can be maintained fully loaded and in a condition of readiness with all of their springs relaxed, and that is certainly a plus in a gun which is to be carried regularly and used only occasionally. Both are simple to operate, to load and fire deliberately, and it is easy to determine positively whether they are loaded. The single action, which must be cocked manually for each shot, usually has a solid frame and is loaded and unloaded one chamber at a time through a loading gate — a procedure which is very slow and somewhat awkward for anyone but an expert. If for no other reason than this, a single action revolver should never be considered for defensive use.

The double action revolver is commonly made with a swing-out cylinder, allowing simultaneous ejection of its empties; and, with a good speed-loader and much practice, it can be reloaded almost as fast — for six shots — as the auto. Although quickness can be developed, speed loading of the swing-out cylinder revolver seems to me not as reliable as inserting a fresh magazine into the auto-pistol. Even an adept speed-loader fumbles occasionally with the revolver, particularly if effective bullets such as the wadcutter and semi-wadcutter are used, because they tend to hang up on the chamber mouths when inserted quickly and in a group. Further, any revolver must be taken out of action while it is being reloaded, but the auto can fire the round in its chamber even while a fresh magazine is being inserted. One must usually take his eyes from the target while reloading the revolver, but an auto can be quickly recharged by feel alone, even in the dark.

For a working gun, however, the cylinder loaded gun has distinct advantages. An autopistol, in order to function properly, requires relatively uniform, full powered ammunition, and the farther one strays from conventional, round nose bullets, the likelier one is to have feeding problems. Within its stress design limits, however, a revolver will fire almost any load you care to drop into its chambers, and this is an important feature in a working gun. You can, for example, load a shot cartridge or two, a couple of moderate, small game loads and a pair of bear stoppers side by side and encounter no problems in functioning, since the cylinder is rotated mechanically for each shot either by cocking the hammer or pulling the trigger, instead of relying on the power of the previous shot fired to actuate its mechanism, as in the auto.

It is a well perpetuated myth that single action revolvers are more rugged than their double action counterparts. Although the Ruger will certainly withstand a great deal of hard use, most of the other single actions which copy the lockwork of the original frontiersmen's guns — designed in the 1800's — contain numerous fragile parts and brittle leaf springs which are subject to frequent breakage. Another common assumption about single actions is that they are inherently safer in the hands of a novice than any other kind of pistol. There are two errors here: 1) no pistol is safe in the hands of a person who does not fully understand it, and 2) for reasons which I don't entirely comprehend, there seem to be more accidents with single action revolvers than with any other type of firearm.

Beginning in 1973, Ruger took a step toward greater safety in these guns by designing a new action featuring a transfer bar which transmits the blow of the hammer to the firing pin. Only when the trigger is pulled, can the primer be struck, causing the gun to fire. In other makes, and in early Rugers, it has been a common and wise practice to load only five rounds in the cylinder, leaving the hammer down on the empty chamber. In the current Ruger and in all reasonably modern American made double action revolvers, it is safe to load all six chambers, since even an impact hard enough to break the hammers will not cause these guns to fire accidentally.

The chief advantage of both types of revolver is that they are made for cartridges of considerably greater power than those commonly used in autopistols[3], and when you need a gun to stop a charging grizzly, you need all of the power you can handle efficiently. Some of these rounds, however, are unnecessarily powerful for combat use, and with increased power comes greater recoil, which interferes with precisely controlled rapid fire — often a necessity in combat.

Revolvers, when compared to the best examples of autopistols, are extremely complicated mechanisms, and they are much more delicately fitted. While this often contributes to the great accuracy of which the best ones are capable, it also makes them more susceptible to breakdowns or malfunctions than properly set up autopistols. A few grains of unburned powder in the crane can make a swing-out cylinder revolver inoperable until it is cleaned, and even dust and congealed oil from carrying in the glove compartment of an automobile often freeze the cylinder. Several noted firearms authorities have opined that revolvers are superior to autopistols because the latter are dependent for reliable functioning on perfect ammunition. In the case of revolvers, particularly those of heavy caliber, recoil from the first few shots tends to cause the bullets in the remaining cartridges to move forward from their cases, through inertia; and if this movement is sufficient, it

[3]The single modern exception to this statement is the Auto Mag pistol which will be discussed in the chapter on special purpose weapons.

will tie up the gun, making it inoperable until the offending rounds are removed and replaced. Although I have no figures on the matter, my experience is that lack of sufficient crimp, which allows this condition to occur, is probably the most common flaw in commercially manufactured ammunition, as well as in beginner's handloads.

Since only a few shots at a time are usually required from the working gun, this characteristic is relatively unimportant, but it does make the revolver a decided second choice for combat use.

Perhaps the most decisive feature of revolvers in determining their proper function has to do with their ignition systems. Double action revolvers, when properly tuned and fired single action, can have superb trigger pulls: they can be made very crisp and much lighter than would be safe in an autopistol, and this is a necessity for the kind of accurate shooting which one needs in a working pistol. Hitting a rabbit at 50 yards or the vitals of a deer at 100 yards calls for great precision in a pistol as well as a high degree of skill from the shooter.

In fact, the trigger mechanism of a double action revolver only poses a problem when the gun is used for defensive purposes. Since these guns can either be trigger cocked with a single, long, relatively hard pull, requiring much skill and practice to be effective, or cocked with the thumb, allowing for much less disturbance upon firing, the shooter is faced with a choice each time he prepares to shoot. Does the situation call for precision or speed? In a working gun, when there is usually ample time to get off a shot, the choice is simple and made in advance — always fire single action. Such decisions in a combat situation, however, complicate — and may well shorten — one's life. Most really expert combat shooters who use the revolver (and there are *very* few) solve the problem in the only sensible way that allows sufficient speed. They fire at

A selection of .357 Magnums. From top to bottom, left to right: S&W Model 27, 8 3/8″, S&W Model 27, 5″, S&W Model 27, 3 1/2″, Ruger .357 Blackhawk Single Action Old Model with factory stag grips, nickel finish Colt Python, 4″, Colt Python , 6″, S&W Model 19, 4″, S&W Model 19, 2″ with round butt.

24

Solid frame, single action revolver with loading gate open.

Swing-out cylinder double action revolver.

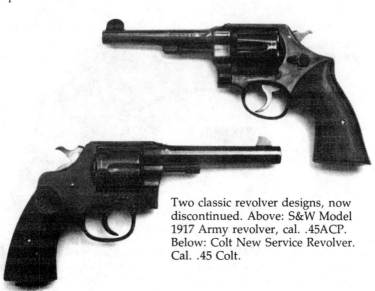

Two classic revolver designs, now discontinued. Above: S&W Model 1917 Army revolver, cal. .45ACP. Below: Colt New Service Revolver. Cal. .45 Colt.

25

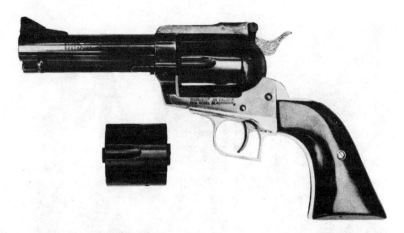

A highly modified Ruger .45 Convertible with cylinders in both .45 ACP and .45 Colt. King's Gun Works has fitted a nickel-plated steel dragoon back strap from the Super Blackhawk, a steel ejector rod housing from a Colt Frontier and an all steel Micro-Sight. The frame is color case hardened and the hammer, jeweled.

The S&W Model 25 .45ACP, shown here with a spare cylinder supplied and fitted by Miniature Machine Co., a ramped colored insert front sight by King's Gun Works and custom grips by Guy Hogue.

all ranges and under all circumstances, double action only; and some even remove the mechanism from their guns which allows thumb cocking. While this is a workable solution, it is not an easy one, since it takes about five times as long to become a marksman using double action firing techniques than it does to develop equal skill with the single action autopistol.

The single-action-only revolver has a different set of parameters. It usually has very slow lock time and an extremely heavy hammer fall, neither of which contributes much to accuracy in use, but with some careful gunsmithing and a lot of practice, good shooting can be done with it. You will either love or hate the grip on a single action. It cramps my hand, but many users rhapsodize about this feature, claiming it absorbs heavy recoil better than any other and is quicker to grab from the holster. In fact, and I have conducted many tests on this point with experts in all three types, there is no significant difference in speed among the single action revolver, the double action revolver, and the autopistol — so far as getting off the first shot is concerned — when all three are carried in suitable holsters in a safe condition.

The three chief advantages of the single action revolver are, as I view the matter: 1) it is by far the safest pistol to use while riding a horse that may react unfavorably to gunfire: if you have to grab the reins or saddle horn with both hands, an uncocked SA is not likely to discharge, 2) changing cylinders is a simple matter — you simply drop one out and drop in the other, thereby enabling you to use a wide variety of ammunition having substantially the same bore diameter: a not insignificant feature for a survival gun[4], 3) a good single action revolver sells new for much less than a quality double action.

[4]Ruger makes three "convertible" models — .22 Magnum-.22 long rifle, .357 magnum-.9mm, and .45 Colt-.45 ACP.

In determining the proper use for a revolver, then, as a part of your survival battery, these seem to be the most salient factors:

1. The revolver is simple to operate.
2. There is a wide choice of ammunition available for it, including the most powerful, suiting it well for outdoors-field use.
3. Heavy, light and shot loads can be mixed at will in its chambers.
4. It can remain loaded and ready for long periods of time with no strain on its springs.
5. It is slow to reload without lots of practice — not a significant drawback for a working gun.
6. Double action is harder to learn and takes longer to master — again, only a factor in combat.
7. The barrel lies higher above the hand than it does in the autopistol, thereby increasing the leverage of recoil: only significant in a situation which calls for fast repeat shots.
8. Revolvers are bulky because of their cylinders, but only defensive pistols usually need to be concealed.
9. Cleaning revolvers is more of a chore than cleaning autopistols because each chamber in the cylinder requires attention, and revolvers are difficult to reassemble if they have to be taken completely apart as they might after being drenched.
10. Barrel-cylinder alignment is critical and it tends, through wear, to need the attention of a competent gunsmith from time to time under heavy duty use, particularly extensive double action firing. This is a critical factor in deciding whether to choose a revolver for defense, since you may fire more ammunition in one day, if you are under siege, than you would fire from your working pistol in a lifetime.
11. Revolver cylinders may seize from unburned powder grains, dust or other foreign matter as well as when bullets jump their crimps — a simple matter to remedy in the field, possibly fatal under fire.

To me, these considerations seem conclusive: I would not consider a revolver as a combat weapon under retreat circumstances, and I would not be without one as a working gun.

Autopistols

The United States Army proved beyond reasonable doubt, during extensive tests conducted in 1907, that a properly designed, well-constructed autopistol is superior to the best revolvers for heavy duty combat use, particularly under conditions of serious neglect and almost continuous fire which such use often requires. Just any auto will not do, however. It must be reliable, easy to repair and maintain, sufficiently accurate for its intended purpose, easy to handle in rapid fire, and it must employ a cartridge which will almost certainly stop a determined opponent instantly with a single hit on the torso. Such a pistol is superior to a revolver of equivalent power for defense purposes because it is easier to learn to shoot, it is more compact, and it can be more easily controlled in aimed rapid fire.

The only handgun in current manufacture which meets all of the above requirements is the Browning designed Colt in .45 ACP. or, possibly, one of its foreign import look-alikes. Although there are four models of the Colt, they are sufficiently similar that their differences can be disregarded until we review individual pistols later in this chapter. Extensive use of millions of these guns by the U.S. military through two world wars and several limited ones, as well as civilian combat matches at the highest levels of skill, have proved the suitability and reliability of the design. The .45 auto can be completely disassembled without tools in minutes for thorough cleaning, and replacement parts can be substituted, without fitting, by relatively unskilled persons. Even replacing a worn-out barrel can be accomplished in less than 60 seconds by an experienced user. Although comforting to have, spare guns are not absolutely necessary, since a thoughtfully selected spare parts kit will keep the Colt firing for several ordinary lifetimes. It can be reloaded faster — reliably — than any other type of pistol, and it is not rendered inoperative during the process: the round in the chamber is ready to fire whether or not the magazine is in place. Furthermore, one does not need to take his eyes from the target while reloading — it can be done swiftly even in the dark or while running or taking cover.

There are two categories of problems, however, which are characteristic of autopistols: one which can be overcome by custom gunsmithing, and another, which makes it undesirable as a working gun. In the first group, we must include poor sights as issued, usually poor triggers, awkward safeties, and sensitivity to non-military style ammunition. In the second, observe that it lacks flexibility in terms of the power and type of ammunition it will use; it throws away and often damages its brass; it requires more critical reloading techniques and, with one exception (previously noted), it is not available in calibers as powerful or as easy to hit with at long range as the revolver; and when it is tuned for maximum reliability of functioning, it may be somewhat less accurate than the very best revolvers.

Fortunately, some expert custom work can provide the auto with sights as good as are available for any handgun, its trigger can be made as crisp — if not quite as light — as a revolver's, it can be made to feed semi-wadcutters reliably, and its safeties can be modified satisfactorily. We will discuss some of these modifications in detail elsewhere in this book.

The auto cannot, however, be set up to feed light loads,

heavy loads, bird shot and full wadcutters, interchange-ably; and a working gun should have that flexibility. We can lessen, but not completely eliminate the damage which the auto causes to its empty brass, and we cannot break its habit of tossing spent cases in the underbrush or a nearby mud puddle; but when you are shooting for your life, brass scrounging tends to drop several notches in priority. Finally, although the autopistol can be tuned so that it will equal or exceed the accuracy of any other hand-gun, such precision is achieved by fitting the parts so tightly that reliable functioning is endangered. If I were forced to make the choice, it seems obvious that it would be wiser to make do with a combat ready auto as a work-ing gun than to rely on a working revolver for defense, but both are needed for flexible survival planning.

Unfortunately, all autopistols do not share the qualities which make the .45 ACP Colt the clear choice as a de-fensive pistol. Aside from reliability, which many of them lack, most have features which render them unsuitable for combat, and double action is one of these. Whatever its value in a revolver, double action in an autopistol is an unintelligent solution to a non-existent problem. Despite its proven superiority in decades of actual use as well as in combat competition at the highest level, not to mention its unparalleled safety record in both circumstances, there are apparently a vast number of people who know little about defensive shooting — some police departments among them — who believe either that 1.) the single action auto is unsafe carried with a round in the chamber, the hammer cocked and the safety on (called "condition one" or "cocked and locked") or 2.) it would be safer and faster to be able to carry the auto with a round in the chamber and the hammer down (known as "condition two"), using trigger cocking to fire the first round. If you have never tried using a double action auto under practical conditions, the theory sounds fine. In practice it is unusable.

To begin with, neither I nor anyone I have ever seen or heard of, has been able to master the trigger action necessary in rapid fire. If you are shooting a double action revolver, it remains in double action mode unless you choose to thumb cock; but the auto shifts, after the first shot, to self-cocking, single action. You are, therefore, obliged to shift from a double action grip with your finger well into the trigger guard for leverage against the long, heavy, double action pull to a single action grip with only the pad of the first joint of your finger on the trigger. Arguments on matters like this are fruitless. If you don't believe my evaluation, try shooting a fast two-shot burst from a double action auto in safe condition. Better yet, try it several dozen times. If you master it, you may well be the first who has. To ice the matter, most of the double action autos are unsafe to carry in condition two unless the safety is also engaged, and without exception, these safeties are slow and awkward to release with the gun in firing position, and none of them can be satisfactorily reworked. One metropolitan law enforcement agency, headed by a notably incompetent, rabid, anti-gun administrator, hails this latter deficiency as a major virtue, stating that the slow awkward safety could save officers' lives, in the event that their guns were taken from them and turned upon their owners.

The magazine disconnector is another flaw in autopistol design which is becoming rapidly more popular among manufacturers. This feature provides you with a gun which will not fire when its magazine is removed, preventing you from covering an assailant while you are in the process of reloading — one of the basic advantages of the better autopistols. Further, if you become separated from your magazine(s), you can't even use your gun as a single loader. Under these circumstances, its only tactical value is as a short, heavy club. The theory behind including this quirk in so many autos seems to be that persons unfamiliar with the functioning of autoloading arms may forget or not know that a round may be in the chamber after the magazine has been removed, and an accident could result if such people think that by withdrawing the magazine they have rendered the weapon harmless. In essence, this kind of thinking is an attempt to alter reality so that it coincides with what the ignorant think it ought to be. That philosophy may sell pistols to the unwitting, but it does not produce a practical defense weapon. My own view is that people who don't know what they are doing are going to have accidents with any tool that is potentially dangerous, whether guns, power saws or can openers, regardless of how many safety devices are hung on them. The only effective preventer of accidents is an aware human being with sense enough to become familiar with the implements he uses.

Another common failing among autos is either a magazine release which cannot be operated easily with the gun in firing position, or else one which does not eject the magazine completely from the pistol — requiring that it be withdrawn manually by the hand which should be drawing and inserting the fresh magazine.

The one factor which most limits the selection of suitable autopistols for defense use, however, is relative power. Only the Colt and its closely similar rivals are available in a caliber suitable for serious defensive use.

Stopping Power

With the advent of smokeless powder, a trend toward higher velocities and smaller calibers began, and despite overwhelming contraindications, the trend persists and has even gained some currency among those whose practical experience in the matter is limited. Handgun power, particularly as it relates to stopping power against human beings, is the subject of much speculation, largely because direct laboratory experimentation would be somewhat strenuous on the subjects. There are two extensive bodies of evidence available, however, which, if taken together, seem conclusive.

The first derives from the U.S. military experience during the Philippine Insurrection at the turn of the century. We had just retired the venerable .45 Colt single actions when the fighting broke out, and our troops were equipped with .38 caliber double action revolvers, which offered, so the army believed, a tremendous ballistic improvement as well as a logistic advantage, since the individual soldier could carry more rounds of the lighter, less bulky .38 ammunition. Unfortunately for our men, something was wrong with the theory. The insurrectionists, and particularly the Moro tribesmen, frequently continued their attacks after absorbing six or more .38 caliber bullets, leaving behind them dead soldiers with empty revolvers in their hands. The fact that the .38's, even when well placed in the vital organs, failed to stop fatal attacks more often than they succeeded, caused the army to convene a board of inquiry in 1904, the purpose of which was to conduct an exhaustive investigation into the factors which determined stopping power.

Colonel John T. Thompson of the Army Ordnance Department and Colonel Louis A. LaGarde of the Medical Corps conducted a series of tests in depth on corpses and living tissue of flesh and bone, so extensive and so grisly that they will probably never be duplicated. Consequently, our best evidence of the actual effects of pistol bullets on human flesh under precisely controlled circumstances is likely to remain the Thompson-LaGarde inquiry. If you have a strong stomach and you wish to make your own analysis of the data, two books by General Julian Hatcher, *Pistols and Revolvers*, 1927, and *Textbook of Pistols and Revolvers*, 1935, should provide the information you will need.

Readers who possess some background in physics and little in practical ballistics may not understand why the question of handgun power is subject to so much controversy. After all, it is a simple matter to determine the kinetic energy of a projectile; it is equal to one half the product of its mass and the square of its velocity, and if you are not fond of mathematics, there are muzzle energy tables to be found in almost any textbook on firearms. Surely the projectile with the greatest energy is the most powerful. That conclusion would simplify the lives of those of us who write about guns, if it were true, but kinetic energy concerns only the flight of a projectile and it has nothing to do with impact, which is the determining factor of stopping power. Parenthetically, the Thompson-LaGarde tests demonstrated conclusively that, in practical experimentation, kinetic energy and stopping power are virtually unrelated, and that velocity — the most influential factor in the kinetic energy formula — was the least important of the five influences on stopping power which they adduced.

Of the remaining four — bullet material, bullet shape, bullet weight and bullet diameter or caliber — the latter was determined to be the single most important element. It is impossible, of course, in practice to divorce diameter completely from weight; and enough momentum must be provided to achieve adequate penetration of the target for the effect of caliber to be observed, but this much is clear from the tests: extreme variations in velocity caused less difference in stopping power than minimal variations in the diameter of the bullet. The conclusion is inescapable. If you want to select a pistol which has stopping power, it must fire a large caliber bullet, probably .40 caliber as a minimum, and .44 or .45 optimally.

In the interest of objectivity, I should tell you that the conclusion stated in the preceding paragraph is not universally accepted, it is even unpopular in some circles — particularly law enforcement — despite the fact that I, and every writer in this field whom I know, have files bulging with documented cases of police officers who are dead because their small caliber, high velocity weapons failed to stop armed felons.

I don't mean to suggest that the opponents of large caliber bullets are nefarious or even particularly stupid, but they are confused. Some of them will point to the tremendous killing power of the .30 caliber rifle as an example of the decisive effect of velocity and they are right — about rifles. When a bullet begins to exceed twice the speed of sound (2258 feet per second at 68°F.) velocity does become a decisive factor, because the phenomenon of hydrostatic shock — the driving of fluids from vital tissue — is introduced; but pistol velocities range between about 650 fps. and 1600 fps. — far below the threshold of hydrostatic shock.

Other small caliber adherents who recognize the *de facto* evidence against such cartridges for serious defensive purposes, argue that the effectiveness of large diameter projectiles can be realized in small caliber weapons by employing expanding bullets. There are at least two errors inherent in this point of view. First, human tissue is not homogeneous; it is made of soft flesh, offering little resistance to penetration, muscle, having several degrees of density, and bone. This fact creates a problem in that if a bullet is so lightly constructed that it will expand in soft tissue, it may go to pieces before it penetrates sufficiently to cause a stopping wound, if it encounters heavy muscle or bone. Conversely, if the bullet is more heavily constructed, it may penetrate the target entirely without expanding at all, and we are right back where we started — with a small caliber bullet. To further complicate matters, the expansion of bullets in *any* medium at pistol velocities is a sometime thing. One thousand feet per second seems to be the threshold of expansion and 1300 fps. is better, even for very fragile bullets, and such speeds are not easy to achieve in short, reasonably handy barrel lengths. Further, it is not uncommon for expanding bullets to self-destruct on meeting no more resistance than a wallet full of credit cards. Certainly, they cannot be depended upon to penetrate even light barriers such as car doors.

The other factor which seems to be so often ignored in this argument is that the energy used to deform or expand the bullet is used against the bullet and not the target. The frequently advanced contention that a bullet which expands and stays in the target delivers its full energy against that target is, therefore, clearly untrue.

Finally, survival planning requirements suggest an additional consideration. If the caliber you choose will not do the job you intend in its most commonly available or least effective form, you should choose another caliber. You may not be able to get your favorite brand or load under difficult circumstances, or you may run out and have to make do with what is available. I know of several poorly advised people who bought .380 autos based on their belief in the adequacy of the high velocity, hollow point Super Vel cartridge. Now that Super Vel is no longer in business, they are left with expensive noisemakers.

To bring the results of the Thompson-LaGarde tests and General Hatcher's analysis of them down to a point where useful comparisons of relative stopping power between various calibers can be made, I have drawn a chart which gives Hatcher's figures, my own — based on a simplified version of his formula — and the raw data necessary for you to make your own calculations.

Hatcher's method is lengthy and complicated, but it fits the observable facts better than anything else I know. For example, his RSP for the .38 Special is 30.8, and for the .45 ACP, 60; and from extensive data on actual gunfights, it is demonstrable that the .45 is just about twice as likely to stop a fight with one shot as is the .38. (It does not follow, incidentally, that two shots from the .38 equal one from the .45).

A simpler method of comparison, which will provide essentially the same relationships, can be derived simply by multiplying the weight of the bullet, in grains, times the muzzle velocity, times the sectional area of the bore, moving the decimal three places to the left for convenience.

For example:

.38 Special   158 gr. × 855 fps. × .102 = 13.77 Comparative Stopping Power
.45 ACP   230 gr. × 850 fps. × .159 = 31.08 Comparative Stopping Power

If you want even a more realistic evaluation, you should use actual velocities from your pistol — or at least one of your barrel length — and then add or subtract an arbitrary factor, based on experience, to reflect the bullet shape. I call this element the "E" factor, for empirical efficiency. I use .9 for round nose bullets, 1.0 for blunt or slightly flat points and 1.25 for semi-wadcutters of the Keith type. The formula then becomes WAVE when W = bullet weight in grains, A = cross sectional area of the bore in square inches, V = projectile velocity, and E = empirical efficiency evaluation of bullet shape. Easy to remember and easy to do with modern calculators. Not only do the results of this formula correlate well with the more complex Hatcher method, they are also substantiated by my own experience and that of others. Finally, they allow me to inject a bit of humor into an otherwise deadly study: I can call my system, the WAVE theory of comparative stopping power, certainly the most pompous title yet devised for this measurement.

In his excellent book, *Cooper on Handguns* (which everyone serious about using a pistol should read), Jeff Cooper outlines a technique almost exactly like mine, but easier — so much so that it can be done in your head. Whichever you choose to work with, you will be led to the same conclusions.

Minimum one shot stopping power in a defensive round is indicated on the Hatcher Scale by a figure of about 45 and on my CSP scale by 22. Bear in mind when using any of these figures that they are based on ballistic data supplied by the factories — and these are often optimistic under practical circumstances. The factories frequently determine velocities from unvented test barrels considerably longer than those which are in common use on handguns. For example, the actual velocity of a 158 grain .357 Magnum bullet when fired from a 4″ revolver is much closer to 1250 fps. than it is to the 1550 fps. claimed by some factory tables. If you choose the popular 4″, the CSP drops from 24.97 to 21.75. It is well to avoid marginal cartridges in combat pistols unless you are willing to settle for marginal results.

Just as stopping power, reasonable accuracy, controllability and availability in quantity are the primary requirements for a defensive cartridge, other factors must be considered in choosing a caliber for the working gun. Fine accuracy, flat trajectory, availability of a variety of loads, including those of extreme power and penetration ability in large animals, are some of these. Since one ought to choose the cartridge that suits his needs before selecting a gun to fire it, perhaps we should briefly examine some of the popular centerfire calibers.

Cartridge	Hatcher's Calculation of RSP	Factory Ballistic Data			Comparative Stopping Power
		W gr.wt.	V FPS	A BSA	
.25 ACP	3.7	50 x	810 x	.049	1.98
.32 ACP	10	71 x	960 x	.076	5.18
.32 S&W Long	12.5	104 x	772 x	.076	6.10
.380 ACP	16.2	95 x	955 x	.102	9.25
.38 S&W	23.8	146 x	685 x	.102	10.20
.38 Special	30.8	158 x	855 x	.102	13.77
9mm. Parabellum	29.4	115 x	1140 x	.102	13.37
.38 Super Auto	31.8	130 x	1280 x	.102	16.97
+.357 Magnum	55.24	158 x	1410 x	.102	22.72
.41 Magnum	not included	210 x	1050 x	.126	27.78
.41 Magnum HV	not included	210 x	1500 x	.126	39.69
.44 Special	60.6	246 x	755 x	.146	27.11
.44 Magnum	not included	240 x	1470 x	.146	51.50
.45 ACP	60.0	230 x	850 x	.159	31.08
.45 Colt	87.4*	255 x	860 x	.159	34.87

RSP = Relative Stopping Power

gr.wt. = weight of bullet in grains

FPS = bullet velocity in feet per second

BSA = Bore Sectional Area

*based on then current load of 910 FPS and bore sectional area of .163

†This cartridge had not been developed when Hatcher made his calculations, but my figures have been extrapolated from his formula. Actually, Hatcher's own figures seem to contain an error. He states: "Note — if the energy and velocity of a bullet are known, the momentum is obtained by dividing the energy by the velocity." He should have said, "twice the energy by the velocity."

Centerfire Handgun Cartridges

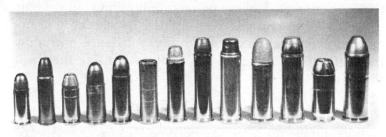

The most popular centerfire handgun cartridges. From left to right: .32 ACP, .32 S&W Long, .380 ACP, 9mm., .38 Super, .38 Special Wadcutter, .38 Special Semi-wadcutter, .357 Magnum, .41 Magnum, .44 Special, .44 Magnum, .45 ACP, .45 Colt.

.25 ACP (6.35 mm. Browning)

There is certainly very little use for this cartridge, and some experts, like Cooper, feel that there is none at all. It is neither accurate enough to be used in a working gun — even one confined to the smallest game — nor powerful enough to be used for defense. It will kill, certainly, but its impact usually causes the person hit by it very little immediate discomfort. Still, the guns made for it can be tiny and there are occasions when the choice lies between having a .25 and having no gun at all. If you are really aware of its extreme limitations, you use it at little more than arm's length and are cool enough to shoot for the eye sockets, it may give you a 5% chance of stopping an attack from a single assailant. If your unarmed chances are zero, that is an improvement in the odds. Perhaps one might view the .25 as a tertiary backup gun — a backup to your backup. The .25 is only available in autopistols, many of which are not well made, reliable or even reasonably accurate. The best is probably the stainless steel Budischowsky, but the no longer imported Browning is even smaller and it functions well. The pre-war Colt hammerless and the tip-up barrel Beretta are both possibilities on the used market. Hollow point ammunition is now being made in .25 ACP but the samples I have tried will not expand even slightly in any known substance, including concrete construction blocks; but then, neither will the solids.

.32 ACP (7.65mm.)

In the pistols which are designed to fire it, this cartridge is very little better than the .25; however, it does have some limited survival use in rifle sub-caliber devices, as discussed in the chapter on accessories. Only autopistols are presently designed for this cartridge, but it will fire in revolvers chambered for the .32 S&W Long. Neither the cartridge nor the guns made for it offer any practical advantages in survival planning, except, perhaps, widespread availability. Hollow points are also manufactured in this caliber and my remarks on those made for the .25 apply to them with equal force.

.32 S&W Long

Not impossible as a small game cartridge within its range limitations, but the .22 long rifle will do about as well and the .22 Magnum is distinctly better. The .32 Long is a little better in the stopping power department than either of the preceding rounds, but not enough to matter. I would not choose this cartridge for any purpose. It is available in revolvers only.

.380 ACP (9mm. Short, Kurz or Corto)

This is probably one of the three most overrated cartridges in existence (the other two being the .38 Special and the .357 Magnum). Even with the no longer available Super Vel round, it was not even marginally adequate as a defense load, and without it, it is spectacularly useless. Although the .380 is quite accurate, it offers little penetration and almost no shock at all; it is not even up to taking small game except at very close range, and then, not reliably. Only autopistols are made for this cartridge, and some of them are very well made indeed, notably the Walther and recently, the TDE Back Up.

.38 S&W

This is a revolver cartridge which falls in the same power range as the .380 ACP, and it has about the same range of usefulness. If you are tempted to select a gun in this caliber, don't. The .38 Special mid-range wadcutter is almost identical in power and recoil, but it is more accurate. The wadcutter is better for both defense and small game, and guns chambered for it can use more powerful ammunition as well. The .38 S&W, deservedly, is not popular and ammunition for it is increasingly hard to find.

.38 Special

The .38 Special is extremely accurate and a pleasure to shoot. Along with the 9mm., it is one of the world's two most popular and easily available centerfire handgun cartridges. In an accurate, well-sighted revolver it makes more sense to me as a small game pistol — at the ranges where you can hit reliably — than any of the rimfires, including the .22 Magnum. There is a wide variety of factory ammunition available, from light target wadcutters to high pressure, high velocity rounds, as well as the good Speer shot cartridges, and it is very easy to reload. Whatever its virtues, it is not an adequate defensive cartridge, however, despite its widespread use for that purpose by law enforcement agencies. At its best — and that means a maximum load in a long barreled revolver — the .38 will stop an attack with a solid hit on the torso about one half of the time, a fact which can be documented from hundreds of available case studies. Under some circumstances, however, such as in the case of a frail, elderly person with severe arthritis who cannot handle a suitable defense pistol, the .38 may have to serve, since there is nothing else available that is easier to handle than the .45 ACP which will do as well (except the .44 Special, which will be discussed later). The .38 Special represents the absolute minimum power range that should be considered for a primary defense pistol, and then only if there is a compelling reason why something more effective cannot be chosen. Whatever purpose you choose the .38 Special for, except hideout use, buy a .357 Magnum revolver to fire it in. It will provide a greater margin of safety and the potential of greater power, should you need it. The external dimensions of the two cartridges are the same, except that the .357 case is 1/10" longer, and the bullets are identical (although the powder charges are not).[5]

9mm. Parabellum (9mm. Luger)

Outside of the Communist bloc, the 9mm. is the world's most popular autopistol cartridge. Ballistically, it is very similar to the .38 Special, although it is usually loaded with a lighter bullet to a slightly higher velocity. Because of its flat trajectory, hitting with it at unknown ranges is relatively easy, but it does not make as good a small game cartridge as the .38 Special because of the usually ineffective round nose, semi-pointed bullet designs with which it is loaded in order to make it function reliably in the autoloading action. It is completely inadequate as a serious

[5]Although the less powerful .38 Special can be fired in the .357 Magnum revolver, the reverse is not true. Some of the older .38's, however, may have deep enough chambers so that the .357 could be loaded and fired. Don't. Some gunsmiths have been known to deepen the chambers of a .38 Special to allow the .357 Magnum to be used in it. Don't buy such a revolver and if you have one, don't use it.

defensive round, having less than half the stopping power of the .45 ACP; and, curiously, its very abrupt recoil makes it actually more difficult to handle in aimed rapid fire than the .45. As I write this chapter, factory loaded 9mm.'s sell for $10.55 per box of 50 or $2.55 more per box than .38 Specials, and since the 9mm. has no real advantages over the .38, its case is smaller and much less flexible for reloading, the choice of effective bullet designs is more limited and there are no shot cartridges made for it, there seems little to recommend it except widespread availability. If you should choose a .357 Ruger Convertible for your light working gun, the extra cylinder in 9mm. which the factory provides could be useful to have in the event that no other ammunition is around. As a defensive load, the 9mm. is one of the most unsuitable selections you could make, despite its extensive use for that purpose among the military of foreign governments. The light weight and compact size of the ammunition and the fact of its almost universal use in submachine guns are more important considerations leading to its popularity in military pistols than its effectiveness.

.357 Magnum

In essence, the .357 Magnum is nothing more than an overloaded .38 Special. Its case has been lengthened by 1/10″ so that it cannot be chambered and fired in guns designed for the .38 — and a wise idea that is, since the pressures in the .357 soar as high as 42,000 pounds per square inch and those in the .38 are usually held between 14,000 and 20,000. This fact is the Achilles heel of the .357: such pressures are very hard on any gun and they will shorten its life significantly. Without those high pressures, however, the Magnum loses its magic, and whatever you choose to call it, it is nothing more than an anemic .38. For survival use, therefore, I would not recommend the .357 if that is to be the only working handgun chosen. It is, nevertheless, a useful item because it is very accurate, its ammunition is plentiful, you can use .38 Specials in it for practice and small game shooting, and it is a very good cartridge, with proper bullets, for either varmints or game up to 125 pounds weight, or a bit more. As a deer load it is marginal at more than 50 yards, fired from a pistol, and even then, it is better confined to small deer. It is at its best in longer barrels since it depends almost entirely for its effect upon velocity instead of bullet diameter. For defensive use it is marginal in power, particularly in the 4″ and shorter barrels in which it is normally employed for that purpose, and it is only available in revolvers. Its recoil is noticeably greater than the .45 ACP, making it less suitable for controlled rapid fire. If you are fond of compromises and the dissatisfactions which usually accompany them, this is the cartridge to choose.

.38 Super (ACP)

This is another in the .36 caliber family, and it stands in relation to the 9mm. somewhat as the .357 does to the .38 Special. In fact, it is close to being a .357 Magnum adapted for use in autopistols. It is a much better cartridge than the 9mm. for any purpose, but it is so much less popular that it hardly merits consideration in survival planning except for singular circumstances. Like all of the other .36's, it is less than optimal for defensive use, and since it is available only for autopistols, it is less than perfect for a working gun. Further, its lack of popularity has contributed to the limited number of loadings available. Presently, no domestic factory provides anything other than a full metal jacketed, round nose bullet — the least effective form for either defense or hunting. Shortly before going out of business, Super Vel produced a superb soft point and an excellent hollow point load, and if you insist on having a

Super, you might see if there are any of these still left on the dealer's shelves; otherwise, you must handload if the cartridge is to be useful for anything other than punching holes in paper. In my gun, 7.7 gr. of Unique and the 125 gr. Speer soft point bullet is a fine combination that can be used under any circumstances where the .357 Magnum would be suitable.

.41 Magnum

This cartridge was designed to give those police departments who are wedded to the revolver something more effective than the .38 Special. Except for that use, I can see very little reason for the .41 Magnum. In its maximum loadings it is just as hard to control as the .44 Magnum and it is in every way ballistically inferior to it. The lighter police load — a well shaped 210 gr. lead semi-wadcutter at 900 foot-seconds from a 4" revolver — is accurate and pleasant to shoot but it leads the barrels of every gun I've tried — badly. The .41 is a new cartridge and it has not become popular; therefore, the ammunition is not widely available and the variety of factory loads is limited. If you have a .41 and you are willing to put up with the factory ammunition problem or to handload, it will probably serve you well as a heavy working gun; and, within the limitations of the revolver action, it it is adequate for defensive use. It is not the best choice for either purpose.

.44 Special

Only one revolver is currently being manufactured for the .44 Special, and that is a small pocket pistol: the Charter Arms Bulldog. Even used guns in this caliber are hard to come by because both the cartridge and most of the guns which used to be chambered for it are excellent. The Special is still a popular cartridge, however, because it can be fired in the .44 Magnum guns. Unfortunately, there is only one very mild load being produced by the factories, propelling a 246 gr. round nose lead bullet at 755 fps., but the cartridge is a handloader's delight. There are a variety of bullet shapes available and the large capacity case allows maximum flexibility in loading. Even the factory load is a proven manstopper, but since only revolvers are available, the .44 makes a more suitable working gun than it does a combat weapon. If you own a .44 Special in good condition, by all means consider handloading for it and using it in your survival battery.

.44 Magnum

This is unquestionably the best revolver cartridge ever designed, and the finest revolvers made in the world today are chambered for it. No pistol cartridge is more accurate or more flexible, and no standard production round is as powerful. Its case is identical to that of the .44 Special, except that it is 1/10" longer; therefore, the Specials can be fired as a sub-load in a gun chambered for the Magnum. There are only two serious drawbacks to the .44 Magnum that I can see. The recoil in full power loadings is so great that not everyone can handle it, and the guns made for it are bulky and heavy. The first problem can be tempered somewhat by handloading. Reduced loads can be used for most of the shooting you will need to do because, unlike the .357 which relies for its effect solely on velocity, the large diameter, heavy bullet of the .44 is effective even on large deer at only 65% of its potential power. Loaded to around 1000 fps., the .44 is easy to handle, its muzzle blast is not uncomfortable, even in a 4" gun, and it will still handle animals the size of black bear reliably. While I prefer the 8 3/8" barrel when shooting full power loads — both for maximum effectiveness and ease of handling — a 4" gun can be used without greatly sacrificing performance, in order to lessen the bulk and weight.

Considering the fact that the .44 Magnum, in practical terms, will give you performance equivalent to a .30-30 rifle in range, power and accuracy, even the long barreled gun is convenient by comparison. For defensive use, the .44 Magnum is more than most people can handle in aimed rapid fire; it is also probably more than you will need. If you plan to handload and if you are willing to practice enough to handle it well, the .44 Magnum is the prime choice for your working revolver.

.45 ACP

Clearly the best choice for defense use, since it is the only cartridge available for the autopistol which has decisive stopping power. There are three widespread myths abroad regarding this round which should be dispelled. 1) Myth: it is inaccurate. Truth: the .45 ACP provides target grade accuracy — in accurate pistols — to the limits of its useful range. 2) Myth: it is impossible to control. Truth: the .45 ACP recoils little more in an auto than a hot .38 Special does in a light revolver, and what recoil there is can easily be managed, even by children, with proper shooting techniques. In fact, I have seen high speed photographs which clearly show that the sudden, sharp rap of the 9mm. is much more difficult to control in rapid fire than is the slow push of the .45. In the premier combat shooting club in this country, the South West Pistol League, more than 90% of the competitors use the .45 and almost all of the winners do.

As a cartridge for the working gun, however, the .45 ACP — while usable — is not optimal. Its case is too small to provide the best flexibility for handloaders, and its practical velocity limit with 200-230 gr. bullets is between 1000 and 1200 fps.; therefore, its trajectory is somewhat high for hitting small targets at long, unknown ranges. Even with round nose, full metal jacketed bullets, however, it will take small game reliably, and with the new 200 gr. Speer hollow point loaded to 1100 fps., it is a respectable deer cartridge at reasonable distances. I would not like to be limited to one handgun under survival conditions, but if I were, it would be a suitably modified Colt autopistol firing the .45 ACP.

.45 Auto Rim

During World War I, the U.S. was unable to manufacture .45 autos fast enough to equip our troops and the government contracted for revolvers to be built by both Colt and Smith & Wesson which would fire the ACP cartridge. Since the auto case has a rim which does not extend beyond the body diameter, to insure smooth feeding from the autopistol magazine, the revolver extractors were unable to remove the empties without using small, "half-moon" clips. After the war, when a large number of these .45 revolvers found their way into civilian hands, the ammunition factories designed a case identical to the .45 ACP, except for a projecting rim which allowed it to be extracted from revolver cylinders. The rim is thick enough to compensate for the absence of the clips and is particularly strong in the head area; therefore, even though the case capacity is no greater than that of the ACP, the Auto Rim can be carefully handloaded to provide slightly higher velocities. The only current factory load propels a 230 gr. lead round nose bullet at 810 fps. — 45 fps. slower than the ACP. You should note that although the Auto Rim is not very popular and may be hard to find, any gun which uses it will also fire the ACP. The Ruger SA .45 ACP cylinder, however, will not accept the Auto Rim.

.45 Colt (often mistakenly referred to as the .45 Long Colt)

This is a fine working gun cartridge, second in that category only to the .44 Magnum among factory loaded rounds and perhaps to the .44 Special, when handloaded. Unfortunately, it is presently available only in single action revolvers, but a few master gunsmiths, such as Miniature Machine Co., can rechamber certain other revolvers for it. If the .44 Magnum is too strenuous for you, the .45 Colt would be a fine alternate. For survival planning, it is particularly useful since you can have a revolver with two cylinders: one firing the .45 Colt and the other the .45 ACP. Even in its distinctly mild factory loading, the .45 Colt is considerably more potent and a much better field cartridge than the ACP; and it can be handloaded to duplicate .44 Magnum ballistics in guns which are strong enough to withstand the pressures. Someone should make a modern, heavy frame double action revolver for this cartridge; it is one of the best.

Choosing Your Handgun Battery

There are essentially three categories from which to select handguns to fire the cartridges you have chosen from the preceding list: defense or combat pistols (usually autopistols), working guns (usually revolvers) and pocket pistols. The first two are both holster guns, relatively large and intended for heavy duty use. The pocket pistol should be small enough to go unnoticed when carried without a holster, and, although its uses are limited, they could be essential.

Working guns can be divided into light and heavy calibers, and for convenience you may wish to own examples of both, but unless your retreat is in an area which offers only small game, the heavy caliber is the more necessary, and with suitable handloads, it can serve a variety of purposes. Following are some brief reviews of the revolvers which I have found to be likely candidates in the working gun classification.

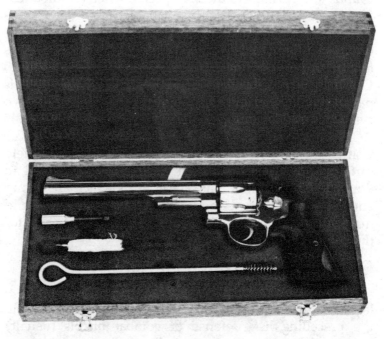

The most powerful regular production revolver in the world: S&W's Model 29, shown here in nickel finish with the 8⅜" barrel and Guy Hogue's custom grips, cased with its accessories.

Smith & Wesson Model 29 .44 Magnum

In my opinion, this is the finest revolver made in the world today. The lockwork, and particularly the single action trigger pull, is usually superb as the gun comes from the factory, the white outline rear and red insert front ramp adjustable sights are the best regularly available on any handgun, and the finish — either nickel or blue — is flawless. The gun is heavy — 47 oz. with the 6 1/2" barrel — but that is a blessing when you fire it. Although it is regularly supplied with oversized factory stocks which feel comfortable while you are aiming, most people find that custom stocks are a must because the prodigious recoil causes the cylinder release latch to bark the joint of the right thumb. I have 1/8″ trimmed from the rear edge of the hammer to keep it away from the web of my hand and I remove 1/16″ from each side of the trigger and grind it smooth on the front surface, re-casehardening the parts after the surgery. The .44 Magnum will probably not be used much double action, but when it is, I think you will find that you have much better control with a slightly more narrow, smooth trigger. Three barrel lengths are offered: 4″, 6 1/2″ and 8 3/8″. Naturally, the longer barrel provides the maximum performance with this cartridge and should probably be chosen by people who intend to use this gun often as a substitute rifle. The long version is also the easiest to shoot by a considerable margin because the extra weight and length seem to dampen the recoil. I am personally quite fond of the 4″ because of its convenient size, but both the recoil and the muzzle blast are so substantial that I would not recommend it to a novice.

Ruger Super Blackhawk .44 Magnum

Another, and less expensive .44 Magnum is the single action Ruger. At 48 oz. and 13 7/8″ overall length, this is a *big* handgun, but the weight helps with the recoil, and the 7 1/2″ barrel balances the massive frame and unfluted cylinder very well. The Super Blackhawk is also the most nicely finished of all the Ruger pistols and mine is very accurate, despite the slow lock time and heavy hammer fall which is characteristic of single actions. I do not like the aluminum sights which are furnished currently on this gun, but they can be replaced by an identical model in steel made by Micro Sight Co. While you are at it, you might want to have the rear leaf white outlined and a colored insert placed in the front ramp, for better visibility. For those of us who didn't teethe on the single action and grow up believing that the plow-handle grip shape supersedes sliced bread as man's greatest invention of the 20th century, the Ruger needs custom stocks. Single actions roll up in the hand, regardless of how hard you grip them and it is difficult to achieve uniformity in your hold from shot to shot without altering the handle configuration to some extent. The Ruger is offered only with a 7 1/2″ barrel, which most people will prefer, but for those who insist on a handier gun, it is a simple matter for a good gunsmith to trim the length and recrown the muzzle. Cutting the bar-

Three double action Model 29 S&W .44 Magnum double actions are shown on the left with the three standard barrel lengths available: 4″, 6½″, and 8⅜″. On the right is Ruger's Super Blackhawk with the dragoon style grip, also in .44 Magnum.

rel to the same length as the ejector rod housing makes a very well balanced gun for my taste.

Smith & Wesson Model 25 .45 Cal.

This is the only revolver in current production which I would consider using as both a combat and a working pistol. It is chambered for the .45 ACP, the best factory loaded defense round we have, and by using three shot half-moon clips, it can be reloaded almost as fast as an autopistol. For combat one would have to master double action shooting, of course, and it would be nice to have a bit more power than the ACP provides, for field use, but as compromises go, this one is not out of the question. Since the .45 Colt and the .45 ACP are both loaded presently with .451 or .452 diameter bullets, an extra cylinder in .45 Colt can be custom fitted, making the Model 25 truly a dual purpose gun.[6] The front sight, which is an upright post, can easily be altered to a snag-proof ramp with a colored insert, and the rear sight leaf can be exchanged for one with a white outline. The trigger and hammer modification which I suggested for the .44 Magnum Model 29 is also a good idea for this gun, as is a good set of custom stocks. A muzzle brake is available which could be a useful, if cumbersome, accessory for those who are exceptionally sensitive to recoil. Even if you choose another pistol for your primary working gun, it might be worthwhile to consider acquiring a Model 25, since in its dual caliber form, it could serve as a spare to either your combat or your field pistol. The only thing wrong with this gun is that it is extremely hard to find. If you want one, you will probably have to pay a large premium over the list price to get it.

[6]The .45 Colt was originally loaded with a .454 diameter bullet but most factories have recently standardized on a bore diameter of .451 for both of these popular .45 calibers. Details of this modification are covered in the chapter on custom modifications (Chapter 8).

Ruger New Model Blackhawk Convertible

If you like single actions and Rugers, this is certainly one to consider. The factory supplies this gun in .45 caliber with interchangeable cylinders for both the .45 Colt and the ACP. A companion model, which could be used as a lighter duty working gun, is offered in .357 Magnum (which also fires the .38 Special) with a spare cylinder chambered for the 9mm. Parabellum. Two guns that will fire five different cartridges is not a bad idea for survival planning; however, there are some problems with these. First, recent quality control seems quite poor. In the last two months I have seen three of the convertible .45's — including my own test gun — which had serious chambering problems. The .45 Colt cylinder for my gun, as an example, had each chamber counterbored to recess the case heads at different levels, and some factory cartridges rode so high that the cylinder would not turn. The .45 ACP cylinder on a friend's gun gave insufficient clearance from the recoil plate and also would not turn. In a third gun, the bottom of the aluminum grip frame was fully 1/8" longer on the left side than the right. Now, the Ruger factory, in my experience, is very co-operative about repairing such things under warranty, but I would suggest that you examine the guns you want to buy very carefully, if you are an expert, or have it done, if you are not. In the chapter on custom modifications, you will find a detailed description of other alterations which I would recommend for these guns.

Colt New Frontier Single Action Army

Except for modern metallurgy and the addition of adjustable sights, which are essential on any working gun so that it can be zeroed for whatever load you are using in it, this Colt is virtually identical to the model first developed in the 1800's which "won the West." That is a pity, nostalgia notwithstanding, because a great many advances in firearms design have been made in the last hundred years. The "New Frontier" shares all of the faults of ignition and grip design which are common to single actions, and, in addition, it is fragile. Its leaf springs are subject to breakage and so are the delicate hammer notches. This is a beautifully made and finished gun but I do not recommend it for survival use because of its design shortcomings.

S&W Model 57 .41 Magnum

In every aspect except caliber, the Model 57 is identical to the Model 29, and my remarks about the latter gun apply here with equal force, except, of course, those regarding the desirability of the cartridge.

S&W Models 27, 19 and 66

These three guns are not identical, but since they are all .357 Magnums and alternatives to one another, I will discuss them together. The Model 27 is built on the same frame as the .44 Magnum Model 29 and consequently it represents the same bulk and it is only 3 oz. lighter. If you want to get maximum performance from the .357 cartridge, however, this gun with the 8 3/8" barrel is your best choice. No portable firearm will withstand the consistent use of a load developing pressure of 42,000 pounds per square inch indefinitely, but this gun will certainly do it longer than more lightly constructed competitors such as the Model 19, which is built on a .38 Special frame. If you expect to do a lot of shooting with maximum loads, this is definitely the best double action revolver to choose. You will lose some velocity with the shorter barrels, but if you need a lighter, more compact gun, get this one in the 5" model instead of going to a smaller frame. On the other hand, if you want a light, easy to carry .357 as a backup gun to your rifle and you expect to carry it more than you will fire it, the 6″ version of the Model 19 will give you excellent performance. Four inch barrelled .357 Magnums make very little sense to me because they offer so little at the target in comparison with the recoil and muzzle blast delivered to the shooter, but if you must have one, you might as well have the advantages offered by stainless steel, so buy the Model 66, which is identical in every way to the Model 19 except for the material from which it is constructed.

Colt Python

Falling in between the S&W Models 27 and 19, in terms of frame size, is the Colt Python — the top of the Colt revolver line. My test gun in the 6″ barrel length is one of the most superbly accurate handguns I have ever fired, the sights are excellent — though not as good as the white outline-red ramp on the S&W — and the trigger pull is as good as anything that any firearms factory is ever likely to produce. The Python features a ventilated rib, a feature which I think is an affectation on a pistol, and its double action is not quite as good as the best examples of the S&W, but overall, I like the gun about as well as I am ever apt to like a .357 Magnum. In the 6″ version it is a good

Two versions of the Colt Python. The 4″ nickel finished version on left is fitted with Guy Hogue's custom grips. For most purposes, the author prefers the 6″ barrel model shown on right.

compromise in size and weight, but I would definitely prefer the S&W 19 or 66 in a 4″. If you want a double action .357, think hard about the circumstances under which you will use it and at least look at both the Python and the S&W's in a store, if you cannot actually fire them; then choose the one you like best. They will all give satisfactory service as light duty working guns, and they will all last longer if you fire maximum loads only when you really need them.

Autopistols

Colt Mark IV/Series 70 Government Model, and Variants

Colt produces four versions of the Browning designed auto which has been the standard service pistol of the U.S. military forces since 1911. Three of these models, the Mk IV, the Combat Commander and the Lightweight Commander, can become, with some modifications, the very best pistols for personal defense it is possible currently to obtain. Although all three are chambered for the .38 Super and the 9mm. Parabellum as well as the .45 ACP, only the latter cartridge should be considered in a fighting gun. With some judicious smoothing of the feeding ramp and the barrel throat, any one of these autos will function reliably — given good ammunition — under conditions of extreme abuse; and, with a well chosen spare parts kit, they will continue to do so almost indefinitely.

The fourth model, called the Gold Cup, was designed as a target pistol to use light loads, and while it will function with hardball, a steady diet of heavy combat ammunition will almost certainly cause damage. The rear sight, for example, is attached with a hollow roller pin which tends to shear, causing the sight to be ejected under an inconvenient bush along with the empty brass. The slide has also been lightened considerably so that it will provide less inertia when using light loads; therefore, it tends to batter the slide stop with full power ammunition. Although some of its shortcomings can be remedied by a master gunsmith, one of the other models would be a sounder choice for heavy duty use.

The Mk IV is the full-size, somewhat improved version of the service pistol. It is of all steel construction, and because of a new collet barrel bushing, is usually acceptably accurate for combat use as it comes from the box. The excellent and very useful .22 caliber conversion unit will fit this model or the Gold Cup, allowing for inexpensive practice, and low cost G.I. surplus parts, including barrels and slides, can be used for repairs or modifications. For these reasons, if I could have only one .45 pistol for personal defense, this is the one I would choose.

The Commanders are in every respect as serviceable as the Mk IV, and they have the same eight round capacity, using identical seven round magazines, but since they are 3/4" shorter, surplus barrels and slides will not fit them, nor will the .22 conversion unit. I understand that Colt intends to provide the new collet bushing for the Commanders, but presently, they are supplied with the old style which often needs some attention from a gunsmith before the guns will shoot as accurately as they are capable of doing. One excellent solution, if you want a Commander, is to fit it with one of the stainless steel match grade barrels made by Bar-Sto, since they are factory mated to a special tight bushing. Many people find that the Commander balances better for them than the Mk IV, and certainly it is more compact to carry. The Lightweight model, built on an aluminum frame, weighs only 27 oz. in comparison to 40 oz. for the Mk IV and 36 1/2 for the Combat Commander.

Whichever model you choose, be prepared to spend at least as much as the original cost of the gun to make it fully

1. Colt New Frontier single action "Buntline" .45
2. Ruger Super Blackhawk .44 Magnum single action
3. S&W "Bodyguard" .38 Special
4. Modified Ruger Convertible .45
5. Colt Commander, Lightweight
6. Colt Python .357 Magnum
7. S&W "Combat Masterpiece" .38 Special 2"
8. TDE Back Up .380
9. S&W Model 29 .44 Magnum
10. S&W "M&P" 2" nickel
11. WW II 9mm. Luger
12. Budischowsky .25 ACP
13. Modified Colt Combat Commander .45 ACP. hard chrome finish
14. S&W Model 27 .357 Magnum 5" bbl.
15. S&W Model 39 9mm. with Miniature Machine sights
16. S&W Model 25 .45 ACP
17. S&W Model 29 .44 Magnum
18. Combat modified Colt Government Model .45 ACP
19. S&W Model 29 .44 Magnum, 8 3/8" barrel, nickel finish
20. Walther PPK .380

61

An array of popular 9 mm. autopistols. Top to bottom: Browning P-35 with full combat modifications by King's, including feather hammer, sights, removal of magazine disconnector plus wrap-around Pachmayr Signature grips, S&W Model 39 double action with excellent adjustable sights by Miniature Machine Co., Colt Combat Commander unaltered with satin nickel finish, German S-42 Luger.

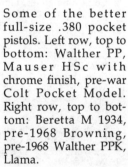

Some of the better full-size .380 pocket pistols. Left row, top to bottom: Walther PP, Mauser HSc with chrome finish, pre-war Colt Pocket Model. Right row, top to bottom: Beretta M 1934, pre-1968 Browning, pre-1968 Walther PPK, Llama.

A panoply of .38 Special "Snubbies". Clockwise from one o'clock: square butt S&W Chiefs Special with custom installed Kit Gun sights and Herrett's Detective Series stocks, S&W Model 60 stainless steel Chiefs with Guy Hogue's grips, Airweight Chiefs Special without hammer spur, S&W Bodyguard nickel finish, old model Colt Cobra with hammer shroud and custom grips, old model nickel finish Colt Detective Special with ivory stocks and Tyler-T grip, Colt Agent with hammer shroud, S&W Centennial, new model Colt Detective Special with oversize factory stocks.

The diminutive TDE .380 stainless steel "Back Up" is almost lost in the author's hand.

63

An assortment of excellent pocket revolvers. Top row: S&W Model 19 .357 Magnum with Guy Hogue grips, S&W "M & P" in nickel finish with Herrett's rosewood Detective Series stocks. Second row: S&W Combat Masterpiece .38 Special with Guy Hogue grips, Charter Arms "Bulldog" .44 Special with factory oversized stocks. Bottom row: old model Colt Detective Special 3" barrel .38 Special with Herrett's Detective Series grips and Colt Police Positive Special with 4" barrel.

Seven versions of the world's finest combat pistol: the COLT .45 AUTOPISTOL. Top: an unaltered G.I. MODEL 1911 A1. Second row: from left to right: COLT MARK IV GOVERNMENT MODEL with S&W adjustable sights and full house combat modifications by King's, pre-World War II COLT NATIONAL MATCH with combat modifications by King's. Third row: from left to right: PRE-MARK IV GOVERNMENT MODEL with full accuracy job by Micro-Sight Co., Auto-Grip adapter, speed safety designed by the author, "melted" Micro Sights and custom grips, early Colt LIGHTWEIGHT COMMANDER with gold shotgun bead front sights and fixed red rear, Pachmayr Signature grips. Bottom row left to right: COLT COMBAT COMMANDER with S&W sights, stainless steel Bar-Sto barrel and bushing, full combat modifications by King's, Pachmayr Signature grips and an industrial hard chrome finish, LIGHTWEIGHT COMMANDER with King-Tappan Combat Sights, King's speed safety and long trigger shoe.

combat ready. Good as the basic design is, it can be greatly improved by careful gunsmithing, and in a gun which your life may depend upon, anything less than the very best is foolish. Who will enjoy the money you save?

Star, Llama and Other 1911 Look-Alikes

Some of these Spanish made autos which look very similar to the 1911 pistol are cheaper than the Colts. If you are interested in buying one, I suggest that you place it side by side with the Colt and examine each gun carefully. Even if you are quite inexperienced in selecting firearms, the chances are that if the relative appearances of the respective models do not lead you to make the correct choice, you won't be able to tell the difference in using them either.

Browning P-35 ("Hi-Power")

The Browning P-35 or the "Hi-Power," as the company curiously prefers to call it, is one of the two pistols which gun store clerks are likely to recommend to you for personal defense (the other is a .38 Special "snub nose" revolver). It is a reasonably well made and very well designed autopistol which has several nice features, such as a comfortable grip for almost any medium or large hand, notably simple disassembly, and a magazine which holds 13 rounds. Unfortunately, it also has some serious flaws which make it an unwise choice as a fighting pistol. For one thing, the trigger mechanism is a nightmare, with more bends, angles and bearing surfaces than a teen aged girl learning to curtsy, making it almost impossible for even a master gunsmith to provide a proper trigger pull. And all of this unfortunate ingenuity has been expended to achieve a feature which is not at all desirable in a combat pistol: a gun that will not fire when its magazine is removed. This feature prevents you from covering an assailant while you are in the process of reloading — one of the basic advantages of most autopistols. Further, if you become separated from your magazine(s), you can't even use the gun as a single loader.

This magazine disconnector is not a fatal flaw, however, for it can be — somewhat laboriously — removed, and the P-35 is not the only autopistol with this design quirk. All currently produced handguns need some gunsmithing before they are suitable for protecting your life, and the P-35 is no worse than most in this respect. Its one irredeemable flaw is that it is made only in 9mm. Parabellum caliber — a cartridge which provides only about one half the stopping power necessary in a serious defensive pistol. If it were made in .45 ACP, or some yet to be developed caliber which would provide sufficient power, this gun could give the Colt autos a very close race.

Smith & Wesson Models 39 and 59

There are few guns on the market which I consider less suitable for defensive use than these. Except for magazine capacity and workmanship, these two models are virtually identical. According to the factory, the 59 holds 15 rounds in the magazine, (my test gun holds 16) and the 39 holds eight. My 39 shoots remarkable 2 1/2" groups at 50 yards from a rest; the 59 barely keeps them inside 8", and the workmanship on it, compared to the 39, is crude. Both guns are saddled with magazine disconnectors similar in function to that on the Browning P-35 (though, mercifully, they are easier to remove). Both have sights which are adjustable for deflection only, and both badly need an adjustment for elevation, since they shoot low with every factory load I know. Both are available only in a completely inadequate defense caliber, the 9mm. Parabellum. If these were not enough shortcomings to make any self-respecting pistol bearing so illustrious a name as Smith &

Wesson blush, they have at least one more: double action — a malady discussed earlier in detail.

Mab P-15

Although it is somewhat crude in appearance, all of the French manufactured Mab pistols I have fired have functioned reliably, and their accuracy, while not of target grade, was well within the practical limits required for combat use. Like the Browning P-35 and the S&W 59, the Mab sports a large magazine capacity — 15 rounds — but, also like the Browning and the S&W, the Mab is available only in 9mm., and that one factor removes it from serious contention as a defensive pistol, so far as I am concerned.

Walther P-38

9mm., double action, poorly balanced, bulky and *too* expensive.

Sig Neuhausen Model 210-1

This is probably the most finely constructed 9mm. autopistol in the world — and it should be, in view of its price. It is accurate in the extreme, for a service pistol, but its design is somewhat awkward for defensive use. It is made in Switzerland and carries an eight round magazine.

An array of better quality .25 ACP autopistols. From left to right: Browning Baby, pre-war Colt Pocket Model hammerless, Beretta Minx with tip-up barrel, stainless steel double action Budischowsky.

Pocket Pistols

Pocket pistols may be regarded as having two primary functions in planning for self-sufficiency. Defensively, they serve as backup guns if you are disarmed of your primary weapon or if it becomes inoperative, and for the hunter who is carrying a rifle or a shotgun, they may take the place of a heavier holster weapon for close range, small game pot shooting or to provide finishing shots on wounded game which do not cost as much or destroy as much meat as rifle cartridges do. For these purposes, they should be as compact as possible and provide power at least equivalent to the .38 Special.

Charter Arms Bulldog .44 Special

Although it is more concealable than many .38 "snubbies," the Bulldog fires a really effective cartridge, the .44 Special. When this gun was first announced, I eagerly test fired three of them and I was greatly disappointed in their performance. All of the guns were very inaccurate — groups ran between 7" and 18" at 25 yards from a rest — and two of them keyholed, sending their bullets sideways through the target. I wrote to the factory about the matter, and Mr. Robert L. Green, Executive Vice President of Charter Arms, told me that some of the first guns had been assembled with too much torque on the barrels when they were screwed into the frame, and he assured me that the factory was prepared to satisfy all legitimate complaints. Graciously, Mr. Green sent me a new gun from current production which I have been using for several weeks, and if it is representative, Charter Arms is now producing one of the most practical pocket pistols I have ever seen. Mine groups under two inches at 25 yards and its wide, easy to see fixed sights are perfectly adjusted for both Winchester and Remington factory loads. I have not had the opportunity to work up a handload for this little revolver, but even the mild factory cartridge is effective in this caliber. With a Keith type bullet loaded to, perhaps, 850 fps., the Bulldog should do all that anyone could reasonably ask of a pocket revolver.

Star PD .45 Autopistol

This is a very good idea, but I do not know how well it has been executed. I have seen the PD and it is small and neat, but I have not been able to fire one, since they are not yet on the market and the importer is uncooperative. Spanish autopistols are not noted for the sophistication of their metallurgy nor the excellence of their workmanship, and I would be cautious of the PD until it has been on the market for some time, and reports begin to come in from the field. I hope that we will be pleasantly surprised; it would be nice to have a good small backup gun in the same caliber as one's serious weapon.

TDE .380 Back Up

Probably the smallest and one of the most practical pocket pistols I have seen in a reasonably substantial caliber is the all stainless steel .380 Back Up, manufactured by the makers of the .44 Auto Mag. Designed as a hide-out gun for police officers, this miniature auto is only 4.75″ long and 3.48″ high and it weighs only 19 oz. Its diminutive magazine holds only five rounds but with one in the chamber, it equals the capacity of most revolvers. The .380 is not my idea of a perfect man-stopper, but it is worlds ahead of the .25 ACP, and this pistol is no larger than many .25's. It just might fit under circumstances where nothing else except a .25 would. The prototype, which I have fired, functioned flawlessly with mixed brands of ammunition and was startlingly accurate, even at long range.

Smith & Wesson Chiefs Special

Within the limitations of the .38 Special cartridge — and it certainly is limited when fired through a 1 7/8" barrel — the Chiefs Special and its variants, the Bodyguard and the Centennial, are very satisfactory pocket pistols. The Airweight Chief with a round butt and aluminum alloy frame is the least burdensome to carry and it works out of a pocket easily if the fishhook shaped hammer spur is ground off. Identical models are also available in all steel and in stainless. A three inch barrel option can be had in all but the stainless version and it adds noticeably to the performance of the cartridge but little to the overall bulk of the gun. The Bodyguard is simply a Chief with protective "ears" extended to shroud the hammer and prevent it from catching on clothing when it is drawn, but which still allow the piece to be cocked for deliberate single action fire. The Centennial completely encloses the hammer, permitting double action fire only. The grip safety which it incorporates can easily be deactivated without tools — and it should be. All of these little revolvers are five shooters, which some count as a disadvantage, but the smaller cylinder does make them extremely compact. I once had one of the all steel, square butt Chiefs fitted with a set of adjustable sights and custom grips, which made it bulkier and less snag free in the pocket, but it could then be zeroed with any load and it was accurate. I have carried that gun on almost every camping and fishing trip I have made for 15 years and it has certainly accounted for its share of rabbits, grouse and snakes. The three inch version, similarly modified, would probably be even better.

Colt Detective Special, Cobra, Agent and Police Positive

If you prefer a pocket revolver that holds a full six rounds and is only a little larger than the Chiefs, consider the Colt Detective Special, Cobra or Agent. These guns are all essentially the same except that the Detective Special is all steel, the Cobra has an aluminum alloy frame and the Agent has both the alloy frame and a smaller butt. The grips supplied on the first two are somewhat bulky and not particularly attractive, but they are quite functional and they do a good job of keeping these diminutive guns from squirming in your hand when hot loads are used. The sights on all of these models are fixed as they are on the Chiefs, but the Colts' are wider and much easier to see, especially in poor light. On the other hand, the double action lockwork on the S&W's is smoother and lighter. Both makes are reliable and both can be improved by careful gunsmithing. If you want a gun of this type, handle several models of each and pick the one that feels best in your hand. If you want the same small frame but a four inch barrel, you will have to choose the Colt, under the name Police Positive Special.

Smith & Wesson Model 19 "Snub" and Colt Lawman "Snub"

The largest revolvers that could reasonably be termed "pocket pistols" are the 2 1/2" versions of the S&W Model 19 and the Colt Lawman. Since velocity diminishes rapidly in the .357 as the barrel is reduced below 6", and since that cartridge is almost entirely dependent for its effectiveness upon velocity, it would seem that such abbreviated Magnums had little usefulness. And I think that evaluation is valid in terms of the purpose for which these guns were designed: defense. With maximum .357 loads their muzzle blast is fearsome, they are almost impossible to control in rapid fire, and the most they can offer is performance equivalent to a hot-loaded 6" barreled .38 Special. These shortcomings notwithstanding, however, there is a place for such guns in some survival batteries, if they are regarded simply as heavy duty .38 snubbies. Either gun will withstand a great deal more firing with .38's than any of the lighter guns will, and there may be times when high-end .38 Special performance is called for without the size of a long barreled gun. The S&W comes with excellent adjustable sights and a round butt which badly needs custom stocks. The Colt has fixed sights — a disadvantage if a variety of different loads will be used — but its grip is usable as issued. If you think you need a gun of this sort, look at both before you decide.

Miscellaneous

There are a variety of medium sized pocket autopistols on the market, most of them chambered for the .32 ACP and the .380 ACP. Probably the best made are the Walther PP, PPK and the Mauser HSc but, with the exception of the .380 Back Up mentioned earlier, all of them are too large for the level of power which they offer. It's just as convenient to carry a .38 Chiefs Special as it is a Walther PPK, and the .38 Special, properly loaded, is a lot better than any .380 for defense purposes, anemic as it is. For field use in a pocket pistol, the .38 Special is vastly superior to the .380, and its ammunition is less expensive, easier to reload and a much better choice of bullets is available.

In choosing a pocket pistol, I think it is advisable to opt for an all steel model, unless weight is absolutely critical; partly because they recoil less than their lighter weight counterparts and partly because they will probably stand more abuse and wear longer. Unless you select a stainless steel model, you should consider industrial hard chrome or nickel plating for any pocket pistol, since it will usually be subjected to perspiration or other corrosive influences.

One final thing which you should think about before you buy a pocket gun is that all small pistols, since they are lacking in power, must be used with greater accuracy; and they are harder to learn to shoot well than any other firearm. If you decide that you need one, be prepared to spend the time necessary learning to handle it effectively.

I do not want to leave you with the impression, because of the size and forward placement of this chapter, that handguns are necessarily the most important items in your survival battery. I have written at length about them because they are probably the least understood of all guns by the general public, and their proper selection is, for most people, the most difficult. Also, the radical legislators and the uninformed are allied in a concerted effort to make them illegal to purchase. If you want a handgun, buy it now. Later may be too late.

The TDE .380 Back Up dwarfed by a selection of full-size .380 pistols. From left to right: pre-war Colt Pocket Model, Walther PPKS, TDE Back Up, Walther PP, Beretta M 1934.

3 Rifles

The need for a good centerfire rifle is probably the most universally recognized firearms requirement among those who live outside the cities; and for most of us, the rifle will be virtually an indispensable tool in our planning for self-sufficiency. It will put more meat on the table per ounce of ammunition expended than any other gun, and no other portable weapon can provide the reliable long range defense potential which the rifle offers.

These statements seem obvious to the point of being trite, but they are disputed so often that some comment may be called for. It seems that every time I lecture, someone who has neither hunted nor loosed a shaft rises to contend that the bow and arrow constitute the perfect survival weapon, rendering rifles and other firearms unnecessary. Although I intend to discuss the role of archery in some detail later in this book, one or two observations seem appropriate here in order to put such romantic speculation to rest. For one thing, the level of skill required to make bowhunting a practical means of food gathering is enormous. Most people require two or three years of diligent practice before they can regularly hit a target the size of the vital area of a deer — even at 50 yards — using a hunting bow with at least a 45 pound pull. Hunting wild animals is not easy even now, and there is no reason to believe that it will become less difficult under survival conditions. Stalking close enough for a sure bow shot is not a regular thing, even for an experienced woodsman. Finally, even the most enthusiastic archer will tell you that an arrow is a far less reliable game-getter than a bullet; and in survival planning we are concerned with practical probabilities, not fortuitous potentialities.

The necessity of rifles for defensive use is also occasionally questioned, since shotguns are easier to hit with and pistols are more convenient to carry. When I counter with the facts that shotguns are strictly short range weapons and that hitting rapidly and consistently at more than 50 yards with a pistol cannot be relied upon, people who have never been under fire often remark that a.) an attack launched from several hundred yards away is not dangerous, or b.) you have plenty of time to escape and hide. I can only reply that even if the first contention were true, which it isn't, determined attackers seldom *remain* at long range if they do not encounter effective return fire; and running away — assuming that you were willing — might not be an option allowed by your opponents. Looters tend not to be bound by the Geneva Convention.

Although it could be done — and I have no doubt that

some will attempt it — stalking a deer in the woods with an assault rifle sporting a 20 round magazine, dangling a bipod and crowned with a flash-hider is not particularly convenient. On the other hand, a scope-sighted, bolt action sporter is not ideal for standing off an attack on your retreat by a dozen or so armed men. Furthermore, the heavy magnum which you might need if you settle in bear country would leave very little of a cottontail for the stew pot. Consequently, unless yours are very unusual circumstances, you are going to need several different kinds of rifles, and I suggest that if you must economize or improvise, do it in some less essential area of your planning. Don't skimp either in quality or quantity when you choose your rifle battery.

If you are a novice, selecting the proper rifles may seem bewildering since the variety available, both in caliber and type of action, is considerably greater than with any other firearm, and also because the circumstances under which a rifle may be required are so numerous and varied. The principle involved in determining your choice, however, is the same as it is with any tool — purpose. Perhaps, then, it may be helpful to describe briefly the uses and essential characteristics of rifles for survival planning before discussing calibers and types of actions in detail.

The defensive rifle must be utterly reliable, capable of sustained rapid fire, accurate enough to hit a man at several hundred yards, powerful enough to stop him with one fair hit and capable of withstanding rough handling and abuse. Regardless of your economic circumstances, you should not even consider compromising in the choice of your battle rifle. Defending your life, after all, is a competitive activity, and if you are to win, you need every edge you can get. At least some of the people who may attack you will probably have very sophisticated weapons indeed, and facing a *sturmgewehr* with an inadequate sporting rifle may prove embarrassing, to say the least.

There are two kinds of hunting terrain for deer-sized animals and larger — dense cover and open range or mountains — and each calls for a different rifle. The woods rifle should be short and handy so that it doesn't hang up on every branch, and it should mount and point quickly. Ideally, it should be capable of firing two or three quick repeat shots in case the first is deflected by brush, and it should employ a cartridge of moderate velocity with a relatively heavy bullet that will not explode on, or be as easily interfered with by, the surrounding cover. Moderate short range accuracy and power are enough for deer under these circumstances.

A rifle suitable for use in open country where shots may be taken at game up to the size of moose or elk at ranges extending three or four hundred yards has almost exactly the opposite characteristics. It should be fairly heavy, to provide steady holding and the utmost accuracy; the barrel should be long enough to allow maximum velocity to be attained with the cartridge being used — and that cartridge should be at least in the .270 - .308 - .30/'06 class.

Since predators and pests are usually relatively small targets and often only present themselves at considerable distances, the ideal rifle for this purpose must be extremely accurate and flat shooting, but it need not be of heavy caliber — in fact, it should not be, since increased recoil, which detracts from the finest accuracy, accompanies caliber and bullet weight. Further, pests and predators, almost by definition, are a nuisance or a menace because they invade your living space to threaten your crops or livestock, so most of your shooting of this kind will be done near your retreat. Under those circumstances, a lightly constructed, small caliber bullet driven at extremely high velocity is desirable, because such a projectile will disintegrate when it hits either the target or the ground instead of glancing and causing ricochets which might endanger your own animals or buildings.

Special circumstances might require additional special purpose weapons such as extremely heavy caliber double-barreled rifles for African residents who could encounter elephant, rhino or Cape buffalo; but for most of us, a versatile battery of centerfire rifles would include at least one of each of the following: a defensive or battle rifle, a big game rifle designed for use in open country (a plains rifle), a brush rifle (if conditions in your area make one necessary or desirable) and a varmint rifle to be used for predators, pests and small game at long range. Within each of these classifications there are sub-categories — such as light and heavy varmint rifles — and there are some multi-purpose guns, such as the .243, which can — with suitable bullets — be used successfully as either a light plains rifle or a varmint gun; but generally, these are the needs — and the characteristics generated by those needs — which you should consider. Only a careful analysis of your particular circumstances — location, available game, type of terrain, your physical make-up and condition — can determine how extensive your personal rifle battery needs to be and whether compromises would seriously impair the viability of your plans for self-sufficiency. It would seem to be more prudent to err on the side of too much rather than too little. Should you find that you have more than you need, your extra firearms and ammunition will probably make the very best trading goods you could ask for under survival conditions.

Given this orientation, let's examine the types of repeating actions available in current production rifles: the bolt, lever, pump and semi-automatic.

Types of Rifle Actions

The bolt action offers the greatest strength and potential

for accuracy, with its rigid lockup and one-piece stock. It is the easiest of all to maintain and repair, it has the greatest ability to extract swollen or dirty cases, and it can be adapted to any practical rifle caliber. Although it is inherently somewhat slower in operation than any of the other repeating actions, it is fast enough — with practice — for almost any hunting situation except, perhaps, use in very dense cover where one or more shots at game may be deflected by brush, requiring the fastest possible follow-up.

If you plan to reload — and you should — the bolt is clearly the action of choice. It takes very good care of cartridge cases, locking them up tightly so they cannot stretch when they are fired, and providing maximum life for reuse. As a hunting rifle for open country, or for the long range precision shooting required in pest control, the bolt has no peer. It also makes an excellent sniping weapon, should it ever be needed for that purpose.

The very best, and, in fact, most bolt actions are of the Mauser type, which is unquestionably the strongest as well as the simplest. The bolt can be easily removed and dismounted for cleaning and maintenance, usually without tools, and the barrel can be cleaned, as it should be, from the breech and not from the muzzle where a cleaning rod can cause serious loss of accuracy through damaging or wearing the rifling at its most critical point. The Mauser-type extractor is the best ever designed; it will remove stubborn cartridge cases that would remain hopelessly stuck in lesser actions, and it offers better control of the ejected case than any other.

Just as we are told that certain foods are "enriched" when, in fact, nutrients have been removed, many firearms manufacturers would have us believe that the Mauser action has been "improved" when it has only been made cheaper to manufacture. Presently, every

Mauser-type action manufactured in the United States is "improved." Extractors which take less of a grip on the case rim have been employed and the bolt face is no longer slotted for an extractor. A plunger is now used as an ejector which almost launches the brass into orbit.

It is claimed that these and similar changes make the actions stronger and better able to handle escaping gasses in the event of a ruptured case. Since brass begins to flow at approximately 60,000 pounds of pressure per square inch and the old actions would handle such pressures, I question the need for such advances which, just incidentally, offer the opportunity for substantial manufacturing shortcuts. But perhaps I am cynical. The fact is that most of the new actions work quite well and they are very strong indeed.

There are four sizes or lengths of actions, each suitable for a different group of cartridges. The short action is adaptable to the .22 Hornet, .222 Remington, .223 and similar sized ammunition. The medium is suitable for the .243 - .308 length cases, and the long action will accept cartridges such as the .270 and .30/'06. The magnum actions are designed for the .375 H&H Magnum as well as certain African calibers. In my opinion, the very best short and medium actions currently made anywhere in the world are the Sako brand, manufactured in Finland and widely distributed in this country. Fabrique Nationale of Belgium produces the finest long Mauser action I have ever seen, and it was recently incorporated in the now discontinued Browning High-Power. The Swedish Husqvarna (Carl Gustav) actions are on a par with the FN, and the addition of guide rails may make them even more desirable. Winchester Model 70 actions made before 1964 are highly regarded and military actions in good condition are also well worth considering, particularly for those on a tight budget. The Model 98 Mausers of Belgian,

Czechoslovakian or peacetime-early war production German manufacture are as sound as any bolt action ever built. A notch below, but still highly satisfactory, are the Swedish 6.5 Mauser, the Model 93 and 95 Mausers, the U.S. Enfield and Springfield and the 6.5 Japanese Arisaka. Most of the middle European wartime actions, and especially the Italian Carcano, are junk and may even be unsafe to fire. Frank de Haas's excellent book, *Bolt Action Rifles*, provides a detailed description of these and numerous other bolt actions, together with illustrations and exploded diagrams.

Although tremendously popular as a shotgun action, the pump or slide action rifle has never been a favorite with American shooters, except in rimfires, and, in my opinion, there are some very good reasons why this is true. For one thing, the pump does not lock up the cartridge case as securely as the bolt does and the brass is allowed thereby to stretch on firing. Full-length resizing of the brass is necessary each time the case is reloaded, and that practice leads neither to the best accuracy nor to long case life.[1] For another, in all of the pumps I have ever used, there is a tendency for the pump handle (forearm) to rattle and frighten the game you are stalking. Also, the two-piece stock of the pump is less rigid, and, therefore, less conducive to fine accuracy than the one-piece stock of the bolt action. Although the pump is accurate enough to use as a brush gun and it is certainly faster than the bolt or any other action except the semi-automatic, it tends to be somewhat fragile and I would not recommend it for survival use. If you really need firepower you might just as well

[1]In bottle necked high power rifle cases it is best whenever possible to resize the neck only since the body of the case will have fire-formed to the exact dimensions of the chamber, and only the tension of the tight neck is required to hold the bullet in the case. This practice should not, however, be followed with straight sided pistol or rifle cases. They should always be full-length resized after every firing whether they are to be used in revolvers, autopistols or rifles.

opt for the semi-automatic and get recoil reduction in the bargain.

Lever actions, which vie with the bolt for popularity, are plagued with many of the same problems as the pump. With few exceptions, the cartridge lockup of the levers allows case stretching and most of them have two-piece stocks. They are, however, streamlined in appearance and flat, making them the most easily carried of all rifles in a saddle scabbard. Except for the Sako Finnwolf, the Savage 99 and the Browning, lever actions are not designed for modern, high intensity loads and the cartridges which they fire are suitable only for short range use against animals no larger than deer. A distinct advantage which some of the levers have, however, is the outside, visible hammer. In addition to the fact that one can see at a glance whether the gun is cocked, the outside hammer on half-cock[2] is probably the fastest and most noiseless safety available — a feature which you may appreciate when you are hunting in woods so quiet that your own breath sounds like a decelerating freight train.

Many lever actions have tubular magazines, and you must use only flat or round nose bullets in them in order to avoid the possibility of the nose of one round detonating the primer of the round ahead of it, upon recoil. Such bullet shapes are excellent for brush hunting but they do not hold velocity well and they will limit the range of your rifle. The handiness and reliability of some lever models, however, mitigates sufficiently against these shortcomings so that you may want to include one in your

[2]The half-cock safety on rifles is designed to preclude the possibility of an accidental discharge if the gun is dropped; that is not the case with pistols. Never under any circumstances use the half-cock notch on an autopistol as a safety. It is not designed for that purpose and it usually will not withstand the stress of dropping or even relatively mild jostling. The sole purpose for the half-cock notch on a pistol is to catch the hammer if your thumb should slip inadvertently while you are cocking the piece.

battery. Several of them will be evaluated in some detail later in this chapter.

As working guns, semi-automatics have several drawbacks, but for self-defense they are without peer. After reading this chapter, some of you may conclude that an auto sporter would be a good compromise for all uses. If so, I urge you to reconsider; you will not have the best defense weapon, nor will you have the most versatile hunting rifle. Autoloading sporters are not really suitable as battle rifles. Their magazine capacities are too limited and they are not designed for the rough handling and sustained fire to which a defensive rifle will likely be subjected. Although some of them are very finely made indeed, no sporter is designed to withstand the frequent firing of several hundred rounds of ammunition at a single sitting and their convenience and accuracy oriented mechanisms may rebel. Assault rifles, on the other hand, are constructed for exactly that purpose and, as fighting rifles, the best ones are superior to anything else.

Most of the better semi-automatic rifles available today, whether for hunting or defense, are gas operated, and that is a distinct advantage to the recoil-shy. Gas operation, although it does not reduce the power of the cartridge as many people believe, does reduce recoil — in some cases as much as 45% — and, in the better designs, it is extremely reliable.

Case stretching is a factor to contend with in autoloaders, since, like many levers and pumps, most of them do not lock the breech bolt at the head, and most of the sporters have two-piece stocks. If I needed a good, fast firing brush rifle, however, or if recoil bothered me and I needed a very heavy caliber, I would certainly buy a gas operated auto rifle — and under no circumstances would I willingly be without at least one assault rifle in my personal survival battery.

Calibers

The most popular — and some of the best — rifle cartridges manufactured in the United States. From left to right: .22 Hornet, .222 Rem., .223 Rem. (5.56mm.), .243 Win., .270 Win., .30 M-1 U.S. Carbine, .30-30, .308 (7.62 NATO). 30/'06, .375 H&H Magnum.

At least as important as the type of action you choose for your rifle is the ammunition you will use in it, and even a hasty glance at the list of currently manufactured cartridges is awe inspiring. Remington, Winchester and Norma — to name only three manufacturers — together list 65 separate centerfire rifle calibers. In addition, there are dozens of "wildcats" for which no commercial ammunition is made, but which shooting enthusiasts happily handload for their custom-built rifles, in an attempt to improve upon factory performance. Whatever the viability of this superabundance of calibers under ordinary circumstances, we must consider popularity and availability in planning for survival, and those criteria reduce our choices to a handful. No one can possibly determine exactly the amount of ammunition that will be needed under a variety of circumstances and for an indeterminate period. Consequently, most of us will have either too much or too little and we will need to get more or trade our excess for other things which we may need. For that reason, the calibers you choose should be the most common available that will suit your needs, even if a more exotic cartridge gives slightly better performance. Fortunately, however, we will have to make few sacrifices because most of the popular calibers became popular because they are good. If the budget permits, some of us will even include an extra caliber or two — such as the .30-30 — just because it is so widely used, even though others in our battery may serve the same purpose as well or better.

Because of the way in which factory manufactured cartridges are sealed, they will last longer in storage than either handloads or components, all other factors being equal; therefore, another element which we must consider is the variety of factory loads available for a given caliber. Several different combinations of bullet weights, shapes and velocities make for greater versatility. For example, the .30/'06 has half a dozen different factory loads which adapt it for varmints at long range, medium-sized plains game, or bear in dense cover, whereas the obsolescent .351 Winchester has but a single mild loading. If you have a particular favorite caliber which is not very popular and you already own a rifle for it, by all means keep it and buy some ammunition for it if you wish, but don't include it in your planning as anything but a secondary backup — unless you are willing to buy several thousand rounds which you may never be able to unload on anyone else if you don't have occasion to use them.

There are only three cartridges which I would consider for primary defensive use: the .223, the .308 and the .30/'06. Each of these is now, or has been, a U.S. military cartridge, and good G.I. surplus ammunition can be had in quantity at fairly reasonable prices — an important factor since you should plan to store at least five times as much ammunition for defense as for hunting. With care, you may expend no more than 10 or 15 rounds of big game hunting ammunition for an entire year's supply of meat; but if you ever have to defend your retreat, you may need to fire several hundred rounds in a single day. Further, precisely because military ammunition is comparatively cheap and readily available it tends to become popular and remain so for years after it is no longer used by the military. If you have a working gun in the same caliber as your battle rifle, the storage considerations will be simplified, and the ammunition can be put to use efficiently for the most needed purpose.

The cartridges in the following list are from three categories: those most often thought of for survival use, those most recommended in the gun stores, and those which I consider from my own experience to be most suitable. By combining these into one list, you will hopefully avoid my personal prejudices to some extent and you will be prepared to make a decision from a fairly broad base.

Caliber	Use
.22 Hornet	Varmint-Small Game
.222 Remington	Varmint-Small Game
.223 Remington	Varmint-Small Game and Defense
.243 Winchester	Heavy Varmint — Light Big Game (deer and antelope)
.270 Winchester	Big Game — open country
.30 U.S. Carbine	Small Game — close range
.30- 30	Deer-sized game — close range
.308	Big Game — Defense
.30/'06	Big Game — Defense
.375 H&H	Large Dangerous Game

Anyone whose hunting is confined to the North American continent will find that cartridges drawn from this list will meet his needs admirably. One could certainly argue that the .22/250 is the best of the .22 caliber varmint cartridges and I would be inclined to agree, but it is not as widely available as the .222 or .223 and with those and the .243 with light bullets, one would hardly miss it. Similarly, the .264 Magnum has a slight ballistic edge over the .270, but I can think of no practical hunting situation in which it would matter, and one can hunt from one coast to another for years without seeing a single user of the .264; the .270 is one of the two or three most popular big game cartridges in the country.

Assuming that we can agree that our choices for a survival battery should be confined to the most widely available and popular calibers, let's take a more detailed look at those on the eligibility list.

.22 HORNET

I am including a discussion of the Hornet here primarily because if I don't, I will receive a flood of letters asking me why it was omitted. Aficionados of this caliber are a devoted lot, and not completely without reason. At one time, the Air Force experimented with the Hornet for survival rifles in bailout kits, but that was before some of our better .22 centerfires were developed. Introduced in the late 1920's, this is our oldest small bore centerfire "varmint" cartridge. It is accurate, has virtually no recoil and a light report. The typical factory load drives a .224 diameter jacketed bullet of 45 gr. weight at a nominal 2680 foot seconds velocity, making it slightly more potent than the .22 Magnum rimfire (40 gr. HP at 2000 fps.). Ten or fifteen years ago, it was virtually impossible to find a new commercial rifle chambered for this round, because the Hornet has been greatly overshadowed in performance by the .222 Remington, the .222 Remington Magnum and others, but recently, there is a resurgence of interest in the cartridge. It is still not sufficiently popular to be a prime choice for the survival battery, however, and its performance limits its use to small game and pests within 150 or 175 yards. It is by no means a reliable deer cartridge, even with handloads, although it has been used for that purpose. It is not available in rifles suitable for defensive use.

.222 REMINGTON

This may be the most accurate centerfire rifle cartridge ever developed and, since its introduction in 1950, it has been a prominent winner in benchrest target matches. The standard factory loading propels a 50 gr. .224 jacketed bullet at 3215 fps. and it is suitable for any small game animal, pest or predator up to but not including deer, out to 225 yards or so. It is a near perfect choice for wild turkey, but in factory loads it is much too destructive for small edible game. Lighter handloads using cast lead or non-expanding bullets can easily be developed, however, making this caliber superbly versatile. It has little value for defensive use, since it is available only in bolt action or single-shot rifles, but it could be effective against a sniper, within its range limitations.

.223 REMINGTON
(5.56 mm. U.S.)

The ballistics of this cartridge are identical to the .222 Remington Magnum: a 55 gr. jacketed bullet at 3300 fps., but the cases are different enough so that one should never attempt to fire a .223 in a .222 Magnum rifle. A case separation due to excessive headspace would be almost certain to result. I have omitted a discussion of the .222 Magnum because it has been completely eclipsed by the .223, since the latter has been adopted, under the designation 5.56mm., as an official U.S. military cartridge.

The .223, which is also used extensively by elite SWAT police units, comes about as close to an optimal light defense rifle caliber for survival use at moderate ranges as I have found. It is flat shooting and very accurate to about 300 yards, it has negligible recoil and offers reasonable stopping power at reasonable ranges. Further, since it is a current U.S. military cartridge, it is popular and readily available. Surplus ammunition as well as once-fired brass can often be obtained at reasonable prices. Both light assault rifles for defensive use and fine bolt action sporters for hunting are chambered for this cartridge and, for that reason, the .223 is my choice for survival use in its power range. Commercial factory loads are suitable for all predators and pests as well as game up to deer size. As in the .222, light handloads are preferable for pot shooting. Although marginal in power for the purpose, many people use the .223, handloaded with the Speer 70gr. semi-spitzer bullet, for small deer and antelope — where it is legal. That same load, incidentally, is deadly on mountain lion.

.243 WINCHESTER

If your hunting is almost never in dense cover and if the largest game in your area is deer and black bear, this is an excellent cartridge to consider. The 80gr. bullet at 3500 fps. is explosive on pests and the 100gr. soft point at 3070 fps. is excellent to 275 yards for deer and antelope. Recoil is inconsequential and accuracy is remarkable. Barrel lengths less than 20 inches, however, produce a tremendous muzzle blast.

The .243 is quite popular enough in its own right to be considered for survival use, and since its case can be simply made by necking down 7.62 NATO brass (.308 Winchester commercial), it might be particularly useful as a light hunting round for anyone who chooses the .308 for defense. On the negative side, the .243 is entirely too vigorous for edible small game and it is too light for reliable performance on moose, elk or grizzly and, because it is only available in sporting rifles, it is not the best choice for defensive use. If you are going to have both a heavier and a lighter caliber rifle, you don't need a .243, but you may want one because it is so accurate and pleasant to shoot. It is a very good choice as a hunting rifle caliber for youngsters and small statured women. Its accuracy potential is best realized in bolt action rifles, but it is available in levers, pumps and semi-autos as well.

.270 WINCHESTER

This caliber is a particular favorite of mine and it comes close to being the mythical "all around" hunting rifle cartridge. With 100-110gr. bullets at 3480 fps. it is excellent for varmints, and the 130gr. at 3140 or the 150gr. at 2900 fps. provide enough power for any animal on the North American Continent, if expertly used. In fact, it is the lightest recoiling rifle that could reasonably be used for our largest game, but it is considered marginal — even with the 150gr. bullet — for moose, elk or grizzly. The .270 is only slightly less potent than the .308 or .30/'06 in striking energy, and its trajectory is flatter, making it easier to hit with at unknown long ranges. Along with the .30/'06, the .30- 30 and the .308, the .270 is among the most popular and easiest to find cartridges in the U.S. Further, its cases can be made by necking down plentiful .30/'06 brass.

Because of its high velocity and pointed bullets, the .270 is not a good choice for hunting in dense cover, and since only sporting rifles are chambered for it, its usefulness for defense is limited; however, it is my idea of a near perfect anti-sniper cartridge. For optimum performance, select a rifle with at least a 24" barrel, and under no circumstances should the length be less than 22". The full potential of the .270 as a highly accurate, long range, big game hunting cartridge is best realized in a good bolt action rifle with a suitably powered scope.

.30 CARBINE

Largely because of the once inexpensive and very handy G.I. carbines which fire it, this is an immensely popular cartridge. So much so, in fact, that a rather strange paradox has developed. Neither the guns nor surplus ammunition is currently plentiful or cheap and commercial cartridges are quite expensive, particularly in the light of their limited usefulness. Nevertheless, vast quantities of both have been purchased over the past 20 years, and presumably stored, so that although ammunition availability now is somewhat limited, a great deal of it could show up during a crisis period.

At best, the .30 Carbine is strictly a short range small game round, for it has neither great accuracy, flat trajectory nor much power. It is inadequate even for small deer and its stopping power for defensive use is not even marginal. Many people who have never used one in a fight are impressed with the carbine's handling and the ease with which it can be managed in rapid fire. They seem to believe that shooting a lot makes up for inadequate power in a combat situation. It does not.

Because so many people have squirreled away so much .30 Carbine ammunition, you are likely to encounter some of it in the event of civil disorders and you may, for that reason, want to have something around which will fire it. If so, consider a sub-caliber device that will allow it to be fired in one of your .30 caliber rifles such as the .308 or .30/'06. If you must have a Carbine, get a U.S. G.I. surplus model and not one of the commercial copies with a cast receiver. There is a large amount of South American military surplus ammunition on the market currently which should also be avoided. Some of it is dangerous and some is so poorly made that primers are seated sideways.

.30- 30 W C F

This is another cartridge whose great popularity is based almost entirely on the light, short, handy rifles which fire it. The .30-30 was the first American small bore round designed for smokeless powder, and since its inception the "thutty-thutty" has been practically synonymous with "deer rifle." Throughout Mexico and Latin America, as well as in many backwoods country stores in the U.S., the .30- 30 may be the only rifle cartridge to be found on the shelves. For this reason alone, one should give serious consideration to including a rifle for this caliber in any survival battery. If you decide to buy one, get the shortest, handiest one you can find. There is no need to seek the accuracy and strength of a bolt action, and scopes on a .30- 30 seem unnecessary to me, since the cartridge should be limited to use on deer-sized animals at ranges no greater than 150-175 yards.

.308 WINCHESTER
(7.62 x 51 NATO)

After World War II, the Army began experiments to produce a cartridge which would develop approximately the ballistics of the proven .30/'06, but in a shorter case with a stronger rim, better adapted to use in automatic and semi-automatic weapons. Known as the T-65 during its development, the cartridge as finally adopted in 1954 was designated the 7.62, and it is interchangeable with the .308 Winchester commercial cartridge which is loaded by all of the major U.S. ammunition companies.

The designers succeeded very well in their assigned task. The .308 is shorter than the '06, it is admirably suited to autoloading actions and, with the 150gr. bullet the .308 is only 110 fps. slower than the same bullet in the .30/'06 —

a ratio which is closely maintained throughout the range of bullet weights shared by the two cartridges. It is superbly accurate to fully 1000 yards, although its remaining energy at that distance is not overwhelming.

The fate of the .308 as a U.S. military cartridge is uncertain, because the M-14 rifle, which was designed to fire it, never completely satisfied the Army and is now out of production. The Southeast Asia encounter was fought with the .223, and only our NATO forces — so far as I know — are still being issued .308's. Nevertheless, our government has stockpiled millions of rounds of this ammunition, some of which could become available on the surplus market — unless Washington, in its usual frugal stewardship of the taxpayers' money, decides to destroy it as they have so often done in the past.

For defensive use, this is the best rifle cartridge yet developed anywhere in the world. There are a number of highly sophisticated assault rifles chambered for it, notably the BM-59, the SIG AMT and the FAL. It is sufficiently powerful for almost any tactical use and yet it is eminently controllable in rapid fire, particularly when used in a gas operated autoloader.

As a hunting cartridge, it is almost as powerful as the world standard .30/'06, and its only handicap in this category is that, because of its shorter neck, the factories load no bullets heavier than 200 gr. for it. Virtually every high power sporting rifle manufactured in the U.S. and Europe is currently chambered for the .308.

.30/'06 SPRINGFIELD

This is certainly the most versatile and probably the most popular centerfire rifle cartridge in the world. Adopted by the U.S. military in 1906 (hence the '06 designation), it has seen service in two world wars, and probably every species of game in the world has fallen to it at some time during its almost 60 years. And there is hardly a corner of the globe where ammunition in this caliber cannot be had. Bullets as light as 100 gr. are available for it for use on varmints, and 220 gr. soft points may be obtained for elk, moose and bear. Unless you expect to encounter the largest species of African game, Indian tigers, or perhaps, Alaskan brown bear, you will never need a more powerful cartridge for hunting. Recoil is not unpleasant for most healthy adults and accuracy is superb in good rifles.

Except for the Garand, there are no suitable defense rifles available in .30/'06, because the .308 is better suited to autoloading actions. A good gunsmith can make a sound Garand into one of the best fighting rifles to be had, however, and spare parts are easy to come by. As a plains rifle cartridge, the '06 is not quite as good as the .270, but it will serve, and it is a fine brush round. The very light varmint bullets give neither the best accuracy nor trajectory as flat as one might desire, but again, the '06 will serve. With cast bullet handloads or a sub-caliber device enabling you to use .32 ACP or .30 Carbine ammunition, the .30/'06 will even do for edible small game. All things considered, this would be a hard cartridge to do without in a well balanced survival battery.

.375 HOLLAND and HOLLAND MAGNUM

This is more cartridge than most people will need and more than many can handle. I am including a brief discussion of it because of the relatively large number of people I know who are planning retreats in exotic locales, particularly Alaska, where extremely large, dangerous game abounds.

If you need this much power, if you can cope with the

significant recoil or are willing to carry a heavy enough rifle to counteract it — say 9 1/2 or 10 pounds, there is nothing better, in my experience, than the .375 H&H. Either the 270gr. bullet at 2740 fps. or the 300gr. at 2550 fps. delivers smashing power — and with target-grade accuracy, in a good rifle. The 270gr. load almost duplicates the flat trajectory of the 180gr. .30/'06.

In Africa, the .375 is considered by most professional hunters to be the optimal cartridge for lion, and it is probably the all-round most useful caliber on safari. Even though many believe it is too light for elephant, Cape buffalo and rhino, it has enough power for the very difficult frontal brain shot on elephant and many have been killed with it.

In Alaska and parts of Canada, the .375 would be my first choice for a working rifle. It has the necessary power for the huge Alaskan brown bear and the really large Canadian moose; and, handloaded to moderate velocity, it is probably the best brush cartridge made for rifles. Also, with handloads, it is suitable for deer, causing less meat destruction than many high velocity small calibers, and it is pleasant to shoot with these reduced loads.

Although not as popular as some lesser cartridges, the .375 is certainly the most widely known and available cartridge in its class worldwide and, I think, the best. The only practical drawback to using it is recoil — something like 45-50 foot pounds with full factory loads versus perhaps 19 or 20 pounds in the .30/'06. Now this is not enough punishment to cause injury — unless you plan to do a lot of shooting from prone — but many people find it distinctly unpleasant, and recoil does adversely affect accuracy. If you think you need a rifle this powerful, borrow one that you can fire and see whether the recoil is severe enough to be a serious problem. If you find you can handle it without difficulty, have a master custom gunsmith make one for you to your exact measurements as heavy as you can conveniently carry under the circumstances you envision. Both the stock fit and the weight will reduce the felt recoil. Also make certain that the stock design has very little drop and insist that the comb and cheekpiece be conservative and slope *toward* the action, not away from it; otherwise you will be belted in the jaw every time you fire. If you cannot afford a custom rifle, look around for a pre-1964 Winchester Model 70 or a Safari grade Browning with the long Mauser extractor and have either weighted to your requirements. Install a thick, fairly hard rubber recoil pad and be sure that the stock is cut or extended to fit you — at the same time. Poor stock fit is one of the chief culprits in apparent recoil, so make certain it is correct. Finally, mount a rugged three power scope, like the Weaver K-3 in Jaeger quick detachable side mounts and fit a good auxiliary set of iron sights and you will own one of the most useful and reliable rifles in the world.

In order to forestall, as much as possible, letters from readers whose favorites I have ignored in the foregoing list, I will touch briefly on a few of the candidates who missed the cut. The 6mm., which is very similar to the .243, is probably a slightly better cartridge but it is much less popular and available, and its brass cannot be made from .308 military. The 7mm. Remington Magnum, which attemps to provide the striking power of the .30/'06 with the trajectory of the .270, is less popular than either, recoils quite a bit more than either, and, for me, does not perform well on large game at close range, since the bullets in all of the factory loads I have tried tend to break up when driven at such high velocity. The .22/250, the .257 Roberts and the 7mm. Mauser are all omitted from consideration solely because they are less popular than their listed rivals. All of them are superb cartridges and if you can afford the money, storage space, ammunition and reloading dies for extra calibers, all of them are well worth having. In fact, the only rifle cartridges currently factory loaded in the U.S. which I would recommend against solely on the basis of their ballistic inefficiency or poor design are the .32 Remington Special, the .300 H&H Magnum and the .351 Winchester SL, together with all of the obsolete pistol-rifle rounds such as the 38-40, 25-20, 25-35, etc. The .264 Winchester Magnum and the .350 Remington Magnum are also less than ideal choices for survival use, in my opinion.

Those who plan retreats outside of the U.S. should give some consideration to the "wine of the country." In Canada and other countries with a pronounced British influence, you may want to own a rifle chambered for the .303 British (not to be confused with the .303 Savage). With the 215 gr. round nose bullet, this is an excellent brush cartridge, and it is only slightly less powerful and flat shooting than the .308. In other areas, find out what the most popular hunting and military rounds are and compare the information in the ballistic tables with that for the cartridges which I have discussed here in detail and you should have a reasonably accurate knowledge of their suitability for your plans.

Recoil

I have mentioned recoil several times in this chapter as a factor in determining a suitable rifle. Newton's third law of motion states that for every action there is an equal and opposite reaction; as this physical law applies to our considerations here, it means that as the power of a cartridge increases, so does the recoil. The three primary factors involved are the velocity and weight of the projectile versus the weight of the gun from which the projectile is fired.

For any given combination of bullet weight and velocity, the force of recoil is the same; however, felt recoil — which is all we are concerned with in practical shooting — may be diminished by a number of factors. Increasing the weight of the gun is one of the simplest methods of reducing apparent recoil and it has the further advantage of providing steadier holding for greater accuracy; however, if the rifle must be carried a great deal, this may not be the best solution to the problem. Muzzle brake devices work on the principle of venting the explosive gasses, after they have done their work of propelling the bullet down the barrel, in such a way that they exert a jet-like effect in the opposite direction to that of the recoil. I have not personally had much experience with any of these devices, but a number of people whose opinions I respect like them very well, particularly the Magna-Port and the Pendleton Dekicker. The greater the inherent recoil, the better muzzle brakes work, I am told. The use of some of these devices increases muzzle blast to a marked degree.

A good stock design which fits you and a recoil pad, if it is not too soft, will both give some relief. Gas operated semi-automatic actions which use a small portion of the propelling gasses to cycle and exert a force opposing recoil are often quite successful in lowering the level felt. Perhaps the greatest single element in unpleasant recoil among novices results from the failure to hold the rifle firmly against the shoulder. Holding the gun loosely or away from your body only allows it to get a running start before it belts you.

People differ greatly with regard to the amount of recoil which they find comfortable, and *machismo* should not influence your decision concerning the level of punishment which you are willing to accept from a rifle. If you choose a gun that kicks too much, you will never shoot it well, and hitting a deer with a .243 is much likelier to put meat on the table than missing it with a .600 Nitro Express.

Most adult males of average build who are in reasonably good health will not find recoil in the area of 20 foot pounds disconcerting, and that will allow them to handle rifles in the .30/'06 class comfortably — assuming that the gun weighs about 8 pounds. If you are interested in computing exact recoil figures for the rifle-cartridge combination in which you are interested I suggest that you consult chapters XI and XII in *Hatcher's Notebook*. The rather complex formulas together with the theory behind them are given in full detail.

For those who are not mathematically inclined, I am including the following approximate comparative figures:

Cartridge	Weight of Rifle	Approximate free recoil (in foot pounds)
.222 Rem.	7 lb.	3.5
.243 Win.	7½ lb.	14
.270 Win.	8 lb.	17
.308 Win.	8 lb.	20+
.30/'06	8 lb.	20+
.300 Weatherby	8½ lb.	30
.375 H&H	8 lb.	45
.458 Win.	9 lb.	60
.600 Nitro Express	10 lb.	100+

Choosing Your Rifle
BOLT ACTIONS

By now, you should have some idea of the types and calibers of rifles that will best meet your needs, and, probably, one or more of your hunting rifle choices will be a bolt action. If so, I suggest that you give serious consideration to having at least the one which you expect to use most built for you by an expert custom maker such as

Arnold Capone of King's Gun Works, Al Biesen or P.O. Ackley, to mention only a few whose work I know personally and can recommend. Such a custom rifle, although it will probably cost from 20% to 50% more than the better off-the-rack guns, is neither extravagant nor an affectation. If you exercise some discretion, you will acquire a gun that fits you exactly, weighs what you want it to weigh, is superbly accurate and will last through several lifetimes of extensive use. The possible combinations of actions, barrels, triggers, stock designs and material would require another book as long as this one to detail, but you will not be misled by the better custom makers, and if you explain to them exactly what your requirements are — and if they are within reason — most gunsmiths will guarantee to produce what you ask for. Only the time factor mitigates against this approach, and only you can determine whether you can afford the often considerable wait involved in having a rifle built to order.

If you decide, for whatever reasons, not to seek a custom gun, you will not suffer greatly if you choose carefully from among the commercial bolt actions. In fact, some of them are better made than some custom-builts. I cannot possibly evaluate in detail all of the currently available commercially manufactured models in a book of manageable length, so I will confine my remarks to the better known brands, the ones I personally prefer, or the rifles which will most likely be touted in the gun shops.

Browning High-Power

Quite recently, Browning discontinued this superb line of bolt action rifles which were made to their specifications by Fabrique Nationale in Belgium, but as I am writing this chapter in mid-1975, a few may still be found on dealers' shelves. The short and medium actions used in these guns are made by Sako in Finland and the long action is the

One of the finest production sporting rifles ever made, the Browning Safari Grade .30/'06, shown here with a Leupold 2 x 7 variable scope in Weaver mounts.

F.N. Supreme by Fabrique Nationale. All of the Sako actions are excellent, but I prefer only the early version of the F.N. which has the long Mauser extractor. The wood and workmanship on these guns is likewise flawless and every one I have shot has been exceptionally accurate. In my opinion, there is no finer production rifle on the market.

Sako

Of the commercial bolt actions currently manufactured or imported into this country, the Sako and Husqvarna are my first choices. Both are modified Mauser-type actions and both have excellent wood — though it is not as good as one generally finds in the Brownings. The short Sako

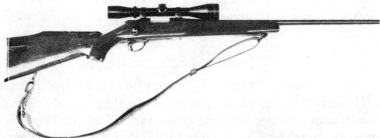

Bad medicine for pests, predators — or snipers: Sako's superb .223 (5.56mm.) bolt action sporter with a Leupold 3 x 9x in Sako rings. This one shoots ½ minute of angle groups with factory ammo.

A top choice for any survival battery: the short action Sako .308 sporter, Leupold 2 x 7 variable scope, Whelen sling in QD swivels.

action, designed for cartridges in the .222-.223 class, is the finest of its kind ever designed, in my opinion. Heavy barrels for added accuracy are available in some calibers and all of these rifles are so constructed that bases for the scope mounts are unnecessary. Sako makes excellent rings of three different heights which fit in a tapered dovetail on the receiver.

The Sako trigger, which is adjustable both for weight of pull and overtravel, is one of the very best ever used in a commercial rifle. The mechanism also incorporates a sliding tang safety which locks the bolt and trigger. Some of the other Sako features which I particularly like are the extremely fast lock time, the one-piece firing pin, and the bolt guide rim. The materials used throughout these rifles, as well as the workmanship, are as good as you will find. My only criticisms are of the extractor and ejector in the latest models; I believe that the older, one-piece spring

This classic full-length stocked Sako .243 mounting a 3 x 9 Leupold variable is deadly on small vermin to 300 yards and, with heavy bullets, is adequate for deer and black bear. Recoil is so light that even a youngster can handle it easily.

Now discontinued, this full-length stocked .222 Rem. by Sako is one of the most desirable rifles of its kind ever made. Shown here with a Leupold 3 x 9 variable.

extractor is better and I would like to see an ejector used that did not require a slot to be cut into the locking lug. Unless the stock is a seriously poor fit, I can think of no reason why a Sako would not admirably satisfy your needs for a bolt action rifle. It is presently available in the following calibers: .222, .223, .243, .270, .308, .30/'06, 7mm. Rem. Mag., .300 Win. Mag., .338 Win. Mag., .375 H&H.

Husqvarna (Carl Gustav)

This fine rifle, made in Sweden, has changed importers several times and has been known under both the name Husqvarna (meaning "handmade") and Carl Gustav. I believe that the latter is the current designation, but some fine bargains may be found among new rifles still on dealers' shelves bearing the earlier name. I have found nothing on the market with a smoother operating bolt

This Swedish built, Mauser-type bolt action is one of the world's finest, whether it goes under the name of "Husqvarna" or "Carl Gustav." The model shown here carries a Bushnell "Lite-Sight," which projects a pinpoint of light at the intersection of the cross hairs to allow accurate shooting under otherwise impossible circumstances.

106

A long range hunting rifle with few peers: pre-1964 Super Grade Winchester Model 70 .270 Win. with Redfield 3 x 9 variable in Redfield Jr. mounts and military style sling. A Canjar custom trigger has been installed by King's Gun Works.

action than this one and it is extremely rugged as well. The trigger mechanism, although very good, is not quite up to that on the Sako, but I like the ejector and extractor better. In fact, these two parts are more easily replaced by a layman in a design of this type than in any other with which I am familiar — a useful feature on a survival rifle. The firing mechanism is also easily removed and replaced because the bolt sleeve completely covers the cocking piece and it is made with a long stem which fits inside the body of the bolt, retained by an inside groove which fits over a lug at the end of the bolt body.

Because of the non-binding guide rails which make this action so smooth even when a long bolt throw is required, I think I would choose the Husqvarna over any other for cartridges of the .30/'06 and .270 length, while I would prefer the Sako for the .243-.308 family and the .222-.223 group. For the utmost in performance, you might want to install a custom trigger, such as the Canjar, in this rifle. The calibers currently available are: .22/250, .243, .25/'06, 6.5x55 Swedish, .270, .308, .30/'06.

Winchester Model 70

When it was introduced in the late 1930's the Model 70 was an instant success and it remained the top quality American bolt action until 1964 (up to serial number 700,000). At that time a number of changes were made in the action which made it easier to manufacture and the stock design was changed greatly. Pre-1964 70's usually bring a premium over current models — with justification, I think. The rifles being produced now, however, are substantially better than those which appeared between 1964 and 1968 (serial numbers 700,000 to 866,000) and they are serviceable, popular and easy to find.

One thing which has not changed with the transition from the pre-'64 to the current models is the trigger mechanism, and that is fortunate because it is excellent. Indeed, it is very likely the best to be found in a bolt action rifle of current U.S. manufacture. Because of the way in which the sear-cocking piece leverage is arranged, an extremely light, short let-off can be achieved which is completely safe.

In short, the pre-'64 is one of the finest rifles ever commercially manufactured and its action is one of the best to use in building a custom rifle; the current model is adequate, and if you want an American made bolt gun, it is probably your best choice, all things considered. Personally, I would prefer to pay a premium for the older model in like new condition. Calibers: .222, .22/250, .243, .25-'06, .270, .308, .30/'06, .375 H&H, .458 Win.

Remington 700

This is a strong competitor to the Model 70 Winchester, both in popularity and quality. It has an extraordinarily strong action and a fairly well designed stock. In fact, if it were not for the extractor mechanism which takes an inadequate bite on the case rim and often fails to remove the fired cartridge, I would probably rate it slightly ahead of the Winchester.

The trigger mechanism is quite complicated and not as good as that on the Model 70, but it seems rugged and several gunsmiths report that it seldom requires repairs.

Remington's finest bolt action, the Model 700 BDL shown in the Magnum version, cal. .375 H&H Magnum. A good receiver sight, a 3x scope and a sling are all that is needed to make it survival ready.

The few of these guns I have fired have all been more accurate than one expects of a mass produced rifle nowadays. One further advantage is that the 700's are often seen at sale prices substantially below list. The factory offers chamberings in the following calibers: .222, .22/250, 6mm., .243, .25/'06, .270, .308, .30/'06, .375 H&H. Two basic models are available, the 700 ADL and the 700 BDL: the latter is much to be preferred.

Remington 600

This is a much less expensive offshoot of the 700, in carbine form, which has recently been discontinued. Quite a few of these guns can still be found in new condition at prices in the neighborhood of a hundred dollars. Despite the fact that they have a curious and awkward bolt release and are without a hinged floorplate, I like these little, un-

Power in a small package. This Remington 600 in .308 Win. is one of the soundest small carbines ever built in the U.S. It carries a Weaver 3x scope in Jaeger quick detachable mounts.

pretentious guns quite a lot. Their actions are very strong and with their 20″ carbine barrels they are handy. If your main rifle is a .30/'06 or a .270 but your defense weapon is a .308 (as it probably will be) and you need an inexpensive but sound working gun in that caliber, the 600 is one to consider. Mine has a Weaver K-3 in quick detachable side mounts so that either the scope or open sights can be elected at a moment's notice, and I find myself reaching for it more often than some of my "better" rifles. In .243 Winchester, this would make an excellent first centerfire for a youngster. It was also chambered, I think, for the .222 Remington. An earlier version with an often sagging ventilated rib of "structural nylon" (whatever that means) was made in several additional calibers including a masochist's special in .350 Magnum, which weighed less than 7 pounds.

Ruger Model 77

For my taste and shooting style, this rifle has the very best stock design of any rifle in current U.S. manufacture, and it is provided with an easy to maintain oil finish. The action is a revolutionary design by the prolific firearms genius, Bill Ruger, who has given us the Blackhawk single action revolver, the Mini-14, and some of the finest .22 rimfire rifles and handguns in the world. Essentially the M77 has an extremely modified Mauser-type action with the bolt turned upside down, although its appearance is

Another example of Bill Ruger's fertile genius, this Model 77 has classic lines and, possibly, the most practical stock design of any commercial bolt action rifle made today. It is available in virtually any caliber you care to name.

quite conventional — even classic.

One of the Ruger's most significant departures from tradition is that the receiver is made from an investment casting instead of being machined from solid steel. The casting is of the finest steel for the purpose, AISI 4140 chrome molybdenum, and I have never heard any reports of weakness in this action; but I prefer machining. There is also quite often some roughness from the mold which is not removed before the guns are released for sale. Another drawback to the 77 is that some of the safeties I have seen are rather rough and hard to move.

Despite these negatives, I have never fired a Ruger Model 77 which did not shoot extremely well. In fact, my experience has been that more of these rifles will shoot into a minute of angle just as they come from the box than any other production rifle I have ever tested. That performance is probably due in no small measure to a patented Ruger feature: the angled front guard screw which pulls the receiver back and down into the stock, bringing the recoil lug into the closest possible contact with the stock.

The trigger mechanism is a good one, fully adjustable from the outside for both weight of pull and overtravel, and on every gun I have examined, it seems to have been carefully set at the factory. The single feature which I most appreciate in the Ruger is the long Mauser-type extractor, although I am fond of several others as well, such as the buffered bolt stop, the gas escape mechanism and the integral scope bases — complete with a set of scope rings.

This rifle has been made for so many calibers — including limited runs of some not readily available elsewhere such as the .257 Roberts, 7x57 Mauser, .358 Winchester and .220 Swift — that I cannot keep track of them all, but certainly all of the standard chamberings are available.

If the cast receiver doesn't bother you, the Ruger M77 is an exceptional value.

In addition to the models described in some detail above, there are several other bolt action rifles on the market which look as if they are worth investigating for survival use, but which have been very difficult to find for testing and evaluation. Among them are the H&R Model 301 Ultra Carbine, which is built on the fine Sako action. It is the only full-length stocked big game rifle currently advertised, and if it is well made, it should be very useful in .308, although I would question its desirability in calibers such as the .270, 7mm. Remington Magnum and .300 Winchester Magnum — all of which need more than its 20″ of barrel to perform well. Another gun which intrigues me, but which I have not fired, is the Ithaca LSA. This is a handsome and quite small rifle made in Finland, and if it is good, it should make an ideal .243 working gun.

Lever Actions

Sako Finnwolf

Unfortunately, I have not had extensive experience with this rifle, although I have fired two examples of it; therefore, I cannot offer anything like an authoritative evaluation. It is included in these listings, however, because it is the only lever action presently available which offers a one-piece stock and a gear driven rotary bolt mechanism — both of which should greatly contribute to accuracy. The Finnwolf has a 23″ barrel, weighs nominally 6 3/4 pounds and is chambered for the .308 and .243 only. It is expensive, as lever actions go.

Savage 99E

This is one of the oldest designs still in production and one of the best. It is much stronger than most levers and it can therefore be chambered for a more useful range of cartridges. Its rotary magazine treats soft nose bullets well

Four reasons why the .30-30 refuses to die. Whatever their theoretical shortcomings, these flat little lever actions are handy to carry and easy to use. More important, they continue to put venison on the table year after year. From left to right: a Marlin 336C, Marlin Marauder, pre '64, Winchester 94 and a similar model shortened and modified by King's Gun Works.

The Savage 99 is one of the oldest, yet one of the most satisfactory of all lever action designs. Its flat receiver houses a rotary magazine and its shotgun type slide safety falls naturally under the thumb.

so that they are not battered by recoil, and since the bullet noses do not rest on the primers of the next round as they do in the tubular designs, efficient, velocity retaining spitzers may be used.

The cartridge lockup is tighter in the 99 than in most other lever actions, hence there is less cartridge stretching, and all of the examples I have fired have had good hunting accuracy despite their two-piece stocks. The Model 99A, which is a straight grip short carbine, is very handy in a saddle scabbard or in the brush. Calibers: 99A-.243, .250/3000, .308. Other models are also chambered for the .300 Savage.

Winchester 94 and Marlin 336

These are the guns which most people think of when you say "lever action." Both are short, handy, flat little carbines chambered for cartridges in the .30- 30 class. If you buy one, you might as well make it as compact as possible by shortening it to the minimum legal barrel length of 16", since the .30- 30 is neither a high velocity nor a long range cartridge.

Of the two, I much prefer the Marlin, which ejects its empty brass to the side instead of out the top as the Winchester does. Either gun should be fitted with a good aperture sight, since a scope is not really needed for the useful range of the cartridge — unless your eyes demand an optical sight.

If you want to scope your .30-30, choose the Marlin (above). It ejects its empty brass to the side instead of straight up as the Winchester (below) does.

More than five million of these little guns have been manufactured since they were introduced in the late 1800's, and most of that unprecedented popularity is based simply on their convenience. They are not particularly accurate or powerful, but they are all you need for deer at short ranges. You will need to full-length resize the cases from these guns for reloading, because there will be some stretching, although there seems to be less in the Marlin than the Winchester.

Semi-Automatics

There are two classes of rifles to be considered in this category: working guns and battle weapons. While there are numerous differences between the two, the principal ones concern the limited magazine capacity of the former — usually no more than five rounds — and its much lighter, less rugged construction. Autoloading hunting rifles are simply not designed to withstand continuous rapid fire or the kind of abuse which a fighting weapon must be subjected to on occasion. This is not a flaw in the design of hunting autos — they would not be as suitable for hunting if they were built like assault rifles — but it does strongly indicate that they should not be expected to fulfill both functions.

At the risk of being thought an alarmist, I must point out that if we have a serious social breakdown in this country, there could be mass desertion by the armed forces and police, together with widespread looting of military bases, National Guard and police arsenals. Logically, the large number of sophisticated and highly efficient fighting weapons which they contain will end up in the hands of looters. You may, therefore, one day find yourself being attacked by determined adversaries armed with automatic weapons, grenades, mortars, tear gas and even flame throwers. In such an event, the very best defensive weapons you can have will be none too good. You will

Three of the best modern assault rifles. Top to bottom: Beretta M-59, SIG AMT, Ruger Mini-14.

simply have to weigh the likelihood of that possibility against the rather considerable expense of acquiring an efficient, highly specialized weapon, the sole purpose of which is to protect your life under extremely demanding circumstances.

Above all other considerations, the rifles which you choose for this purpose must provide reliable firepower: the ability to deliver disabling hits rapidly at reasonably long distances, without significant interruption. No easily portable weapon satisfies these requirements as well as the modern assault rifle and, fortunately, there are several of these available. By "available" I do not mean that they are usually stocked in the local hardware store. You will have to do some searching to find them, but they do exist, and all of those discussed here are legal for civilian ownership in their semi-automatic only versions — despite the fish-eyes and chin-stroking which you may encounter in some gun shops when you ask to see one. If you can't find what you want locally, look through copies of *Shotgun News* or *Gun Week*. Thanks to the Gun Control Act of 1968 you will not be able to order directly from the advertisers in these publications, but your local dealer can — usually for a nominal fee.

Outside the Communist Bloc, the two cartridges for which most assault rifles are chambered are the 7.62 NATO (.308 Winchester) and the 5.56mm. (.223 Remington). Each in its way is as good a round as one could ask for the purpose, but the two are in no way comparable. The 7.62 — a .30 caliber — will penetrate most body armor, substantial barricades, automobiles and dense cover. An expert marksman can deliver a disabling hit with it to 800 or even 1000 yards, and an average shot can stay within the confines of a man-sized silhouette to perhaps 400. The ammunition and the rifles to fire it are bulkier and more expensive than their 5.56 counterparts,

117

but if I could only have one assault rifle, it would be chambered for the 7.62.

There is a trend among the military of many nations, our own included, toward the lighter calibers, primarily, I think, because they are easier to learn to shoot and require less training. That should not be a factor for private individuals who want to stay alive as long as possible, but there is, nevertheless, a place in personal survival batteries for the 5.56mm. In family groups it may not be necessary or even possible for every member to be armed with the heavier weapons. The lack of recoil in the 5.56 suits it well for youngsters, adults of small stature, the elderly or handicapped; and within its range limitations, it is very effective. Barriers and certain types of body armor may withstand it, however, and despite the fact that it will penetrate both sides of a steel army helmet at 400 yards, it does not deliver sufficient shock for reliable stopping power beyond 250 or 300 yards. Assess your own circumstances and retreat plans, then make your own determination of how these two levels of power will best suit your needs.

In 7.62, almost any of the better *sturmgewehre* is acceptable. I personally favor the BM-59, closely followed by the SIG-AMT and the FAL, with the CETME as an outside possibility. Perhaps the cheapest way to acquire a usable fighting gun, if you have an M1 Garand that you bought before they became unreasonably priced, is to have that very reliable weapon modified. The BM-59, made by Beretta in Italy, is based on the Garand action and I am told that there is a source of supply in the U.S. for the parts necessary to make the conversion. Otherwise, a good gunsmith can rechamber the Garand to .308, shortening its barrel from 24″ to 20″ in the process. A 20 round capacity magazine of the M-14 type can then be fitted, replacing the eight round *en block* clip loading. Even without modification, the Garand is a better battle rifle than anything other than the very best modern assault rifle. Its chief flaws are that it is heavy — almost 10 pounds — a little clumsy because of its length, and its firepower is handicapped by an internal magazine. The 7.62, or .308, is a better cartridge for auto actions than the .30/'06 for which the Garand is chambered because it is shorter and it has a thicker, sturdier rim for more positive ejection. Nevertheless, the Garand will do — preferably modified.

BM-59

Of the current crop of assault rifles in 7.62, my choice is the BM-59, partly because I trust the Garand action on which it is based, but also because it is extremely accurate and it handles almost as well as the little G.I. Carbine of World War II. Its kinship to the M1 also makes parts cheap and easy to come by. Mine weighs just under 8 pounds and, with its gas operation and muzzle brake, the recoil is not at all strenuous. It is very stable in aimed rapid fire. It will accept, among others, 20 round magazines and it may also be fed from stripper clips.

The workmanship by Beretta on these rifles is absolutely first class in every respect, and mine is one of the few military rifles I have ever fired that will feed commercial soft nosed hunting ammunition flawlessly without some gunsmithing. I am told that there are a number of these guns on the market, not made by Beretta, which have either investment cast receivers or receivers made by

The author's choice of a heavy battle rifle, the BM-59. Twenty round magazine in place.

welding together pieces that were cut up for scrap. Although I have not personally examined any of these, I would be very wary of buying one. Unfortunately, the genuine Beretta conversions are almost impossible to come by and your only chance will probably be in the used market. Prices at this writing range from about $550 to a high of $750 for a gun in excellent to mint condition.

SIG-AMT

Although many of the parts are stamped, the SIG is a first class assault rifle, and it is very well finished, as its Swiss origin might imply. Like the BM-59, it is one of the few modern battle rifles which still employs a wooden stock. The forearm incorporates an ingenious folding bipod, and there is an auxiliary trigger which unfolds for cold weather use when heavy gloves are worn. U.S. import models come with 20 round detachable magazines which are more than usually sturdy. The recoil is only about nine foot pounds — the least of any .308 assault rifle I have tested. Current U.S. prices for rifles in new condition are just under $600.

The light recoiling SIG AMT 7.62 NATO assault rifle resting on its integral bipod.

FAL

The FAL (Fusil Automatique Legere — light automatic rifle) is made by Fabrique Nationale of Belgium and it is probably the most widely distributed of all the assault rifles outside the Communist Bloc. According to W.H.B. Smith's authoritative *Small Arms of the World*, 10th edition, "It is currently used in Argentina, Austria, Australia, Belgium, Brazil, Burundi, Cambodia, Canada, Chile, Congo, Cuba, the Dominican Republic, Ecuador, India, Indonesia, Ireland, Israel, Kuwait, Liberia, Libya, Luxembourg, Morocco, Mozambique, Muscat and Oman, New Zealand, Paraguay, Peru, Portugal, Qatar, Ruanda, South Africa, Syria, Thailand, the United Kingdom (Britain) and Venezuela." If your retreat plans call for migration, this might be the weapon of choice because of parts availability throughout the world. It is gas operated, fed from detachable 20 round magazines, and it is easily field stripped without tools for cleaning and simple repairs. Despite its folding carrying handle, a scope can be mounted quite low on the side — if you like optical sights on battle rifles. Like the SIG, the FAL is simply constructed using stamped parts almost entirely; however, it is not as well finished as the SIG. The FAL points better than most for instinct shooting, but I like it less for the more effective deliberate aimed fire than any other models tested. This gun seems to be imported into the U. S. for the civilian market sporadically in batches, so it may not be consistently available. Currently it is, and the going price for a new one is about $750.

CETME

The CETME (Centro de Estudios Technicos de Materials Especiale) is made in Spain, largely of stampings. Unlike most other assault rifles, it is not gas operated, but based on the delayed blowback principle. That, and the generally lower level of workmanship on the examples I have examined, cause me to rate it a notch below the others, but still acceptable. One feature that I particularly dislike is the fluted chamber which deeply ridges the empty brass, making it unusable for reloading.[3] Unfortunately, this is an integral part of the design and it cannot be eliminated by gunsmithing.

The CETME also has a built-in folding bipod and 20 round detachable magazines. Prices tend to vary, depending upon your source, but a new or near new CETME goes for between $450 and $550.

5.56mm. (.223)

In open country where its light, .22 caliber high velocity bullet does not have to penetrate dense underbrush, the 5.56mm. can be highly effective, within its range limitations. It is used extensively by SWAT units as well as by the military of a growing number of nations throughout the world. Recoil is practically non-existent, and its trajectory to 300 yards is very flat. Even with rather loosely fitted military weapons, it attains a high degree of accuracy.

Colt AR-15

The most easily available of the 5.56 mm's. is in my opinion the least satisfactory. The Colt AR-15 is the civilian version of the U.S. Military M-16, and all I have ever fired are guilty of the one unpardonable sin in combat rifles: they tend to jam after they have been fired a bit. This design incorporates a tube to feed the gas which func-

---

[3]In order to insure reliable functioning it is better to purchase a large quantity of surplus military 7.62 ammunition than it is to reload for a semi-automatic assault rifle; however, the once fired brass from most of these weapons can be full-length resized and used in a bolt action hunting rifle of the same caliber.

tions the rifle, and a troublesome recoil buffer. Unfortunately, the ball powder with which much 5.56 military and some commercial ammunition is loaded builds up residue very quickly in the chamber area because of the gas feeding tube, and this condition rapidly creates extraction problems. Although this rifle is widely used by SWAT units, where it is — I presume — immaculately maintained, I cannot recommend it for inclusion in a survival battery.

Armalite AR-180

Armalite, who designed the M-16, apparently recognized its shortcomings, and they subsequently developed the AR-18 and its civilian counterpart, the AR-180, both of which incorporate an operating rod which precludes the deposit of powder residue in the chamber area. I have never experienced a malfunction of any kind during the

Visual proof of the penetration ability of the .223 (5.56mm.) cartridge at long range.

Photo courtesy of Burt Miller

firing of many thousands of rounds with these guns; they are also accurate, rugged, easy to repair and very convenient. The magazines made specifically for them are unusually rugged with strengthened feeding lips, and they seat positively, although surplus military magazines can also be used — with varying results. A spring-loaded firing pin has been employed which prevents inadvertent discharge when a round containing a sensitive primer is chambered.

A very convenient folding stock of glass impregnated nylon is used and there is a manual charging handle which assists in ejecting a stuck case, should one occur. The only problem with the 180 is one of availability. Armalite is presently relocating their manufacturing facility from Japan to England and new rifles will not be available until the end of 1975 or the beginning of 1976. The last price before the guns were temporarily discontinued was about $300 and I expect that they will be priced close to that figure when they become available again.

Photos courtesy of Burt Miller

Two views of the Armalite AR-180. The bottom photo shows it with the stock folded and the one above with the stock fully extended and a sniping scope mounted.

Ruger Mini-14

At a distance, this little rifle greatly resembles the popular G.I. .30 Carbine, but the similarity is one of appearance only — the Ruger is a potent fighting weapon. Its action is a finely machined, diminutive version of the rugged Garand, and it field strips quickly and easily without tools into eight basic subassemblies, all of which are large enough not to be easily lost. Only 37 1/4″ overall and weighing less than 6 1/2 pounds, the Mini-14 is made of the best alloys — including heat treated chrome molybdenum — and it employs music wire coil springs throughout for maximum reliability and long life. It is supplied with a flush five round detachable magazine for sporting use, but 20 and 30 shot carriers are being manufactured.

The original front sight was apparently identical to that on the Ruger 10/22 and it was changed because it was too fragile. It should be changed again, because the present sloping ramp looks like an afterthought and it certainly is not the most visible design I can think of. My only other criticism is that it is somewhat muzzle light, but then the Ruger is a true carbine and perhaps it should not be directly compared to much heavier assault rifles. If you also own or plan to acquire a 7.62, the Ruger would make the very finest sort of lightweight, compact companion; and it is also more than a makeshift small game, predator and pest rifle, although I think mounting a scope on it for that purpose would detract from its handiness.

Look again. This is *not* a G.I. Carbine but the efficient new Ruger Mini-14 in .223 (5.56mm.).

The only serious problem with the Ruger Mini-14 is finding one to buy. There are a very few around on the open market, and those usually bring scalper's prices of $400 or more. It is the factory's official position, at present, to make them available only to military and police buyers. Bill Ruger is one of the most highly respected men in the firearms business and I am sure that he has his reasons for this policy; but I find it somewhat puzzling, nevertheless, that efficient defensive firearms such as this one, which are completely legal for civilian ownership, should not be made available to the potential victims of the mounting crime rate in this country.* An effectively armed citizen is a much more efficient deterrent to crime than any gun control law ever written in that he is apt to make a much more severely lasting impression on a lawbreaker than any law is. Now that we are beginning to have full-fledged strikes by the police, as in San Francisco in August of 1975, perhaps some of the factories will reconsider the matter of making efficient tools available to the private citizen who may soon, more than ever before, need to provide his own defense.

Both Valmet of Finland and Heckler and Koch of Germany produce assault rifles in 5.56mm. which I have not yet had the opportunity of testing. The Valmet appears to be a near copy of the Soviet AK-47, and it is also made in the Russian 7.62x39mm.

Working Autoloaders

Turning to working rifles with autoloading mechanisms, I can find only three in current production: the Browning BAR, the Remington Model 742 Woodsman and the H&R Ultra M360. I am not sufficiently familiar with the H&R to comment on it, but both the Remington and Browning warrant consideration if you have a need in your survival battery for a hunting auto.

*The Mini 14 was released for public sale in 1976.

As the Model 740, the Remington was the first success-ful high power autoloading sporting rifle in the U.S. With a few improvements, it was renamed the Model 742 in 1960. It is gas operated, has a two-piece stock and appears reliable in my limited experience with it. It is available in .243, .280, .308, and .30/'06 calibers with either 20 or 22 inch barrels.

The Browning BAR, manufactured to Browning speci-fications by Fabrique Nationale in Belgium, has the dis-tinction of being the only autoloading rifle in the world designed to handle the belted Magnum cartridges. In addition to the standard calibers, .243, .308, and .30/'06, it can be had in either 7mm. Remington Magnum or .338 Winchester Magnum, and the recoil reduction from the gas operated mechanism is amazing — the .338 feels about the same as a .30/'06 in an eight pound bolt action.

The Browning has a very strong lockup although it is still fairly hard on its brass. The hinged magazine is an excellent feature which makes reloading in cold weather with gloves on virtually fumble proof. This is an accurate rifle, particularly for an auto, it has a good trigger and it scopes easily. Of all the working semi-automatic rifles, it is my first choice.

When fast follow-up shots are needed, nothing else quite matches a good autoloader, and this Browning BAR offers gas operation and sub-stantial recoil reduction in the bargain. Side ejection allows low scope mounting.

Automatic Weapons

It should be clear from the foregoing that I consider semi-automatic rifles less than ideal for most working uses, but essential for personal defense. If this were a lecture instead of a book, someone would probably rise at this point to ask whether fully automatic weapons — "machine guns" — wouldn't be the best of all for defensive use.

Aside from the fact that they are, for all practical purposes, prohibited by law from most civilian ownership, hand-held fully automatic weapons are almost always less effective in a combat situation than guns which can provide aimed semi-automatic rapid fire, even in expert hands. Fully automatic portable arms are extremely difficult for most people to use efficiently. They are very wasteful of ammunition — an especially serious drawback in survival use; they lead to poor shooting habits and a false sense of confidence. Firepower is hitting what you aim at, not peppering the landscape with near misses. For these reasons, even if you have legal access to them, I strongly recommend against hand-held fully automatic weapons for any survival use.

Sighting In

Because of the influence of gravity, all projectiles — including bullets — describe an arc when they are propelled. When a bullet is fired, for example, it leaves the barrel below the line of sight, crosses that line, rises to a point above it — called the maximum ordinate or mid-range trajectory — begins to descend, crosses the line of sight again, and finally falls to earth. To the degree that the arc of a bullet is shallow, that is, to the degree that it rises very little above the line of sight, it is said to have a flat trajectory.

The primary ballistic influences on this arc or trajectory are the velocity, sectional density and ballistic coefficient of the bullet — factors having to do with the length, weight, diameter and design of the projectile. Simply put, short, heavy bullets at low velocity have very pronounced trajectories and long, slender bullets driven at high velocities shoot flatter. The practical value of this information has to do with the most basic function of shooting: hitting what you aim at.

Since your line of sight — which is a straight line — does not coincide with the curved flight of your bullet, there are only two distances at which where you aim and where you hit will be exactly the same: the first, when the bullet crosses the line of sight rising, and the second, when it crosses it falling. The rest of the time, your bullet will be either above or below your point of aim. In order to take maximum advantage of the trajectory of any given cartridge, the rifle must have its sights adjusted in such a way that the maximum point blank range will be achieved, so that shots may be taken at a variety of distances without the necessity of aiming above or below the target.

Now the length of your point blank range will vary depending upon the cartridge you use as well as the kind of target you are shooting at. For example, if you sight in a .308 Winchester so that the 180gr. bullet will strike the point of aim at 250 yards, it will be approximately 3.5″ high at 125 yards and 4.5″ low at 300 yards. If you were shooting at a deer-sized target, you could simply forget about trajectory and aim where you wanted to hit, knowing that your bullet would strike close enough to your aiming point, from 0 to 300 yards, to put venison on the table — assuming good marksmanship. If your target were a woodchuck, however, whose vital area was not more than two inches in diameter, you would either have to accept a much smaller point blank range or go to a cartridge which would provide a flatter trajectory.

As a rule of thumb, if you sight in so that your bullet strikes the point of aim at 25 yards, your rifle will be adjusted to provide the maximum usable point blank range

Cartridge	Bullet Weight and Style	Suggested Short Range Sighting-In Point (yds.)	Point of Impact at Various Ranges (in yards)										Velocity (EPS) at Various Ranges (in yards)						Energy (Foot Pounds) at Various Ranges (in yards)					
			50	75	100	125	150	200	250	300	400	500	Muzzle	100	200	300	400	500	Muzzle	100	200	300	400	500
.22 Hornet	45gr. PSP	29.0		+1.5			⊕						2690	2030	1510	1150			720	410	230	130		
.222 Rem.	50gr. PSP	30.0			+2.0			⊕	-3.5				3200	2660	2170	1750			1140	785	520	340		
.223 Rem.	55gr. PSP	30.0			+1.6				⊕	-3.0			3300	2800	2340	1930			1330	955	670	455		
.243 Win.	75gr. PSP	30.0				+2.5			⊕	-3.0	-15.5	-36.5	3500	3070	2660	2290	1960	1670	2040	1570	1180	875	640	465
.243 Win.	100gr. PSP	27.5				+3.0			⊕	-3.5	-16.5	-35.5	3070	2790	2540	2320	2120	1940	2090	1730	1430	1190	995	835
.270	130gr. PSP	27.5					+3.0		⊕	-4.0	-16.0	-35.5	3140	2850	2580	2320	2090	1860	2840	2340	1920	1550	1260	1000
7x57 mm.	139gr. PSP	27.0				+4.0			⊕	-4.5	-18.5	-41.0	2800	2500	2240	1990	1770	1580	2420	1930	1550	1220	975	770
7mm Rem. Mag.	175gr. PSP	25.0				+3.5			⊕	-4.0	-18.0	-43.0	3070	2720	2400	2120	1870	1640	3660	2870	2240	1750	1360	1040
30-30 Win.	170gr. Fl.pt.	23.0			+1.5		⊕	-4.5					2220	1890	1630	1410			1860	1350	1000	750		
.30/06	150gr. PSP	25.0				+3.5			⊕	-4.0	-17.5	-41.0	2970	2670	2400	2130	1890	1670	2930	2370	1920	1510	1190	930
.30/06	180gr. Ptd.	20.0				+4.0			⊕	-4.5	-21.5	-48.5	2700	2470	2250	2040	1850	1670	2910	2440	2020	1660	1370	1070
.30/06	220gr. RN	21.0			+3.0			⊕	-5.5		-41.0		2410	2120	1870	1670	1480		2830	2190	1710	1360	1070	
.308 Win.	150gr. PSP	25.0				+3.5			⊕	-4.5	-20.0	-47.5	2860	2570	2300	2050	1810	1590	2730	2200	1760	1400	1090	840
.308	180gr. PSP	22.0				+4.5			⊕	-5.0	-21.5	-51.5	2610	2390	2170	1970	1780	1600	2720	2280	1870	1540	1260	1010
.308	200gr. RN	22.0			+3.0			⊕	-5.0	-12.0	-35.0	-48.5	2450	2210	1980	1770	1580	1410	2670	2170	1750	1400	1110	875

⊕ = suggested optimal range for zero

+ = inches high   − = inches low

PSP = pointed soft point
RN = round nose
Fl.pt. = flat point
Pt. = pointed

— with cartridges of the .30/'06 class, about 300 yards. The following chart will give you the optimal ranges at which to zero various cartridges as well as the approximate distance at which the bullets first cross the line of sight. You will save a great deal of ammunition if you do your initial shooting at the closer "short range sighting in point," but do not fail to verify that you are also on at the suggested optimal range. Individual rifles and loads all differ slightly, so the figures in the chart can only be approximate.

All of the ammunition manufacturers will provide, on request, free ballistic tables for the calibers which they load, and you will find composites in such general reference books as the *Gun Digest* and the *Shooter's Bible*. For further information on various aspects of working rifles, I highly recommend Jack O'Connor's definitive book, *The Hunting Rifle*. There is nothing readily available of any great value on battle rifles, so far as I know, but you can find pictures, descriptions and takedown instructions for most of them in W.H.B. Smith's *Small Arms of the World*.

Your rifles, both working and defensive, will probably be your most needed firearms, and possibly the most needed tools of any kind under circumstances of long term self-sufficient living — whether or not we have a social crisis in this country. I hope you will bear that fact in mind as you select them. The difference in price between a "bargain" model and the best is usually no more than the cost of a meal for two in a good restaurant and, perhaps, a pair of theater tickets.

4 Shotguns

Virtually every household in America has some sort of firearm about — unless local laws prevent it or the householders are complete hoplophobes — and more often than not, that gun is a shotgun. Most adult males in this country have fired one at some time or other and one young man of my acquaintance who holds himself out as a "survival consultant" believes the shotgun to be the mythical "ideal" survival weapon.

Yet, shooting at birds on the wing is an inefficient method of obtaining food under survival conditions, in terms of the weight and bulk of ammunition expended per ounce of meat obtained, and skeet or trap seems an unlikely retreat activity. Surely small game can be trapped or taken with rimfires or air guns as can sitting birds. Shotguns are bulky and a reasonable amount of ammunition for them occupies a great deal of storage space. For either hunting or defense their range is limited to about 50 yards; they are incapable of the sustained rapid fire necessary in most combat situations because their magazine capacities are limited and they are comparatively slow to reload. What, then, is the role of the shotgun in survival planning?

It is true that the practical uses of the shotgun for food gathering are highly specialized and, some might even say, rather limited; nevertheless, those functions could be critical under some circumstances, and no one with battle experience can deny the conclusive supremacy of the shotgun in a close quarters fight. Although there is no weapon made for hand-held use which will instantly stop a determined opponent 100% of the time with a single hit, a 12 gauge shotgun loaded with buckshot shells comes closer than anything else, at 25 yards or less. Also, don't overlook the psychological value of the shotgun: nothing else is as intimidating. Simply having one may, on occasion, preclude the necessity of shooting, since that gaping 12 gauge muzzle makes a very persuasive, if taciturn, argument against aggression.

Loaded with the best rifled slugs, shotguns make better hunting weapons in dense cover than anything else, assuming that most shots will be taken at 75 yards or less — as they usually are in deep woods. With the same ammunition, they are suitable for defense against dangerous game, even the largest bears. Some authorities maintain that slugs lack the necessary penetration for sure results and that is probably true at distances over 50 yards, but the Brenneke 12 gauge version has accounted for several grizzlies and more than one Cape buffalo to my certain knowledge — all at less than 40 yards. Unlike men, animals only become a threat at close range, and the sharp shouldered, 471 gr., .70 caliber, 12 gauge Brenneke slug traveling at 1600+fps. delivers a blow like the hammer of

Thor at short distances. For most people, in fact, such a slug-loaded shotgun is probably a better choice for the purpose than a heavy magnum rifle because its recoil is so much easier to handle — and, within charging ranges, it is just about as effective.

Quality that should last a lifetime. Below, a superb matched pair of Pidgeon Grade Browning Superposed shotguns in 12 and 20 ga. Above, disassembled in its English style hard case, a Belgian Francotte side-by-side 12 ga.

If you read some of the articles in the gun magazines, you may be led to believe that head shots on running rabbits at 100 yards with a .22 are routine. They are not. Actually, it is very difficult for the average marksman to hit and anchor a rabbit at 50 yards with a caliber small enough to leave some edible meat, even if the animal cooperates by sitting stock still and posing broadside. Small game running at top speed is a challenge to any rifleman, and the odds of bringing home meat are slim in such situations, unless you use a shotgun. Under survival conditions when game is heavily hunted, you may expect a large percentage of running shots.

Of course, some may argue that small game hunting is not really necessary, and while I agree that taking large animals is more efficient — both in terms of the energy and the ammunition expended — there may be occasions when no large game is to be found within a convenient distance of your retreat; or else you may simply want a change of diet. The latter may not be a critical requirement, but it certainly can make living under restricted circumstances more pleasant. Children, in particular, have been known to refuse all nourishment — even when starving — if their diets have been too monotonous and completely devoid of foods they enjoy for long periods of time. Also, there will probably be days when you simply cannot hit anything except with a shotgun, because of illness or fatigue resulting from being constantly on the alert. If you are desperate for food, no other weapon will provide it as surely. It is the optimal pot shooting gun.

The shotgun also provides the most versatile means of using "scrounged" ammunition. There are devices made to fit into the bore of a shotgun which will enable it to fire virtually any pistol or rifle cartridge as well as any smaller gauge shotgun shell. One of my own 12 gauges is set up to use .22 long rifle, .30-30, .45-70, .38 Special, .45 ACP, 20 gauge, 28 gauge and .410 bore. The chapter on accessories will describe these adapters and their uses in more detail.

In planning for long term self-sufficiency, I tend to regard the shotgun as essentially an emergency weapon or occasional gun rather than an everyday working tool, for the reasons outlined above, but it is no less important just because it may only be needed intermittently. Anyone who has ever tried living off the land for long periods knows that there are occasions when the traps are empty for days on end and all of the deer seem to have vanished. Only an occasional flying bird or a rabbit intent on establishing an Olympic record give evidence that wildlife still exists. Under such circumstances a good shotgun is more valuable than any other tool for providing food. And if the time should ever come when your perimeter defenses are broached and you are suddenly under attack inside your own home, the very best gun to have in your hands is a suitable shotgun.

Since many of the more common uses for the smoothbores, such as skeet, trap, flying waterfowl and upland bird shooting do not concern us in survival planning, choosing the right shotguns and appropriate loads is a much simpler matter than it might appear from an examination of sporting goods catalogs and ammunition charts. For one thing, there are only two sizes or gauges of guns which are suitable for our purposes.

Gauges and Bores

Except for the .410 bore, which is measured in decimals of an inch just as rifle and pistol calibers are, all shotgun ammunition sizes are expressed in terms of gauge. That designation is derived from the number of lead balls of a given gauge or bore diameter needed to weigh a pound. A dozen round lead balls which exactly fit inside the barrel of a 12 gauge gun should weigh a pound, for example, or

20 of a size to fit the 20 gauge. Of the six sizes currently manufactured in the U.S. — 10 ga., 12 ga., 16 ga., 20 ga., 28 ga., and .410 bore, only the 12 and the 20 are both popular and effective enough to be considered for survival planning. The .410, though quite popular, has neither the power nor the range to be practical except in a special purpose weapon such as the shot pistol described elsewhere in this book. The 28 ga. is slightly more effective in pattern but no more powerful and it is neither widely available nor popular. The 16 ga. is actually a fine chambering and extremely well-liked by many sportsmen, but, except in Continental Europe where it is quite common, it is not widely used; and it offers no real advantage over the 12 or the 20. Ten gauge Magnums are strictly for pass shooting at ducks and geese.

For the purposes outlined in this chapter, the 12 is the only gauge you will really need but special circumstances, personal preference, or the desire for a lighter backup gun may lead you to choose the 20. The 12 is more powerful and more versatile than the 20 and it is without question the easiest for which to obtain a wide variety of ammunition. I have included the 20 only because some will prefer it for its lessened recoil or because smaller, lighter guns are made for it, and because some very useful special purpose weapons such as the Savage 24C combination gun employ it. For sporting use, the 20 has a great deal to recommend it; I personally use one and like it enormously under the right circumstances, but for survival use, it must be regarded as simply the best imperfect alternative to the 12.

Both gauges are available in 2 3/4" and 3" lengths. Double-barreled and single-shot guns with 3" chambers accept either length shell without adjustment; repeaters usually will not, although some offer interchangeable barrels in both chamberings. If you are buying a double or a single-shot, you may as well get the long chamber if it is available in the gun of your choice. Some say that shooting the shorter shells in the long chambers causes the shot patterns to open up or even to blow, but I have never seen that contention demonstrated successfully on a pattern board. In any event, the 2 3/4" shells in both gauges are the most readily available and, generally, the most useful, so you should make certain that the gun you buy will handle them, whatever its other virtues. In Britain, a number of curious lengths such as 2" and 2 1/2" are made. If you are buying an imported gun, make certain that it is not chambered for one of these.

When you look through the factory lists of current production loads, you will find — in addition to length — three primary variables: shot size, weight of the shot charge and power, which is often expressed in "drams equivalent." Considering these in reverse order, the term "drams equivalent" refers to the power of a particular loading as it relates to an equivalent charge of black powder or bulk smokeless, measured in drams. It simply means that the load described will give approximately the

Left to right: 2 3/4" 12 ga., 16 ga., 3" 20 ga., 2 3/4" 20 ga., 28 ga., 3" .410 bore, 2 1/2" .410. All are high base loads.

139

same pressure as a black powder charge of that weight. It does not necessarily indicate that the shell is actually loaded with the given weight of powder. This is a somewhat archaic method of expressing the information since the modern smokeless powders now used in loading most shotshells are more efficient and bear no relation in terms of either bulk or weight to the older propellants; however, it is an argot of common acceptance and you will quickly learn the designations. As a reference point, you might take a 3 1/2 drams equivalent load with 1 1/4 oz. of shot to be a well-balanced hunting load in 12 ga. About the lightest 12 ga. load you will find generally useful is the standard trap load of 3 drams equivalent and 1 1/8 oz. of shot. In 20 ga., 2 3/4 drams with 1 oz. of shot is a practical hunting load.

Shotgun shell power is also expressed in other terms such as "field," "express," "high power," "low base" and "high base," as well as "Magnum." Low powered shells with light shot charges intended for small birds at close range are often called low base or field loads. High base or express loads are those with the widest use for hunting, and Magnums are needed only for waterfowl at long range or, conceivably with buckshot, for defense. Incidentally, the "high" and "low" base refers to the distance from the base or head of the case that the brass collar extends upward, providing additional strength to the paper or plastic shell in the more powerful loads. For both defense and the kind of hunting which survival conditions demand, the high base or express loadings will be the most useful, although you might want to include a few trap loads in the 12 ga. for occasional use. The 12 ga. Magnum loads produce such heavy recoil in moderate weight sporting guns that I would not recommend including them in your survival supplies under most circumstances, even for defense. Remember, your scatter-gun hunting will be primarily for small game at relatively close range and you do not want your lunch shot to pieces or unnecessarily studded with tooth-cracking bird shot. In most cases only about four pellets are needed for rabbits, birds or squirrels. If you choose the 20 ga. as your only smoothbore instead of as an auxiliary to your 12, you may benefit from having some of the heavier loads on hand — and the recoil in the smaller gauge is not unbearable with them unless you select an exceptionally light gun. The 3″ Magnum 20 almost duplicates 12 ga. express ballistics. With rifled slugs, there is no choice of power ranges; only one is available in each brand and gauge, and here, the 12 ga. greatly outperforms the 20.

Shot Sizes

During the past 30 years I have read more than a hundred articles discussing the fine points of selecting shot sizes for various kinds of hunting, and during that same period I have fired a few thousand shells under a variety of conditions. Although the factors to be considered are highly complex, so far as sporting uses are concerned, I am firmly convinced that only two sizes need be chosen for survival food gathering and one for defense: #6 and #7 1/2 for hunting and #4 buckshot for personal protection. Add a few boxes of Brenneke rifled slugs for hunting large game in dense cover or for bear insurance and, perhaps, a few #4's if there are wild turkeys in your area, and you will be prepared for almost any eventuality which you might reasonably expect a shotgun to handle under survival conditions. You could probably get by with only the #6's, the buckshot and the slugs without serious inconvenience.

The accompanying chart will give you an idea of the various shot sizes in current manufacture, and, as you can see, there are a large number of them. If you had un-

No.	12	11	10	9	8	7½	6	5	4	2
Actual Size	•	•	•	•	•	•	•	•	•	•
Diameter In Inches	.05	.06	.07	.08	.09	.095	.11	.12	.13	.15

No.	Air Rifle	BB	No. 4 Buck	No. 3 Buck	No. 1 Buck	No. 0 Buck	No. 00
Actual Size	●	●	●	●	●	●	●
Diameter In Inches	.175	.18	.24	.25	.30	.32	.33

limited storage space and planned to do a great deal of wing shooting, you might want to include several sizes in order to match your load as nearly as possible to the game you were hunting, but I do not recommend that practice in planning for survival. Most people do not buy enough ammunition, and their problems are compounded if what they do buy is highly specialized and the circumstances under which they need it are greatly varied. Although #4's may be optimal for ducks or turkeys, and #7 1/2's the best for dove and quail, neither of these extremes will do as well for a variety of uses as #6's, which will take anything from turkeys to rabbits, squirrel, pheasant, dove or quail, if the distance is right.

Almost certainly you will be touted onto #00 buckshot for defensive use, because that is the only size which most stores carry. I hope that you will politely insist that they order a supply of #4 buck for you, since it is decisively superior for the purpose. I am certainly not a leading authority on sport shotgunning but I have done more than my share of experimentation with buckshot and I can state categorically that #00 buck is the least effective size available, despite its popularity. There are only nine pellets in the 2 3/4" 12 ga. high power loading, and 12 in the Magnum; the standard #4 load contains 27. When fired from a cylinder bore or riot gun barrel for maximum dispersion at 7 yards — the statistical average range at which gunfights take place — the pattern spread of #00 is only 4" and it increases to less than 20" at 25 yards. Number 4 averages a 7" spread at 7 yards and just over 30" at 25. Guess which one you have a better chance of hitting with? As far as stopping power is concerned, any 12 ga. buckshot load will deliver within 25 yards. In 20 ga., the only buckshot loading is 20 pellets of #3 and it is certainly adequate for the job at close range.

Another subject on which you are likely to encounter a good deal of misinformation is the rifled slug. Some "experts" will tell you that you can't hit your hat with one at arms length and others insist that slugs group like bench rest rifle bullets at vast distances. My own experience with these huge chunks of lead suggests a position somewhere between those two extremes. First, I have found handloaded slugs very unsatisfactory. Usually the ammunition you can make for yourself — even with moderate skill — is better than you can buy, but both commercial and home cast slugs in my reloads and those of others I have tried have never given adequate results for me. Part of the problem, I think, lies in the skill required to execute precisely the critical roll crimp which holds the slug in place. In fact, the only rifled slug ammunition on the market which I can recommend without reservation is the Brenneke, made in Germany. The slug itself is heavier than any of the domestic varieties I know of (1 oz. vs. 7/8 oz.), and it is driven at a slightly higher velocity. The shape of the projectile is extremely effective both in penetration and in causing tissue damage. Perhaps most important, this ammunition is very uniform and accurate. I have fired 12 and 20 ga.

Brenneke's in at least a dozen guns of each bore size and, given a good gun, the 12 gauge will group in 4" to 6" at 75 yards and the 20 will do as well at 65.

In order to achieve this kind of performance, however, the shotgun itself must be optimal for slug use. For one thing, double-barreled guns are unsuitable; they will not deliver slugs fired from both barrels to the same point of aim, except as a fluke, since they are regulated for shot and not solid projectiles. Second, ordinary shotgun sights are inadequate for use with slugs. You must fit rifle type sights — either open or aperture with both front and rear elements or else a low powered scope, if you expect consistent groups. Finally, the most pronounced influence on slug accuracy appears to be bore diameter. Since the development of chokeboring about one hundred years ago, makers have discovered that choking, or the constriction of the shot pattern, has more to do with the difference between the interior diameter of the barrel and the choke constriction at the muzzle than with the size of the bore itself. Consequently, manufacturers have become rather casual about maintaining absolute uniformity in bore size. For example, the standard 12 ga. bore is supposed to measure .729, but I have found that, from one brand to another or even from one model to another of the same make, actual bore sizes run from .722 to .747. Although this variation poses no problem when using shot, so long as the choke constriction is proper in relation to the actual bore diameter, it is critical so far as accuracy with slugs is concerned. The very best slug barrels are those with minimum dimensions having little or no choke constriction. Guns which offer interchangeable barrels, such as pumps and autos, usually have available "Riot Gun," "Slug" or "Deer" barrels especially designed for use with rifled slugs, and these will ordinarily give you the best results. For some reason which I do not understand, oversized barrels with modified chokes and oversized barrels with variable chokes set to "improved modified" seem to provide the next best level of accuracy. Length variations from 18" to 32" seem to have no substantial effect on either accuracy or velocity.

The proper weight of shot charges is another topic which gun buffs debate endlessly. Obviously, the heavier the charge, the more individual pellets of a given size there are and, hence, the likelier you are to hit your target with enough of them to kill cleanly. On the other hand, the more pellets in the charge, the more apt you are to make hamburger of small game at close range and the more your gun will kick. The best compromises I have found for practical pot shooting — and the loads which I recommend for hunting under survival conditions are:

*12 ga. 2-3/4" high base	#6 shot	1-1/4 oz.
12 ga. 2-3/4" 3 drams equiv.	#7-1/2 shot	1-1/8 oz. (standard "trap")
*20 ga. 3" Magnum	#6 shot	1-1/4 oz. (virtually duplicates 12 ga. high base load)
*20 ga. 2-3/4" high base	#6 shot	1 oz.
20 ga. 2-3/4" high base	#7-1/2 shot	1 oz.

    *most generally useful

Chokes and Patterns

The choke is simply a constriction near the muzzle of a shotgun barrel, the purpose of which is to control the spread of the shot pattern, much as the nozzle on a garden hose determines the concentration of the water spray. The standard choke designations and the percentages of the total shot charge which they are supposed to concentrate in a 30" circle at 40 yards are:

Extra Full (X-Full)	75% +
Full	70 – 75%
Improved Modified	65%
Modified (Half Choke)	55%
Quarter Choke	50%
Improved Cylinder	40 – 45%
Skeet No. 2	50 – 55%
Skeet No. 1	40%
Cylinder (No choke constriction at all)	35%

In this country, we seem to be plagued with the notion that the most is always the best, even in the matter of choosing a shotgun choke and, consequently, most people who know little about smoothbores select the full choke for all-around use — a task for which it is entirely unsuited. The reason we use shotguns in the first place is so that we can have a better chance of hitting difficult, usually moving objects, and it should be obvious that the larger the pattern or pellet spread, the likelier we are to get some shot on the target. Too much dispersion too soon, however, and the pattern becomes so thin that our quarry may escape being hit altogether, particularly if the spread of the pellets is not uniform. The following list will give you an idea of the way in which the main body of the shot charge spreads at various ranges with different degrees of choke.

Choke	20 yds.	30 yds.	40 yds.
Cylinder	32"	44"	58"
Improved Cylinder	26"	38"	51"
Modified	21"	32"	45"
Full	16"	27"	40"

Now compare the size of these patterns with the density by looking at the relative percentages of the shot charge that each choke will deliver in a 30″ circle at several distances.

	Full	Imp. Mod.	Mod.	2 Skeet	Imp. Cyl.	1 Skeet	Cyl.
20 yds.	100%	100%	90%	93%	84%	87%	76%
25 ″	100%	95%	87%	91%	76%	66%	57%
30 ″	90%	85%	80%	81%	62%	59%	44%
35 ″	82%	73%	65%	65%	55%	43%	40%
40 ″	70%	60%	50%	50%	41%	33%	35%

For practical use under survival conditions, I think the smoothbore loaded with shot should be regarded essentially as a 40 yard gun with occasional usefulness to 50 yards. As you can see from the charts, any pattern which is broad enough to hit small, fast moving game regularly at close range begins to be too thin for effectiveness much beyond 40 yards, and patterns which would carry a killing density at 50 or 60 yards are simply too small at short distances and they would leave little but feathers or fur if you were lucky enough to connect.

I recommend, therefore, that you avoid the full choke completely and consider either the improved cylinder or modified for hunting, or else buy a double-barreled gun which gives you both. Another alternative, which we will discuss in more detail at the end of the chapter, is the variable choke.

Since the shotgun begins to lose its awesome stopping power at greater distances, I suggest that you limit its use for defense to no more than 25 yards. At such close range, you want the maximum spread possible, so for that purpose, cylinder bore — no choke at all — should be your choice.

Shotgun Selection

The basic shotgun types are the break-action single-shot, the doubles — including both side-by-side and over-and-under configurations — and repeaters: auto-loaders, pumps and bolt actions. I would suggest that you rule out the bolts because they are not well suited to handling the shotgun shell and all of them are somewhat clumsy — not at all the sort of thing you want for quick, instinctive use.

Double-Barreled Guns

Nothing else will last as long or prove as satisfactory for field use as a well made double. It will digest without damage overloads that would put repeaters out of action and it will fire almost anything which you can stuff into its chambers, including old paper shells swollen from age and moisture as well as imperfectly resized reloads. Whether over-and-under or side-by-side, the double is a very simple mechanism which rarely needs repairs. Basically, it is two complete single-barreled guns welded together, which share a common stock, each with an independent lock or firing mechanism; and it has the further advantage of offering the instant selection of either of two different chokes. It has only two drawbacks as a working gun that I can see: limited magazine capacity — not very important in practical hunting — and expense. A sound double will cost a minimum of $300+ these days and the very best can easily carry a price tag of several thousand.

Although I personally prefer the side-by-side, the over-and-under is currently more popular — especially in the U.S. The claimed advantage of the latter is the single sighting plane; however, the rib on a side-by-side provides that feature to my satisfaction and I like the handling better. The side-by is also less expensive to manufacture

A sound double at an affordable price: the Browning B-SS. This one is a 12 ga. with 28" barrels. A 20 is also available.

and therefore, to purchase, all other factors being equal. Further, it is more convenient to use in cramped places, since the over-and-under must necessarily describe a much greater degree of arc when it is opened to eject and reload the bottom barrel. Real differences between the two are small, however, and I would suggest that you make your choice on the basis of personal taste. Pick the one that feels more natural to you.

In my opinion, doubles are unsuitable for defense under survival conditions, not only because they carry only two shots, but also because those without external hammers

Known variously as "coach guns" or *luparas*, these short barreled doubles have external rebounding hammers and double triggers. The Russian-made Universal Baikal, below, wears a lace-on cheek piece, designed by the author, which conveniently carries spare ammunition. The model shown above is the Rossi.

149

may not be safely maintained in a loaded condition. The firing mechanism is cocked when you open the action of a double for loading. For hunting, however, the double and the break-open single-shot are the safest guns to be had since the action can remain open with shells in the chambers until you are ready to fire.

Short side-by-side doubles with external rebounding hammers — often called *luparas* or "coach guns" are a variation which you may want to examine. Most of those currently available in the U.S. are inexpensive and too crudely made to be considered as a primary hunting weapon. Their two shot limitation also makes them less than ideal for defense in situations where you may expect to be attacked by multiple assailants. They are almost perfect house guns for urban areas now, however, because of their simplicity, and you may want to consider buying one for that purpose with the thought in mind of using it for a spare at the retreat. The two most common brands are the Soviet made Universal Baikal and the Brazilian Rossi. Of the two, the Universal seems sturdier; neither will win beauty contests.

If you have the time and the money, the best way to acquire a double is to have one made to order by one of the best English custom gunsmiths such as Purdy, Boss, Holland & Holland or Westley Richards. You can expect a wait of from 18 months to three years and a cost of from $2500 to $11,000 for plain working guns with little ornamentation. A used model by one of these makers will save you the wait but not much of the cost. If you want the best and if you can find a gun that fits, this is probably your best bet.

Some of these makers offer ready-made guns through selected dealers and they are also excellent. About the cheapest utility double that I can recommend is the Browning B-SS, which sells in mid-1975 for $320. It is well made, sturdy and should last a long time. The only serious objection I have to it is that it employs a single, non-selective trigger. I personally prefer double triggers because they offer a simple, instant choice of barrel and choke combination. Most people like single selective triggers better, and they do offer the same choice but neither as simply nor as instantly, in my opinion. The non-selective single trigger of the Browning offers no choice at all; it always fires the right — more open choked — barrel first. This is not a great handicap, however, since your first shot is usually taken at closer range than your second and I have no hesitation in recommending the gun to clients — so long as they understand the trigger limitation. The B-SS is a side-by-side double and it is available in both 12 and 20 gauges. Barrel lengths are 26", 28" or 30" and the choke combinations are either modified and full or improved cylinder and modified. For survival use, I would choose the 12 ga. with 26" or 28" barrels, bored improved and modified. If you prefer the 20 ga., get the 26" tubes with the same chokes.

For about $100 more than the B-SS you can have the Ithaca 200E Deluxe Grade side-by-side, which boasts a number of highly desirable features. The finish on the barrels is black chrome — much more durable and rust resistant than the customary blue — and the bore interior is hard chromed to reduce leading and to prevent oxidation. A single selective trigger is standard, as are automatic selective ejectors, which throw empty shells clear when the action is opened, without disturbing unfired rounds. I have not had extensive experience with this gun since it is relatively new, so I cannot say how well it holds up under extended use, but it looks good, shoots extremely well and appears to be soundly constructed. The 200E is available in either 12 or 20 gauge. The modified-improved cylinder choke combination in 12 ga. comes with 26" barrels, and in 20 ga. with 25". I like both guns very much. If you pay more for a side-by-side double, you should have one built to order.

If you prefer an over-and-under, the popular standard of comparison in the U.S. is probably the Browning Superposed, made in Belgium to Browning specifications. This is a very superior shotgun in all of its grades, but recently the price has gotten a bit rich, reflecting the decline in value of the dollar on world markets. You can have virtually any gauge, choke combination and barrel length you prefer in any of the three progressively more expensive grades: #1, Diana and Midas. The features and basic quality are the same in all grades, only the engraving and figure of the wood differ. All models have single selective triggers which allow you to choose the firing order of the barrels by simply deflecting the safety to one side or another as you move it to firing position. Selective automatic ejectors are also standard to simplify and hasten reloading. My personal choice among the Superposed models is the Super-Light, which has a straight, instead of a pistol grip stock and weighs but 6 lbs. 6 oz. in 12 ga. and 6 lbs. even in 20. The light 12 does kick but it is a very handy gun to carry with its 26 1/2" barrels and it is quick on the target. As I write this chapter, the least expensive Superposed is $1,100 and the Super-Light is $70 more. Browning is having a less expensive line, called "Citori," made in Japan, but I have not yet had the opportunity to do more than handle these guns. They are priced around $400. Over-and-unders are expensive guns to make and there are no good cheap ones.

If you like the over-under design, the Browning Superposed is certainly as good a shotgun as anyone really *needs* in a survival battery. There is nothing wrong with wanting the very best, however, if you can afford it; you will not survive any more surely just because your gun is plain and

Spartan. If you are willing to spend several thousand dollars to get the finest over-and-under made, I suggest that you give serious consideration to the Perazzi light game model.

All double-barreled shotguns of quality require a great deal of hand fitting. Merely regulating the two barrels so that they both deliver their charges of shot to the same place is expensive and painstaking work. This kind of workmanship usually contributes both to the usefulness and longevity of the product, however, and if a shotgun is important in your battery, you will probably find the double to be worth its cost. Because there are so many fine doubles on the market — many from small makers in England, Belgium, Italy and Spain — it is impossible in a book of this scope to discuss them all. You will usually find that price is a pretty good indicator in doubles, however, and if you pay from $300 to $1500 and buy from a reputable and knowledgeable dealer, you should get value received. I consider the guns discussed above, plus the recently discontinued Belgian Francotte to be among the best buys available, but if you know shotguns well or have an expert adviser, you may be able to find equivalent quality at slightly less cost from some of the small makers.

Break-Action Single-Shots

These guns are probably the best bargains to be had in firearms. Omitting the high grade trap guns which do not concern us here, you can buy any of a half a dozen single-shot models for about $50. There are drawbacks, of course: they are not finely made, they offer but one choke, and, most important, they allow only one shot. Certainly they are unsuitable for defense, and they are a handicap when hunting because of their limited firepower, but they are nonetheless quite practical from several standpoints. They are cheap enough so that you can have several in various gauges hidden in caches near your retreat, "just in case," and most of them "take down" so that they can be tucked away in very little space. They make good spares and the very best beginners guns for youngsters because they are so safe. I use one in 12 ga. for the adapters I mentioned earlier, and I can think of no better goods for barter in a survival situation. One client of mine whose funds were

A close-up of the sturdy, simple break-action design typical of many inexpensive single-shots, open for loading.

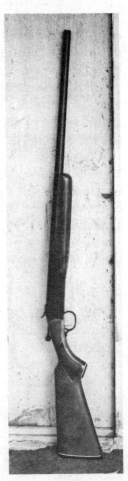

The inexpensive Winchester 37A — a lot of gun for the money and a safe design for novices.

154

quite limited decided to spend the bulk of his shotgun money on a sophisticated High Standard Model 10 for defense and bought a single-shot for all of his hunting — and I did not disagree with his decision. Any farmer will tell you that you can put a lot of meat on the table with one of these inexpensive little guns, and dispatch a few crows and foxes as well; in fact, one nickname for these single scatter guns is "the farmer's friend." You will be surprised how quickly you can learn to reload them by holding spare shells between the fingers of your non-shooting hand.

At one time or another, I have owned examples of all of the makes now on the market and all were satisfactory. I suggest that you buy a model with a visible hammer, however. My first choices would be: the Winchester 37A, the Iver Johnson Champion and the Savage-Stevens Model 94-C in 12 or 20 gauge, with the shortest barrel available and either an improved cylinder or modified choke. You might want to consider putting some inexpensive rifle sights on one of these and using it for slugs. A variable choke will add 50% to the cost of the gun, but it would make it more versatile, particularly if you have no other shotgun. The reliability and sturdiness of these little single-shots belies their modest cost.

Repeaters

Repeaters — autoloaders and pumps — are an American development and their popularity in this country exceeds that of any other shotgun. Although they generally lack the elegance and feel of a good double as well as, perhaps, the ultimate long term durability, they offer a lot for the money, and their firepower is unsurpassed by any other type of smoothbore.

A few years ago, there were only one or two autoloading shotguns which were completely reliable; now there are several. Until the present generation of autos

Note the shorter overall length of the double when compared with a repeater having the same length barrel. On the left, a Browning 2000 autoloader and on the right, a Browning Super-Light over/under. Both are 12 ga.

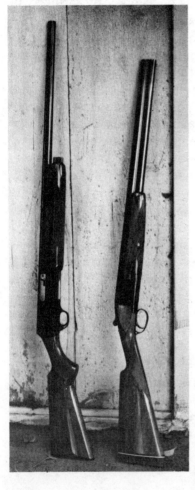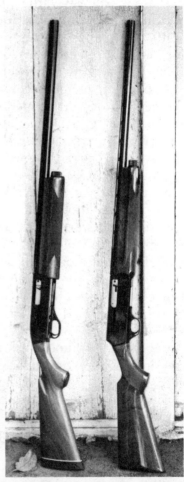

Left: Winchester Super X #1. Right: Browning 2000. Two of the best gas operated autoloading shotguns on the market.

was developed, most advocates of the repeater preferred pumps. The new gas operated semi-automatics, however, add significant recoil reduction to reliability and firepower and they have become practical weapons indeed, particularly for the recoil shy.

One auto in particular is my hands down choice for close range defense — the High Standard Model 10-B 12 ga. gas operated riot gun. This may be the ugliest gun made but in my opinion, it is the most efficient for its intended purpose, as well as the most specialized. One look and you know that it would be virtually useless for hunting. It is equipped with a mounting bracket for a special heavy duty Kel-Lite police flashlight, which serves as a sight in the dark. The shotgun pattern coincides with the beam of the flashlight — an exceptionally useful feature, since the kind of people you may need to defend yourself

Obviously not designed for upland game shooting, this High Standard Model 10B gas operated autoloading riot gun can easily be operated with one hand. It is shown here with the carrying handle raised, the folding slug sight extended and the optional Kel-Lite flashlight installed.

against usually prefer the cover of darkness for their activities; also, you are more likely to be attacked by surpirse within shotgun range in the dark. The overall length of this unconventional looking weapon is only 27 1/4", exceeding the statuatory minimum length by only 1/4", and the barrel, at 18 1/8", is legal with 1/8" to spare. It carries four rounds in its magazine and one in the chamber, but I believe that a good gunsmith could extend the magazine tube forward, even with the muzzle, so that two or three additional shells could be carried, and I intend to have my gun so modified. Operating handles are conveniently placed on both sides of the receiver and there is a handy folding carry handle on top. The gun is also supplied with pop-up rifle sights for use with slugs. Recoil reduction, even with Magnum buckshot loads, is significant and the gun is designed so that it can easily be used one-handed, should the need arise, as it might if you were injured. This last feature alone makes the 10-B the best fighting shotgun available, so far as I am concerned.

If you decide to buy one of these guns, be persistent. They are not easy to find in the average sporting goods store, and many dealers will tell you, erroneously, that they are only available to police and military organizations. Until recently, that was true, but High Standard should be congratulated that it no longer restricts the sale of these efficient weapons. My gun is extremely accurate with slugs and it throws deadly buckshot patterns. I have never experienced a malfunction of any kind with it and none of the clients to whom I have recommended it have reported any difficulties whatsoever. In my opinion, the High Standard Model 10-B is the most efficient close range defense weapon currently available to the private citizen.

Whatever the virtues of the Model 10, it is not a dual purpose gun, and if you want an autoloader that is, you must accept less efficiency in the fighting department.

Nevertheless, there are several guns available which will serve acceptably for both purposes — with accessory barrels and/or some modifications. One of the best of these is the new Browning Model 2000. Available in both 12 and 20 ga., this gas operated auto has a unique loading system which suits it admirably for defensive use. Whether the gun is empty or partially loaded, fresh rounds can be slipped in the loading port of the left side of the receiver without moving the weapon from firing position. Recoil reduction is as good as I have found on any gas operated shotgun and, judging from the overall quality with which the piece is built, its durability should be up to the Browning standard — which is to say, very good indeed. The capacity of the 2000 is five rounds and it does not appear that increasing this capacity would be practical. Like most modern repeaters, the Browning offers interchangeable barrels in various lengths and chokes, with or without ventilated ribs. Presently, there is no riot, deer or slug barrel available, but I am sure that one will be made in the future. In the meantime, you could purchase a plain barrel, have it cut to 18 or 20" and install rifle sights on it. Such an arrangement together with an additional barrel having a rib and a variable choke, measuring about 26" overall, would make an excellent all-around shotgun for the survival battery of those who prefer autoloaders.

If I were buying a new auto for my own use, it would probably be a tossup between the Browning 2000 and the new Winchester Super-X Model 1, although the Browning

A classic, now discontinued: the fine Winchester Model 12 pump in 12 ga.

A selection of fighting shotguns. From left to right: High Standard 7 shot pump, Remington 870 police riot gun, High Standard Model 10B auto riot gun and Universal double *lupara*.

might have the edge because of its convenient loading mechanism and handsome wood. Nevertheless, there is probably no auto on the market that is sturdier or which shows better workmanship than the Winchester Super-X. Like the Browning, it is gas operated and interchangeable barrels are available — including a 22" "deer" model with rifle sights. Some will like the more streamlined receiver of the Winchester and some will prefer the distinctive hump of the Browning. If you want a gun of this type, I suggest that you try both of these and buy the one that handles best for you.

Easily the most popular, and one of the very first, gas operated autos is the Remington 1100. Although these guns shoot very well and reduce recoil significantly, I cannot recommend them for survival use because of the maintenance problem which many of them pose. My own experience has been that, above all other gas operated autos, the 1100 requires more frequent and diligent cleaning to function reliably, and, more important, it is subject to chronic parts breakage — particularly the action bar. I have one acquaintance, a tournament trap shooter, who likes the handling of the gun so much that he owns three 1100's: one to shoot, one as a spare in case of breakage during a match, and one to keep in the shop for repairs. Several gunsmiths have told me that they have more breakage problems with the 1100 than any other current model autoloader, but in fairness I should point out that there are probably more of these guns in use than any of the others. Were it not for the maintenance problem, the Remington would be a good choice.

The recoil operated Browning Automatic-5 has one of the longest and most trouble-free reputations of any autoloading shotgun on the market, and if you like the way it handles, there is nothing of any importance to say against it; however, unless you want the recoil reduction offered

161

by gas operation, I can see no very good reason to choose an auto. Pumps can be at least as fast, with practice; they are less likely to malfunction with slightly imperfect ammunition and generally, they are simpler to repair and more rugged than most autos. Further, they provide the same barrel interchangeability and they usually sell for about 1/2 the price of an auto of equivalent quality.

One of the best examples of modern firearms design and, in my opinion, the very best pump shotgun for survival use is the Remington 870. It is seldom that a product which is designed for simplicity and cheapness of manufacture turns out to be the best of its kind, but that is certainly the case with the 870. It is rugged, simple to repair, contains but a few exceptionally strong parts; yet it handles extremely well and it has one of the smoothest actions of any gun of its type. One of the best things about the Remington is the fact that it uses two guide rails to prevent the pump handle from binding — a common complaint with some other makes — and the bolt assembly locks into the barrel extension — an exclusive feature. I know of no other pump that is as easy to disassemble and barrels can be changed in less than half a minute without tools.

The fact that very little handwork is required accounts for the quite reasonable price of this gun, and such machine-made uniformity is one of the reasons why it is such a good choice for a survival battery. Hand fitted guns often will not accept so-called interchangeable parts with-

The excellent Remington 870 pump is shown here with a 20″ slug and buckshot barrel, rifle sights and a magazine extension.

out some gunsmithing, but the 870 will. A small kit of springs, screws, firing pins, extractors and a few other odds and ends should keep it going indefinitely.

For defense, the exceptional reliability of the 870 makes it one of the best choices, particularly when fitted with the extension magazine tube — an accessory which is curiously available only to police. A 20" slug barrel with rifle sights is offered as well as almost any practical combination of choke and barrel length, with or without ventilated ribs. A good recoil pad is standard, and you may be grateful for it when using heavy loads. Like all other pumps, the 870 does not reduce felt recoil as gas operated autos do. It may be had in 12, 16, or 20 ga. and left-hand models are also made.

The only other pump which I recommend to private clients for survival use is the Ithaca Model 37. It has bottom ejection which some — particularly left-handers — may prefer and it is reliable. Its action is about as smooth as that on the 870 and its Raybar front sight is the very best on any shotgun, so far as I am concerned. It has interchangeable barrels, including one of the most accurate slug barrels available for any shotgun. I am told that the factory bores these tubes slightly undersize for their full length without any choke constriction. Several grades are available in 12, 16 and 20 gauge. There are probably some other sound pumps on the market, but I *know* there are some poor ones. Since there is less than $50 difference in price between the cheapest and the best pumps, I suggest that if you want one, you look at both the Remington and the Ithaca and choose the one that suits you. I should mention, however, that if you already have one of the older Winchester Model 12's in good condition, you needn't shop for a new gun because you already own the best pump ever made, in my opinion. Take it to a good gunsmith and have any worn parts replaced, buy some spares for your repair kit while they are still available and congratulate yourself on your good fortune.

Recoil

I have spoken of recoil several times in this chapter and perhaps it would be useful to provide some comparative figures at this point.

Shotgun Recoil		
12 ga. Magnum	High Base 1-1/4 oz.	40 foot pounds
12 ga. Trap	Low Base 1-1/8 oz.	20 " "
20 ga. 3" Magnum	Magnum 1-1/4 oz.	30 " "
20 ga. 2-3/4"	High Base 1 oz.	15 " "
.410 Bore	High Base 3/4 oz.	12 " "
.410 Bore	Low Base 1/2 oz.	6 " "

When you are evaluating the recoil factor in relation to your shotgun choice, bear in mind that the effect is much less when you are swinging the gun — as you will be when tracking a moving target — than when it is fired from a stationary position. For this reason, you may find that you can comfortably handle 5 or 6 foot pounds more actual recoil in a shotgun than you can in a rifle. Also, you will probably carry your shotgun a great deal more than you will fire it, under survival circumstances, so you may want to put up with a little extra recoil in return for lighter weight. A 12 gauge weighing around 6 1/2 pounds is about right for me.

Most cities and moderate sized towns have a trap or skeet range where you can borrow or rent shotguns for use on the premises, and unless you are already an experienced shooter, I suggest that you visit such a range and do a bit of shooting with various shotguns before you make your choice.

Variable Chokes

If you buy a single-shot or a repeater, you should give serious thought to installing a variable choke device. Even though interchangeable barrels are available for most repeaters, they are rather expensive and not as convenient as a choke device.

There are two basic types of variable chokes: the collet, such as the "Poly Choke" or the adapter with interchangeable tubes, like the "Cutts." The collet works very much like the nozzle on a garden hose. You simply twist the adjusting collar to any of the designated degrees of choke — or any point in between — and the muzzle is constricted accordingly.

The other style requires that you carry several small tubes, each with a different constriction, which may be screwed into an adapter chamber, permanently attached to your barrel. A wrench is usually required to remove or attach the tubes.

Either type of device can be had with recoil reducing muzzle brakes incorporated into them, but I usually recommend against such gadgets because they tend to increase the muzzle blast to an annoying degree. If you must have more recoil reduction than a good pad will supply, you may want to try one of these, but I urge you to do some shooting with one before you have such a deafener permanently installed on your gun.

Although some shotgun authorities maintain that the choke devices employing separate tubes give slightly better patterns, the collet type is certainly more convenient and has proved completely satisfactory for me. Far more important than the type you select is the quality of its installation. Do not assume that a gun shop will install your variable choke correctly merely because it is "Factory Authorized" to do so. One of the worst "Poly Choke" installations I have ever seen was done by a rather large "Factory Authorized" sporting goods store in the Los Angeles area. What these people seem often to overlook is that choke is not an absolute muzzle diameter for any given gauge, it is the *difference*, measured in thousandths of an inch, between the size of the bore and the constriction of the muzzle. Manufacturers of variable choke devices recognize this fact and they make their products in several different sizes within each gauge so that a proper fit can be obtained. Make sure that your gunsmith is also aware of this problem. A "Poly Choke" without muzzle brake, properly installed, will add so much versatility to your survival shotgun that I urge you not to be without one.

Whatever you do about chokes, however, whether you install variables, get extra barrels or buy the finest English double with several additional sets of barrels, the only way you will know what kind of patterns you are getting is to test fire the gun. Unless you perform this simple act, some very unpleasant surprises may await you when you need to use your shotgun in an emergency.

The best way to conduct this necessary pattern test is to obtain some wrapping paper 48″ wide, cut it into 4 foot squares, tack one up on a suitable surface, draw a small

Two views of the Ithaca Model 37 pump: before and after installing a "Poly Choke" variable choke device.

circular aiming point in the center, back away exactly 40 yards and *carefully* fire a shot, preferably while seated at a shooting bench. Shoot at least three separate target sheets with identical loads from the same box; then, with a pencil on a string, draw a 30″ diameter circle around the largest concentration of shot (*not* necessarily the point at which you aimed). Now, you can either find the estimated number of pellets of the size you are using in ballistic tables or, better, cut open a shell and count the actual number of shot. Then count the hits within the 30″ circle you have drawn and determine what percentage those hits represent when compared to the total number of shot in your shell. Turn to the appropriate table in the section on "chokes" in this chapter and you can determine the degree of choke which your gun actually shoots. It may be quite different from the designation marked on the barrel or the variable choke device. Further, you may find that your gun does not show the same degree of choke with different shot sizes. I have seen shotguns that would throw 75% tight full choke patterns with #6 shot and only 45% with #2's. You should, therefore, pattern your gun with each different load you plan to use.

Two additional things which you need to know that you can learn from this test are: 1) how even, or uneven, your patterns are — do they have large holes that game could escape through? — and 2) how well does the densest part of your pattern coincide with your aiming point? Often you will find that the point at which you aim only receives the fringes of the pattern. If either of these factors — or the degree of choke — is not as you would have it, corrections can be made — but only by a very skillful gunsmith who has the proper equipment and who thoroughly understands the ways of scatter-guns.

You may also discover from these tests that your gun will shoot one or more brands of shotgun shells noticeably better than the others. All of the leading makes are about comparable in quality, but many guns will show a distinct preference for brand as well as shot size, and you should buy accordingly when you lay in your survival supplies. Also, modern shotgun shells with their plastic shot cups which lessen deformation of pellets in the barrel on firing, tend to produce patterns one full degree tighter in most guns than the choke marked on the gun barrel would indicate. In case I haven't made my point: patterning your shotgun and the loads you intend to fire is extremely important; please don't neglect it.

Barrel Length

There is an incredible amount of misinformation abroad about shotguns. One bit of nonsense which you may hear is that you need a long barrel to shoot hard and far. Twaddle. The average velocity differential between shot charges fired in 32″ barrels and 26″ barrels is less than that usually found among individual shotgun shells taken from the same box. For that matter, there is no difference that your quarry would ever detect even when the barrel is 22″. Shotgun barrel length, then, should be determined on the basis of gun handling qualities, rather than ballistic considerations. A shotgun should feel almost alive, come to your shoulder quickly and swing onto the target smoothly, and barrel length has a considerable influence on these factors.

Obviously, "feel" is going to be different for different people and I suggest that you borrow or rent guns with different barrel lengths and try them on clay pigeons or actually hunt with them if you can. If not, at least handle a variety in the gun shop before you buy. My own preference runs to shorter barrels; they are handier and I shoot better with them. For defense, I want the shortest legal length — 18″, and I would prefer 16″. For hunting, I like either 26″ or 28″ barrels on a double, depending upon the balance of the individual gun. On pumps and autos, which have longer receivers than doubles, I often go to 24" or 25" and never more than 28". I even prefer 28" on doubles when shooting handicap trap. If you simply can't try some guns before you buy, the following list will probably serve. Assuming that you are using a "Poly Choke" on your repeaters, have the barrels cut so that the overall barrel length, *including the choke device*, measures as follows:

      12 ga. Pumps and Autos   26"
      20 ga. Pumps and Autos   25".

On over-and-under doubles try 26" and on side-by-sides, 26" or 28" in 12 ga.; get 25" or 26" barrels on either type in 20 ga. If I had one shotgun for both defense and hunting, assuming it was a repeater, I would install a "Poly Choke" and cut the barrel to 22" including the choke. If I could have an extra barrel for the gun, I would choose the shortest "slug" barrel and leave my "Poly Choke" equipped hunting tube at 26".

For the most part, you will find the shotgun to be a very forgiving tool. Your choice can be less than perfect and your shooting far from expert, but it will still disable an attacker or fill the pot — and those are its functions in a survival battery. The more skill you develop and the better your equipment is, however, the more likely your survival — and that is the purpose of planning for self-sufficient living. Even though the shotgun may not be your primary survival weapon, it is sufficiently useful to be chosen with some care and, if you live in a city, it may be the one firearm which you have the opportunity to fire regularly at a skeet or trap range. If that is the case, I urge you to engage in a systematic course of practice, because any shooting that you do will carry some skill over to all of your weaponscraft.

5 Rimfires

A "rimfire" is simply a cartridge which has its priming compound distributed around the rim of its case instead of concentrated in a disposable metal cup in the center of the head. When metallic cartridges were first introduced in the last century, rimfires were available in a variety of calibers, but because they were found to be less suitable than centerfires for the high pressures which came with smokeless powder and, when once fired, they could not be reloaded, their numbers waned. Today, the only practical rimfires in widespread use are the various .22's: undoubtedly the most popular and ubiquitous ammunition in the world. According to industry sources, some four billion rounds are consumed annually in the U.S. alone.

There is, perhaps, more controversy surrounding the role of the .22 rimfire in planning for long term self-sufficient living than any other item in the survival battery. Some "authorities" insist that the rimfire is the ideal survival ammunition, pointing out that it is light, compact, cheap, accurate, relatively quiet and very easy to handle since it has no appreciable recoil. Others argue that it has limited range, limited power, limited storage life, compared with centerfire ammunition, and that it is somewhat less reliable in use because it is not well sealed against moisture and oil, both of which are capable of rendering the powder charge inert. These detractors of the rimfire maintain that apart from shooting small pests, squirrels, cottontails and frogs, the .22 is virtually useless. The proponents say that the .22 long rifle cartridge is capable of killing any animal in the world, and some even consider it a suitable combat round, since it can be fired quickly and accurately by the novice and expert alike.

Neither of these two extreme points of view reflects my own experience with the rimfires, but I am certainly further from agreeing with those experts who counsel their clients to spend fully 50% of their firearms budget on .22's than I am from those who find the little rounds less than ideal for most practical uses.

I do not doubt that a .22 long rifle cartridge will kill virtually any animal on the North American Continent — under laboratory conditions. For that matter, I personally know of a case in which a high speed .22 short fired from a pistol accidentally killed a circus elephant. On a practical basis, however, and certainly under conditions where getting the game you shoot means life or death, the rimfire is not reliable on animals larger than cottontail rabbits except at distances of a few feet and even then, only with perfect bullet placement.

Those who favor the .22 for defense argue that because the little cartridge can be fired with such accuracy, even under stress, one can place shots with great precision in the heart, head or a nerve plexus — and if all else fails, one can fire a large number of shots very quickly. Aside from the fact that the "hail of lead" and "placement with surgical accuracy" arguments seem to be inimical to one another, this point of view can lead to serious — possibly fatal — tactical errors. The head is a very poor target to shoot for in a fight, even at modest distances, because it is usually in motion, it is small and, since it is held away from the mass of the body, missing it ordinarily means missing your adversary entirely. Furthermore, a head shot, particularly with a .22, while certainly not designed to improve the overall state of your opponent's health, may not be immediately incapacitating — at least not with any comforting degree of frequency. Further, even though the .22 has a high degree of inherent accuracy and most people can learn to shoot it well, making pinpoint hits on stationary silhouette targets is quite a different matter from trying to stop a live aggressor who is shooting at you. Under those circumstances, you may be fortunate to strike your opponent anywhere on the torso, and the .22 usually will not bring about an abrupt end to hostilities unless a nerve center is hit. There is also the matter of multiple attackers which calls for very quick shooting indeed, with the virtual certainty that not all of your bullets will be perfectly placed. Those who advise dumping a full magazine at your assailant in the vain hope of compensating for inadequate power with multiple wounds seem never to give any thought to the fact that rats often run in packs, and that the domino theory seldom applies to the black-hats.

In short, people who tell you that a .22 is "all you need," that it is the "ideal survival weapon" or that it should be the primary weapon in your battery, simply do not know what they are talking about. Of course, the .22 is a good backpacker's weapon and it is probably the best single choice if you are lost in the woods for a few days (except in bear country), but for *long term* living off the land, it is inadequate because it is not a *reliable* killer of large game nor a dependable defense cartridge. It will — and has —served in both capacities but it is uncertain in either, and, as I have previously observed, practical probability, not chance success, should be the criterion for selecting tools for self-sufficient living.

Although it is not a panacea, it would be folly to do without the .22 in your survival battery, if for no other reason than that the ammunition is the most popular in the world, the cheapest and the most compact. In my view, the rimfires should be regarded essentially as occasional substitutes for more effective weapons, when circumstances permit. They should be chosen as primary tools only for limited small game hunting and pest control — and even then, a suitable air rifle will take frogs, turtles, small birds and cottontails at close range just as reliably and with less damage to edible meat. One of the most important anomalies to bear in mind when dealing with the paradoxical .22 is that although it has little shocking power, it usually creates an extensive wound channel, causing a slow and painful death to wounded animals which escape, and destroying a good deal of meat on those which it does bring down. Yet it often fails to stop even large, tough jackrabbits.

Despite all of these negatives, the rimfires are remarkable cartridges, they have great flexibility, they are offered in a wide variety of power levels and projectile designs — including shot — and they will do some things better than anything else. Up to this point, the majority of my remarks on the rimfires have been made with the most popular cartridge, the .22 long rifle, in mind, but there are others which we should consider as well.

Rimfire Ammunition
.22 BB and CB Caps

Both of these rounds are a direct outgrowth of the original Flobert design, which was the first successful rimfire. Cartridges so designated are nominally powered by the priming compound alone and contain no powder. Some of the recent makes, however, do contain a very small powder charge. The BB caps have a case only about 3/16" long which contains a .22 caliber round ball. They can be superbly accurate at short range in guns chambered specifically for them, having rifling twists designed to handle the short bearing-surface ball. Fired in standard .22's, they still provide adequate accuracy out to 20 yards or so and they will handle sparrows, starlings, small rodents and frogs at that distance. The only source for these tiny cartridges is the import market, and the transportation costs added to the declining value of the dollar in world exchange combine to negate their chief virtue: cheapness.

CB caps usually employ the same size case as the BB's, but a light bullet of conventional design is loaded. Because of the projectile design, they often give better accuracy in conventional arms and they are much easier to obtain. CCI manufactures them in this country, and the Ely brand is imported from England. If you use any of these short bodied .22's in guns designed for longer cartridges, you should clean the chambers thoroughly and often, since prolonged firing can cause enough fouling, and possibly chamber erosion, so that the full-length rounds will not seat completely. Both the BB's and the CB's are very quiet and their primary usefulness is indoor target practice. A large catalog or a metropolitan telephone book is all you will need for a backstop.

.22 Rimfires, from left to right: BB Cap, CB Cap, Short HP, CCI Long CB Cap, Long Rifle HP, CCI Long Rifle Shot, .22 W.R.F., .22 Magnum, CCI .22 Magnum Shot.

.22 Short

Once considered a good cartridge for a hideout gun — particularly a ladies garter or muff pistol — the short is now used almost entirely for target shooting and plinking. Although it employs a lighter weight bullet at less velocity than the long rifle, the high velocity, hollow point short should not be overlooked when buying your ammunition supply. It is cheaper than the long rifle and much more compact, but still quite effective at very close range. If you confine it to use on mice, gophers, rats, prairie dogs, crows, tree squirrels and the like, within 30 yards, it is efficient. The short is certainly no defense cartridge, but at arms length, I would prefer it in the high speed hollow point version to any .25 auto. It is much more accurate than people recognize. Ballistic tables offer the following profile:

Cartridge	Bullet Wt.	Velocity (fps.) Muzzle	100 yds.
.22 Short Std. Vel.	29	1045	810
.22 Short High Vel.	29	1125	920
.22 Short High Vel. Hollow Pt.	27	1155	920

I always carry a few shorts in my emergency kit because of their compactness. The high speed hollow point is the most generally useful.

.22 Long

Less accurate than the short and less powerful than the long rifle, the .22 long is an altogether useless cartridge, except in one version: the .22 long CB cap. For at least 15 years, I have been using rather expensive imported RWS long CB caps for indoor and casual outdoor target practice. Recently, however, CCI has introduced a cheaper, more easily available and vastly superior product made here in the U.S. The chief advantage of the long CB cap over its diminutive brothers is that it employs a standard short bullet loaded into a standard long rifle case, thus combining better accuracy with no mid-chamber fouling or erosion. Further, in a barrel of 22" or longer, the CCI cap is almost totally silent. At a distance of 8 feet from the muzzle of my 24" Anschutz, the sound level from firing was only 9 db. and at 15 feet it was totally inaudible. Not only does this lack of noise make the CCI long CB caps desirable for indoor or backyard target practice, it makes them virtually a necessity for survival use should you ever need to do some shooting without attracting attention or alarming game in the neighborhood.

The accuracy level of these useful cartridges is good. At 75' they will make one ragged hole. Their useful range for small animals is probably about 50 yards and at that distance, groups from my rifles are exactly twice the size of those made with standard velocity long rifles — not match grade, but good enough for the purpose. Head shots on squirrels and grouse should be limited to about 20 yards.

Velocity is only a claimed 675 fps., so you should realize that this is not very powerful ammunition; exact bullet placement is a must. Although it will feed through all of the repeating actions I have tried, autos must be cycled by hand since the caps do not develop enough energy to function them. Maximum performance is attained in short barrels — 16" or so — but there is some noise when the cartridges are fired in such abbreviated rifle tubes or from pistols. I highly recommend that you include a supply of this "silent" .22 ammo in your kit, but be sure to buy enough for practice now as well. There is no more convenient way for a new shooter to become familiar with his rimfire rifle than a program of daily indoor practice with these CB caps; all you need is a 25 to 50 foot range and a thick metropolitan telephone book or an inexpensive bullet trap.

.22 Long Rifle

This is the rimfire round for which most modern guns are chambered; it is the world's standard. There are two power levels generally available: high velocity and target or standard velocity. Solid bullets, hollow points, a new hollow cavity called "dyna-point," and even shotshells are loaded. The two most generally useful rounds are the high velocity hollow point and the standard velocity solid. The bulk of your rimfire ammunition supply should be comprised of these two. I personally do most of my rimfire shooting with the standard velocity rounds because they are considerably more accurate than the hotter loads. There is no question but that the high speed HP does more damage to tissue than any of the others, but that is not an unmixed blessing when hunting small game for the table. Whenever possible, I take head shots with whatever rimfire ammunition I am using, and that is much easier to do with the more accurate standards. If you must take body shots, as with running game, or if you are shooting pests and predators — particularly the larger ones such as coyote — high velocity HP's are a must.

Unfortunately, it is impossible to recommend a brand of long rifle ammunition. Even though the ballistic tables indicate that all of the leading makes are virtually identical, there are subtle differences in bullet design and powder type which will probably cause your particular gun to prefer one brand to another. It is more important than it may sound for you to select your rimfire ammunition supply on the basis of its performance in your own guns. The differences in accuracy between brands in a given firearm can be enormous, and since the rimfires provide very little power at best, we need the highest possible level of accuracy from them. I suggest, therefore, that you buy 100 rounds each of the leading makes, Remington, Peters, Winchester, Western, CCI and Federal in high velocity HP, high velocity solid and standard velocity solid, then do some careful shooting at no less than 75 yards from a bench rest, in order to determine the preference of your guns, before laying in your survival supply. If you can bear the added expense, it would also be a good idea to try a box of the premium target-match ammunition from each manufacturer. Most of the makers listed above also market a bargain brand such as CCI's Blazer or Remington's Mohawk. I have never had good results with any of them for consistent accuracy and I have experienced a number of failures to fire. If you can't resist the lower price, use the bargain brands for plinking and general firearms familiarization, but don't include them in your survival stores, except, perhaps for trade goods. Incidentally, when you decide how much rimfire ammunition to buy, bear in mind that it is so popular and ubiquitous that it could become virtually a standard currency during a prolonged crisis.

For a number of years, various manufacturers have offered a shotshell loading in .22 long rifle for dispatching pests at close range, but unless they were used in special smoothbore .22 shotguns they were quite ineffective and they leaded barrels to an annoying degree. Usually these little shells were loaded with a pinch of #12 "dust" shot and crimped inside a full-length brass case. By the time this book is in print, CCI will have released a new style .22 shotshell which is somewhat more effective and which eliminates the leading problems completely. CCI has encapsulated the shot charge within a transparent plastic, bullet shaped container which keeps the pellets from contacting the rifling while in the barrel and then disintegrates upon emerging from the muzzle. Since the shot are undamaged by their trip through the barrel, there are fewer flyers and the patterns are denser; however, even with this improvement, long rifle shot cartridges have limited effectiveness. I have fired several hundred of the CCI's through a number of test guns and I have concluded that their effective range is limited to about 10 or 12 feet, except in .22 smoothbores which can throw good patterns to 25 or 30 feet. In rifled arms the best results were obtained from short barrels. My 2″ .22 Kit Gun showed the densest and most evenly distributed patterns among the 12 pistols tested and my Charter Arms AR-7 gave the best performance of the 10 rifles used. Apparently, the rotation imparted to the shot capsule by the longer rifle barrels causes the pellets to disperse too quickly. Penetration at 10 feet averaged 136 pages in the Los Angeles telephone directory.

Except in a .22 shotgun, I don't think these shotshells could be used successfully for hunting, but I can think of nothing better to clean rodents out of a barn or other buildings without shooting holes in the walls. Since the range is so limited, they are quite safe to use in settled areas and they are good for practicing with small aerial targets. They are also quite useful for snakes. CCI packs them handily in flat, shirt pocket sized plastic containers of 20 rounds.

The following table will give you some idea of the ballistic performance of the various long rifle loads:

Cartridge	Bullet Weight	Rifle Velocity		Handgun Velocity (6″ barrel)
		Muzzle	100 yds.	Muzzle
.22 LR Std. Vel.	40 gr.	1145	975	950
.22 LR High Vel.	40 gr. solid	1285	1025	1125
.22 LR High Vel.	37 gr. HP	1365	1040	1165

I sight in my scoped .22's at 100 yards with high speed ammunition. Such a zero will put you on the point of aim at 25 yards and 1.6" high at both 50 and 75 yards. At 125 yards you will be approximately 3.1" low. With non-optical sights I zero at 75 yards, which puts my bullet .6" high at 50 and 2.2" low at 100. With the 100 yard zero the bullet first crosses the line of sight at 25 yards; with the 75 yard setting, it crosses at 17 yards. You will save some trouble and ammunition if you do your initial shooting and sight adjustment at the closer distances.

Any rifle or handgun chambered for the .22 long rifle will fire any of the ammunition discussed above, although some of the shorter or less powerful rounds may not function the action or feed from the magazine.

.22 Winchester Magnum

A slightly larger cartridge of considerably greater power which is not interchangeable with any of the above is the .22 Winchester Magnum — often abbreviated as the .22 WRM. Except for the Remington 5mm., which has never become popular enough to consider for survival use, the .22 Magnum is the most powerful of the rimfires. In fact, it approaches the performance of low end centerfires such as the .22 Hornet.

This is a very efficient small game and pest cartridge to about 125 yards and, under certain circumstances, it has some value for defense. The hollow point is much too destructive for use on small edible game, but it is outstanding on varmints and I have found it dependable to the limit of its useful range on game up to 75 or 80 pounds weight. The solid is the best choice for pot shooting but it also ruins too much meat when fired from a rifle at less than 25 yards from the quarry. The smaller and somewhat cheaper .22 Winchester Rimfire, which can be used in any gun chambered for the Magnum, is excellent for pot shooting at the closer ranges. This is *not* a deer rifle caliber, however, with any load, and even under survival conditions I would not attempt to use it as such at any distance beyond 25 yards, and even then, only if I were desperate.

I have read a number of articles by "experts" which insist that the .22 Magnum has only marginal accuracy. That has not been my experience, and I suspect that such reports of inaccuracy were based on using cheap, inaccurate guns. I have a bolt action Anschutz which will *average* minute of angle groups with CCI ammunition and a Winchester 9422M which will do almost as well. There are few rifle-ammunition combinations which will do as well, from the box.

The primary drawback to the .22 Magnum is its cost. It is more than twice as expensive as the .22 long rifle, and unlike the small centerfires which can be used for the same purposes, it cannot be reloaded. I like the cartridge and find it better for small game hunting with a rifle than anything else, but you will have to decide, based on your own requirements, whether to include it in your battery.

CCI is making a very useful shot load in the caliber which I have used extensively in a 3 1/2" Kit Gun. Its range and killing power is about double that of the long rifle shotshell.

For people who cannot, even with proper instruction, handle a more effective weapon for defense because of a physical problem, the .22 Magnum is worth considering. From limited observation of its use for this purpose and from conversations with others who have used it, it appears to be just about equal to the .38 Special with standard ammunition so far as stopping power is concerned, but it will not penetrate chance barriers nearly as well. I would not like to have to defend my life with any rimfire, but if I were forced to, I would prefer the .22 Magnum to anything else in that category.

One plus with this cartridge is that, in my rifles at least, it fires both the hollow point and the solid to the same point of aim. I sight in at 100 yards, which puts the bullet 1 1/2" high at 50 and 1 1/2" low at 125. It is then 4" low at 150 and 16" low at 200 (*not* 5" low as some claim). Both CCI and Winchester produce .22 Magnum ammunition, and I suggest that you buy the brand which groups best in your guns.

Two fine .22 Magnums. Above: the Anschutz bolt action. Below: Winchester's new 9422M lever action.

Choosing Survival .22's

The two most important criteria in selecting rimfire arms for survival use are accuracy and durability: since the cartridges lack power, you must try to compensate by exact bullet placement, and because of the lower cost, you will probably do several times as much shooting with your rimfire guns as with any others. Fortunately, there are a number of guns which satisfy both of these requirements, but there is also a good deal of junk on the market as well, and I suggest that you make your selection with care.

Rifles

Bolt Actions

The better bolt actions are incredibly accurate, easy to maintain and they will last through several lifetimes of heavy use. They are, however, rather expensive because the best are almost all imports. Fifteen years or so ago, there were a number of excellent, very inexpensive domestic bolt actions on the market, but that is no longer the case. U.S. manufacturers have concentrated their ingenuity on autoloaders, in response to American taste, and the bolt guns have suffered both in quality and quantity. I recently purchased a domestic bolt action tubular magazine repeater for testing and I was amazed at how poor the construction had become. The barrel was no longer screwed into the receiver, but was held in place only by a pin. The magazine tube rattled and when I began to look for the reason, I found the metal to be so thin

Bolt action .22's, once plentiful, are now scarce and expensive in quality good enough for survival applications. Top: discontinued Remington 512 with Williams receiver sight and tubular magazine. Middle: fine Anschutz Model 164 with receiver sight. Bottom: Anschutz full-length stocked carbine with double set triggers and Bushnell variable scope.

that the tension screw which should have held it in place could not bear on it without bending it. The bolt itself, which was touted for the strength of its locking mechanism, employed a paper-thin, crescent-shaped spring to retain and operate the extractors and it flew across the room every third or fourth time I opened the action. It shot well enough, when it functioned, but I have seen after-dinner mints that were more durable.

The three best bolt action rimfires on the market today, in my opinion, are the Anschutz Models 54, 164 and the Walther KKJ, but they are all expensive. The Walther may be had with double set triggers for the finest precision shooting, on special order. If you want a bolt action .22 and the price on these seems too high, I suggest that you look for one of the older Remington or Winchester models

Three of the most reliable .22 auto rifles: from top to bottom, Remington Nylon 66, Ruger 10/22, Colt Stagecoach.

on the used market. You can often find a Remington 521 for about $50 or a 511, 512 or Winchester Model 69 for as little as $30, and all of these are very satisfactory guns, in good condition.

Autoloaders

In some circles, autoloading .22's have the reputation of being inaccurate, unreliable and fragile. While those accusations are certainly true of some models, there are a few which are outstanding. Probably the chief drawback of any auto, but particularly the .22, is that it encourages beginners to develop poor shooting habits. When succeeding shots are only a pull of the trigger away, there is a tendency to substitute a volley of shots in the general direction of the target for careful first round marksmanship. This tactic not only wastes ammunition, but it also leads to an empty game bag.

Weatherby Mark XXII

From the standpoint of accuracy, I have seen few rimfires of any action type which perform as well as the Weatherby Mark XXII. It is available with either detachable box magazines or with a large capacity tubular one, which I much prefer. This is a large rifle for a .22, and for that reason it makes an excellent understudy for heavier

In a class by itself, the Weatherby Mark XXII. The "clip" loading model is shown here, but the author prefers the tubular magazine which is available at no extra charge.

caliber weapons, but it is not as handy for some purposes as other models which are scaled to the cartridge. It takes down for convenient storage and it has a unique single-shot selector which is useful in training youngsters. It is also easier to single load than most autoloaders are. A rifle this large and with this accuracy potential should be used with a scope and I highly recommend the one which Weatherby supplies for this model. Sling swivels are standard. The Mark XXII weighs 6 lbs., has a 24" barrel and measures 42 1/4" overall.

Ruger 10/22

My choice for the best buy in .22 auto rifles is the Ruger 10/22. Like most Ruger products, this is an innovative design and a good value. It employs a unique 10 shot rotary magazine, which is far less susceptible to damage than any other on the market. The action is as trouble free as any I know and accuracy is very good. I have never seen a 10/22 which could not benefit from a trigger job, however. All of the pulls seem quite a bit too heavy for the best shooting and most of them have some creep as well. The top of the receiver is smooth and streamlined, but an adapter plate is furnished with the rifle for scope mounting. If you don't mount a scope, you should consider installing the Williams receiver sight which is especially designed for this model. The folding leaf open sight which is supplied is better than the issue sights on most .22 rifles, but it cannot compare with the speed and accuracy of a good "peep" or a scope. I like to use slings on all rifles, even .22's, and I would suggest that you install one with quick detachable swivels on the Ruger. With its 18 1/2" barrel, the Ruger is a handy size and its 5 lb. weight is about average for guns of this type. Sales on this model are quite common, and you may be able to save enough to pay for a trigger job and a sling if you shop around.

Colt Stagecoach

Despite the fact that I do not usually like rifles with aluminum receivers, I am particularly fond of the Stagecoach. The accuracy on my test rifle is outstanding: 3/4" groups at 50 yds. with iron sights — and it is the shortest, handiest conventional .22 auto on the market. It weighs 4 lb. 10 oz. including the sling which is supplied as standard equipment. With its 16 1/2" barrel, it measures only 33 5/8" overall. The trigger on my gun broke cleanly if a bit heavily at 4 lbs. and after two thousand rounds without cleaning, I have not experienced a single jam or mechanical failure of any kind. The receiver is grooved for a scope, but it seems a shame to add such bulk and awkwardness to this compact little gun. I prefer to install a good aperture receiver sight. For me, the "saddle ring," which is supplied as a "Western" feature, needs to be replaced by a plain flathead screw because it interferes with my thumb in firing position, and I could do without the decoration on the receiver, but these are not serious criticisms. The 13 round tubular magazine provides a lot of firepower for a gun this small and it is very convenient to load. For some reason, the Stagecoach has not had good distribution and it is not always easy to find. If you want one, you may have to do some looking.

Browning Automatic

This is a classic design and the workmanship is outstanding, as it should be in a gun of this price. The takedown feature, which allows the gun to be put away or transported in very little space, is simple and positive. Trigger pulls are generally better than average and accuracy, while not outstanding, is certainly acceptable. The 11 round magazine loads through the buttstock — a feature which some like, but I find it awkward. My primary objection to this gun is that it ejects its empties straight down. If you hold the rifle properly with your left arm directly under it, you will receive a shower of hot brass, which is very disconcerting should you happen to be wearing short sleeves. Left-handers often prefer downward ejection, however, in preference to having the empties fly past their noses. The Browning looks smaller and lighter than it really is because of its slender forearm and diminutive receiver. Barrel length is 19 1/2" and weight runs 4 lbs. 15 oz. Balance is excellent and the stock design seems to suit a wide variety of users from youngsters to large men.

Remington Nylon 66

If you want a .22 autoloader with a stock made entirely from plastic and a front sight that looks as if it came from Buck Rogers' ray gun, the Nylon 66 is it. Of all the autos which I rate "acceptable" this is the one I like least, but I should point out that I am obviously in the minority, because this is one of the most popular .22's on the market and it is unquestionably one of the most durable. Like the Browning, the 66 loads through the stock and it is unusually difficult to introduce single rounds into the chamber, should you wish to fire a cartridge such as a short, which will not feed from the long rifle only magazine. Accuracy is just passing with most of the guns I have tried, producing 1 1/2" to 2" groups at 50 yds. The rear sight is fragile and should be replaced with an aperture or a scope, for which the receiver is grooved. The trigger is almost certain to require attention. The 4 lb. weight, outstanding durability and virtually unbreakable stock seem to be the features which most attract purchasers to this gun. Barrel length is 19 5/8".

Charter Arms AR-7

This is one of those designs which makes a writer want to append the unnecessary adverb "absolutely" to the word "unique." Armalite developed this rifle specifically as a survival weapon several years ago and recently licensed its manufacture to Charter Arms. It is certainly one of the most useful guns available for the purpose. The stock is hollow, fitted to accept the action, barrel and magazine, when taken down, and it is waterproof when the removable butt cover is in place. Assembly or takedown can be accomplished in less than a minute and the rifle floats whether assembled or packed away in the stock. I know of nothing more suitable for an emergency kit: taken down, the overall length is only 16 1/2" and weight is just 2 3/4 lbs. Accuracy is better than you might expect with a weapon of this type. I have three of them and the worst groups into 2" at 50 yards. The rear sight is a protected aperture, adjustable, somewhat crudely, by loosening a screw and wiggling the perforated plate up and down. The front sight must be driven right or left in its dovetail for deflection.

During the transition from Armalite to Charter Arms, a

The Charter Arms AR-7 is one of the most useful of all .22 survival guns. It weighs only 2 3/4 lbs. and stows away in its own waterproof stock. Shown here assembled, taken down and packed for transport or storage.

number of very poor examples of this rifle reached the market, and its reputation was tarnished both among dealers and consumers. I examined a number of these "transition" pieces which would not function reliably and the external finishes were terrible; they looked as if they had been dunked in a bucket of paint. I wrote to Charter Arms about the problem and they recently sent me a sample from current production for testing. Since this is such a useful design, I am pleased to report that present quality is at least as high as the best of the original Armalite manufacture — and the magazine supplied is superior. I have now fired several thousand rounds through the new gun with no malfunctions of any kind. If you were put off by the quality control of earlier models, or if your dealer advises against the gun, I urge you to examine one from current stock before you decide. Although I do not recommend the AR-7 as the only .22 in a survival battery, one should be included at least for the emergency kit. There is also nothing better for a hidden cache, since the gun is self-contained in its own waterproof storage stock.

Pumps and Lever Actions

There is no need, from either the standpoint of accuracy or durability to look beyond the better autoloaders when selecting a .22 but, as a matter of taste, some people prefer manually operated actions — and it may be that they do encourage more deliberate marksmanship. Also, a wider choice of suitable models is available and they exhibit somewhat greater versatility in their uses of ammunition. For example, there is only one autoloader in current production chambered for the .22 Magnum, but there are several good lever and bolt actions. Further, most autoloaders are designed to function only with long rifle ammunition,[1] whereas shorts, longs and long rifles can ordinarily be

[1]Other lengths can often be loaded and fired singly.

191

used interchangeably in pumps and levers. Fortunately, many rimfire rifles are sufficiently inexpensive that most people can own several. If you are not in that position, one reasonable approach is to buy an autoloader for the less expensive .22 long rifle ammunition and a lever or a bolt for the Magnum, which will be used more frugally.

The two best rimfire pumps I have ever used — the Winchester Models 61 and 62 are no longer in production, but either may occasionally be found in good condition on the used market and parts are still available for them. The 62, a takedown with an outside hammer, was a favorite with shooting galleries because of its rugged reliability and yet it is a compact design, scaled to the ammunition it uses. Because of its top ejection, it cannot be used readily with a scope, but any of several excellent aperture sights can be fitted. The 61 is one of the most accurate sporting model .22's ever manufactured and later models had grooved receivers to facilitate scope mounting so that its full potential could be realized. Also a takedown rifle, the 61 was briefly offered in .22 Magnum as well as standard rimfire chamberings, but the Magnum version is so scarce that it is almost a collector's item. Prices for a used one in

Classic .22 pump designs, both now, sadly, discontinued. Top: Winchester Model 62, straight grip, outside hammer. Bottom: Winchester Model 61, pistol grip, hammerless.

excellent condition are about twice the original cost.

The Remington Fieldmaster 572 and the High Standard Sport King are the only domestic rimfire pumps in current production and neither exhibits the obvious quality of the Winchester. Although I have fired both, I have tested neither extensively enough to comment on their suitability for survival use. Rossi makes a copy of the Winchester 62, but the sample I had was rather crude and did not feed or eject reliably.

What we lack in quality pumps on the U.S. market is amply compensated for by the panoply of excellent lever actions available.

Marlin 39

The factory claims that the Marlin 39 is the oldest shoulder gun design still in regular production anywhere in the world. Certainly it is one of the best. Marlin uses a special barrel on this gun which employs a larger number of shallower grooves and lands than is customary in order to cause less deformation of the soft lead .22 bullet when it is fired. I do not know whether this "micro-groove" process actually improves accuracy as the manufacturer states, but

Two of the best all-purpose rimfire rifles. The Marlin 39A rifle, above, has a pistol grip stock and a 24″ bbl. The 39M carbine below is lighter, with its straight stock and 20″ bbl. Both take down conveniently.

193

something does. I have used perhaps a dozen of these rifles over the past 25 years and all of them have been remarkably accurate. I have one 39A which is almost 20 years old that has fired more than 25,000 rounds. It still shoots 1/2″ groups at 50 yds. and it has never needed repairs of any kind.

Current production models seem a bit rougher than the older guns and almost all of them will need a trigger job, but they are just as accurate and they appear just as reliable as their forebears. I recently bought a 39M — the short carbine model — and after having the action smoothed and the trigger honed, it is completely satisfactory except for the cheap, crudely adjustable open sights which seem to be furnished on most .22′s these days, regardless of the quality or price of the gun.

Both models of the 39 take down simply by loosening a single screw, allowing the rifles to be stored or transported easily and to be cleaned, as they should be, from the breech. A screw-on plate is provided for easy scope mounting and sling swivels are furnished on both models. Prices are the same, and a choice between the two is purely a matter of personal taste. The "A" model has a 24″ barrel, a pistol grip stock and weighs 6 3/4 lbs. The "M" has a 20″ barrel, a straight stock and weighs 6 lbs. Neither, unfortunately, is chambered for the .22 Magnum, but both will handle shorts, longs and long rifles interchangeably from their large capacity tubular magazines.

Winchester 9422

In my opinion, there are no domestic firearms on the market showing better overall workmanship and quality control than the new Winchester Models 9422 and 9422M (for Magnum). Good triggers and sights are features which seem simply to elude U.S. gun makers and the 9422′s are no exception to this rule, but their actions are smooth and tight, their finish is superb and they shoot very well indeed. Since both Magnum and standard rimfire chamberings are available, you can have a matched pair of rifles with the same feel and handling qualities.

The guns have one screw takedown and receivers grooved for scopes. The tubular magazine of the Magnum holds 11 rounds and the standard accepts 15 long rifles, 17 longs or 21 shorts. Barrels are 20 1/2" and weight is 6 1/2 lbs. If you don't scope them, replace the open rear sights with apertures.

A matched pair of Winchester 9422 carbines, one chambered for the .22 Magnum and the other will handle anything from CB caps to long rifles. Workmanship is superior.

Ithaca 72 and Browning BL22

Both of these guns look satisfactory but, frankly, I have not used them enough to offer a fair evaluation. On the Browning, the entire trigger mechanism moves down with the lever and I suspect that it may prove somewhat fragile in heavy use. Of the two, only the Ithaca is available in Magnum chambering.

Rimfire Handguns

In the abstract, I suppose a .22 pistol is not a necessity in a survival battery, assuming a proper balance among the

Fine Smith and Wesson .22 revolvers, some remodeled and most with custom grips. The bottom pair are: above, Model 48 .22 Magnum and below, "Combat Master-piece" .22 LR. The remaining six are various models of the famous "Kit Gun."

other guns recommended, but it can be a great convenience. I often carry one for pot shooting when I am hunting larger game with a rifle which would make mincemeat of a grouse or a rabbit. Some authorities find handguns unproductive for this purpose and prefer to carry a pocket full of light handloads for their rifles. I have never been able to develop squib loads which would shoot to the same point of aim as my full power ammunition and at the same time offer sufficient accuracy to behead a grouse at 15 yards. On the other hand, I have no trouble filling the pot with a good .22 pistol, and using one saves me hours at the reloading bench. Your choice in this matter is really a question of personal taste and the level of skill which you can develop with the pistol.

I also find the .22 pistol useful for a number of other chores, from running a trapline and routing pests to slaughtering domestic animals more humanely than some common methods, but other guns will serve these purposes as well, if not as conveniently. If you decide to own a rimfire pistol, it will probably get a lot of use, so buy a good one, but keep it fairly small or you will negate the convenience factor which is its *raison d'etre*. Guns as large as the fine S&W K-22 or the target grade autoloaders all seem unnecessarily heavy and bulky for the uses which I anticipate for such a piece in the survival battery, but, again, this is only a matter of personal preference. Such guns, fired carefully from a solid rest, will group almost as well as the average .22 rifle up to 50 yards, and you may envision circumstances under which you would need such performance.

For most of us, however, the following models will do all that is required of them and they are much more convenient to carry. In my opinion, .22 revolvers have one slight advantage over autos because they can fire any standard rimfire cartridge, from CB caps to long rifle or shot, interchangeably. The autos do have more firepower, however, if you consider that a factor in choosing a .22.

S&W Kit Guns

It is difficult to imagine more practical .22 pistols than these little guns. They have excellent fully adjustable sights and, usually, fine single action trigger pulls, although their double actions can almost always benefit from some attention to smooth and lighten them. The basic Kit Gun frame can be had with either a square or round butt and with barrel lengths of 2″, 3 1/2″, 4″ and 6″. An Airweight model with an alloy frame and cylinder is

Variations on a theme — a complete set of S&W Kit Guns. Left, top to bottom: 2" round butt with Guy Hogue custom rosewood grips, 3 1/2" Airweight with Tyler T-grip adapter, 3 1/2" .22 Magnum with S&W rosewood target grips. Right, top to bottom: 6" square butt target model with Guy Hogue custom grips, 4" square butt with factory target grips, 4" round butt with Guy Hogue combat style grips.

also available as is a .22 Magnum version. (If you are ever lost in the woods, the Magnum Kit is ideal for signaling because it is so loud.)

Ruger Convertible

I am not enchanted with single action revolvers. If you are, your clear choice is the stainless steel Ruger Super Single Six Convertible. It is a sturdy, well designed gun with virtually unbreakable coil springs and it provides the advantages of stainless steel as well as an extra cylinder so that the .22 Magnum may be used as well as the full range

198

of standard .22's. It is a good deal larger than the Kit Guns, but depending upon the use you have for it, that may not matter. Adjustable sights are standard. Since the bullet diameter of the Magnum is somewhat larger than that of the standard .22, any gun which is designed to fire both must have a bore size that is a compromise for at least one of them, so you may not receive the very best accuracy. Given the slow lock time and the heavy hammer fall of a single action, however, you may not notice.

Lost or damaged empty cases are not a factor with rimfires since they are not reloadable; therefore, .22 autopistols can be considered without prejudice, even for field use. None of them is presently chambered for the Magnum, however, but in my opinion, that round is far more efficiently employed in a rifle than in a handgun.

Walther PP and PPK

One of the most practical .22 autopistols, and certainly the handiest, is the German made Walther. The workmanship is excellent and the sights are rugged and easy to see. Although this is a double action design, that feature is not a drawback in a small pocket pistol which is not intended for combat use. The guns are safely carried in the pocket with the safety engaged and the hammer down on a live round. The trigger cocking feature should be completely ignored.

There are presently two models of the Walther being imported into the U.S., the PP, which has a 3.86" barrel and the PPK/S with a 3.72". Except for barrel length, these two guns are identical and a choice between them should be based on which feels better in your hand. Thanks to the ill-conceived 1968 Gun Control Act, the more compact PPK, which has the shorter barrel *and* a smaller butt, cannot be brought into this country. I personally prefer the PPK and you may also. Despite the fact that they can no

Two of the best .22 pocket pistols ever made. Above: Walther PPK. Below: S&W Kit Gun 2″ with custom sights and Hogue grips.

longer be imported, they are legal to own and you may be able to find one second-hand — although you will probably have to pay a premium price. I have used a number of these pistols over the years and have found them reliable, extremely durable and possessed of a high degree of practical accuracy. Most of them will only function properly with high velocity ammunition, however. The magazines seem particularly durable. I have one that is 15 years old which has seen much use and it still feeds flawlessly.

S&W Model 41

I have never fired a handgun of any kind that shoots as well for me as the 5″ barreled S&W Model 41. The trigger pull on these guns as they come from the box is usually superb, the grip is outstanding and the sights are as good as you can find. This is a target grade gun and its accuracy

On the left three Ruger autos, considered by the author to be among the best bargains in current handgun models. The standard model, top, carries a Bushnell Phantom scope. Beneath it, another standard — this one with the short barrel option and custom adjustable sights by Miniature Machine Co. Bottom: Bull Barrel Target Model. On the right, the author's favorite S&W Model 41 on top and the Colt Woodsman Target below.

is remarkable. From an arm rest I have been able to keep all my shots on the silhouette of a rabbit at 75 yards — and, for me, that is top pistol performance.

The 41 is not a pocket sized gun even with the 5″ standard weight barrel which I prefer, but some are willing to accept the increased bulk in exchange for optimal accuracy. A conversion unit for shorts which can be installed without tools is also available, as are several interchangeable barrels from a 7 3/8″ model with a muzzle brake to a 5″ heavyweight.

A trio of Rugers. Top: Standard Model, Miniature Machine sights. Middle: Bull Barrel Target Model with factory target grips. Bottom: Long Barrel Target Model, standard grips.

Ruger Autopistols

One of the first, if not the first, Ruger products was their brilliantly designed .22 autopistol. These guns are still available, virtually unchanged, and they represent the best handgun bargain I know. They are outstandingly strong and durable and their potential accuracy is such that several national target championships have been won with them. Their only significant weakness is that the trigger pulls on the standard models are usually gruesome and they are difficult to improve. The target models often do not have really first class triggers but they are better than the standards and easier to gunsmith. King's Gun Works in Los Angeles manages to make either acceptable, however, and they fit a needed stop on the standard which prevents overtravel.

The target model is only available with a long 6 7/8″ tube

or a heavy 5 1/2" bull barrel, but if you don't mind the bulk and weight, these guns are superior in several ways to the standard, which can be had with a more compact 4 3/4" barrel as well as a 6". The bull barrel holds very steadily and shoots very well. I think it is the best choice, all things considered, but you may prefer to buy the long barreled target model and have it cut to a handier length. The standard model with a trigger job and the excellent adjustable sights made by Miniature Machine Co. is also very satisfactory; I have been using one for quite some time with complete satisfaction.

Colt Woodsman

The Achilles' heel of the Woodsman is its notoriously weak magazine which is not only unusually susceptible to damage but seems also to deteriorate from ordinary use. Except for this idiosyncrasy which can, of course, be counteracted by keeping a large supply of spare magazines, the Colt is a nice pistol. For my hand, the grip could be improved and the trigger badly needs a stop, but these are personal preferences. Accuracy is good and, though the Woodsman is a bit more fragile than the other autos mentioned here, it is an acceptable choice for survival use. It is one of our oldest designs and it has been very popular with outdoorsmen.

Colt Conversion Unit

Anyone who has a Colt Government Model .45 or .38 Super for defensive use should own this conversion unit for low cost practice. It consists of a slide, barrel, recoil spring, and a floating chamber which increases the felt recoil of the .22 so that it more nearly simulates firing the heavier cartridges. This kit can be easily installed on the Government Model frame without tools in less than one minute simply by field stripping the gun as you ordinarily would for cleaning. It will not fit Commander Models. Excellent adjustable sights are installed on the slide so that the unit can be zeroed for any .22 long rifle ammunition. Accuracy is not up to the level of the best .22 autos, but it is acceptable for most purposes and it is more than adequate for simulated combat practice. The price differential between .22's and .45's of approximately $22 per hundred will quickly pay for the cost of this unit. I recommend it highly as a training device, but not necessarily as a substitute for other .22 pistols.

The Rimfire in Perspective

As you consider the place of rimfire guns and ammunition in your overall survival plans, here are a few observations which you may find helpful.

There are very few uses for which the rimfires should be considered the weapons of choice. Except for target practice and shooting pests and game which are either too large or too far away to be taken with air guns, there is very little that the .22's will do that cannot be done better with other guns. Rimfires are cheap, however, relative to centerfires and, when used with care, they can often substitute for more effective weapons under non-critical

A matched pair of Anschutz full-length stocked actions with double set triggers and Bushnell variable scopes in .22 LR and .22 Magnum.

204

circumstances. My own strategy is to buy .22's in large quantities because they are cheap and compact, and to use them in preference to centerfires whenever the outcome of the shooting is not vital, saving my more effective weapons and ammunition for occasions when they are really needed. Such voluntary tactical use of the .22, I think, is prudent. Where many people go astray in survival planning, however, is not that they intend to *use* rimfires extensively, but that they intend to *rely* on them; and that, I submit, is a serious error. Whatever you do, don't spend so heavily on rimfires that you fail to buy the more effective weapons and ammunition that you will need. It is one thing to decide to do all of your meat hunting for a week with a .22 in order to be frugal, but it is quite another to be forced to do so because you have nothing else. What you learn about your skill and the power of your weapon in the first instance may be humbling, but in the second, it could be terminal. It has become fashionable among armchair survival theorists to proclaim that .22's can effectively handle all subsistence requirements. Indeed, the non-cognoscenti who overrate the .22 are second only to those who overrate the bow and arrow. I urge you not to rely on these theories of how easy it is to take large, fat-bearing game with a .22 until you have tried it for yourself. Yes, Virginia, a .22 will kill anything that walks, slithers, crawls or flies, but the critical question is whether *you* can reasonably *depend* on being able to make it do so when you must.

Don't forget to buy enough rimfire ammunition to use for sharpening your skills now and for trading purposes during a crisis. Under some circumstances a handful of .22's may be considerably more valuable than a bag of silver coins.

Spend some money on the triggers and sights on your rimfires. These are two areas where most of the off-the-shelf guns fall short. On your iron sighted rifles, install good aperture rears such as the Lyman 48 or the Williams Foolproof. Many of the sights made especially for .22's are too flimsy for rugged use. And if you expect to use your .22 rifle extensively or for critical applications, consider fitting it with a full-sized scope of good quality instead of the inexpensive rimfire only models.

At the risk of appearing more negative about rimfires than I really am, allow me to caution you once more against relying on any rimfire for defending your life. There are only two circumstances in which I can envision the .22's playing a useful role in defense. The most obvious is arms-length protection when no other weapon is available or when the shooter is physically incapable of handling anything more effective. In such cases, the Magnum is much to be preferred, but whatever you use, wait until your assailant is close, then aim for the eye sockets and keep shooting until he is disabled or your gun is empty.

The second circumstance is a tactical ruse. If severe social disturbances come, you may one day be faced by a band of looters intent on attacking your retreat. If they have some superficial military training — and many probably will — they may fire a few rounds from concealment in order to assess the level of resistance which they may encounter from you. Some spaced return fire from your .22 — as if a slow bolt action of limited magazine capacity is all you have — may lead them into the error of careless, exposed attack.

Except for instances such as these, do not expect rimfires to play a prominent role in deterring aggression. Successful defense with a .22 is like holding a winning lottery ticket or making a dozen straight passes in Las Vegas: it is reported often enough to be tempting, but the reliability factor precludes making a career of it.

6 Special Purpose Weapons

There are several very useful tools which, although not requisite in all survival batteries, may be virtually indispensable in some. A few of these special purpose weapons, such as boomerangs or slingshots, are quite primitive and should be regarded solely as means of last resort. Others, in addition to their special uses, also serve as spares or backups for more conventional weapons: combination guns are an example. Still another class is comprised of items which, like the Taser, may have, at best, limited usefulness, and they are reviewed only for the sake of completeness.

Air guns fit into none of the above categories. They are among the most universally useful arms available for survival applications, but because of their unique characteristics and the fact that their practical value is not ordinarily recognized in this context, I have chosen to include them in this chapter.

Air Guns

Until a few years ago, I was, like many American shooters, only casually familiar with air guns, and I tended to regard them merely as plinkers and playthings. The only pellet guns with which I had much actual experience were the toy-like American made arms which are designed primarily for the youth market. As a youngster, I had owned an inexpensive, inaccurate, low-powered BB gun and later I developed an oversized right arm from constantly pumping a Benjamin or a Sheridan pneumatic; but I viewed all of this as simply a prelude to my first "real" gun — a firearm.

In Europe, where firearms restrictions have been, for generations, as repressive as some emotional, short-sighted and, possibly, sinister minorities would make them in this country, air guns have been developed to a point where some of them are actually more durable, more finely made and more accurate than any firearm. When I began to make a systematic study of weaponry from the standpoint of survival use, I was fortunately led to examine many of these precision European *luftgewehre*, and I was amazed to discover how greatly they differ from our domestic products. Having now had extensive practical experience with them, I am convinced that their application to survival planning can hardly be overemphasized.

If you think that last statement is an exaggeration, consider some of the characteristics of air arms which led me to make it. For one thing, ammunition is extremely compact and inexpensive. Ten thousand pellets can be purchased for as little as $35.00 and that entire supply could be contained in a one pound coffee can. Further, pellets can be stored almost indefinitely and without hazard. The guns themselves are complementary to the ammunition in that they require little maintenance and, as air gun specialists are fond of saying, they "wear-in" instead of wearing out. The better ones actually exhibit higher velocity and a smoother firing cycle after extended use than when they are new. Just how long a good one will last I don't know, but one manufacturer asserts that his product does not even require lubrication until six million rounds have been fired. Air Rifle Headquarters, one of the leading suppliers of precision air arms in the U.S., suggests that high quality spring type designs should last indefinitely even under conditions of heavy use, given proper maintenance and the possible replacement of three basic parts every 10 years or so.

To this extraordinary durability, fine accuracy and the low cost of shooting air guns, add the fact that many of them are virtually silent and without perceptible recoil, and you have, obviously, a remarkable class of weapons; but what is their practical value in a survival battery?

Although their usefulness is certainly not limited to training, that is, perhaps, their most obvious niche. Shooting is *not* like swimming or riding a bicycle; even a master will lose the fine edge of his skill unless he practices regularly, and air guns provide an excellent means of doing so even for apartment dwellers in the city. Bullet traps silenced with "ballistic putty" allow safe, convenient air gun shooting almost anywhere. The gestation period of every chapter in this book was made less agonizing by some judicious plinking into the bullet trap in my office, and I regularly fire at least 50 rounds every evening while unwinding before bed. The Air Force found that for men who were totally unfamiliar with the basics of marksmanship — sight picture, trigger control, etc. — coping with recoil and noise was simply too much for them, within the limited training program offered. I have been told that when these preliminaries were taught using recoilless air guns, the number of men then able to pass the program using issue firearms on the rifle range increased by 30%. I am by no means convinced that anything can substitute completely for practice with the gun and ammunition with which you wish to develop skill, but all of the shooting that you do contributes to the development of grip and holding, acquiring sight pictures quickly and trigger control.

In my own case, I have found that practice with air guns is a good method of maintaining the level of shooting skill I have developed by range training with various firearms. I especially recommend "backyard safaris" as a means of sustaining one's timing and speed. If you have never tried it, I think you will be surprised how shooting air guns at insects, pine cones, sycamore pods and other targets of opportunity at various unknown distances and difficult angles will improve your practical marksmanship. After a few weeks, even people who have never fired a gun before are able to hit flies at 25 feet with some regularity; and the confidence which comes with such skill makes the transition to firearms an easy one. The fact that air guns are — except for occasional local ordinances — completely free from government regulations of purchasing, ownership, transport and use makes them a comparatively hassle-free means of learning to shoot. You can order both guns and ammunition by mail if you like, and use them indoors in urban areas without harassment. Because the better guns are all single-shots, they also provide an excellent and safe introduction to shooting for youngsters. Family picnics and other outings offer many opportunities for instruction with air guns when the use of firearms might be prohibited or inadvisable.

Food gathering and pest control with suitable air guns are much more practical than most people realize. In fact, if you are willing to limit your targets to animals no larger than cottontails, proper air rifles will kill almost as reliably as .22's to distances of 50 yards or so. For protecting your garden from crows and other pests, destroying rodents for reasons of hygiene, or any other short range, small target shooting which must be done in and around your dwelling or barn, air rifles are just as efficient as firearms and they are considerably safer. For hunting small game and fish, either for your table or as food for your dogs and other meat eating domestic animals, air guns are far less expensive to use and they usually destroy less edible meat than even rimfires do. I find them better for squirrel hunting than anything else because their extreme accuracy makes the necessary head shots easy and their lack of noise often allows several shots to be made. Air guns can also be used to rout larger pests without causing them serious harm, but be careful about this; foxes and even larger animals have occasionally been killed with powerful air rifles.

Obviously, the kind of weapons which possess the accuracy, durability and power for the purposes discussed here are not the ordinary air guns with which most of us are familiar. Very few of the several hundred different guns available are suitable for survival use. In fact, there is only one type which I consider completely satisfactory: those employing a spring piston for power.

Far more common in this country are the CO_2 gas guns and the pneumatics. The former use compressed carbon dioxide instead of air as a propellant, and their dependence upon commercial sources of gas renders them less than practical as survival guns even if there were no other arguments against them. They are also, however, usually less accurate than other types and because of the

Sheridan pneumatic .20 caliber.

213

delicate and complex valves which meter the gas, they fail more often and they are harder/to repair. For these reasons, there is not a single CO_2 gun which I can recommend.

Pneumatics, such as the Sheridan, Benjamin and Smith & Wesson, operate by forcing air into a storage container, by means of a compression piston, where it remains until released by a trigger-actuated valve mechanism. Usually, several strokes of a lever, pump handle or rod are required to store enough air for firing. The effort involved is often considerable, the process is slow and frequently very noisy. The chief advantage claimed for the pneumatic system is variable power: a few strokes can provide enough velocity for close range target shooting or frightening pests without harming them. Unfortunately, however, the pneumatics have a number of drawbacks. They do not produce very good practical accuracy, much less the level of precision which the best air guns are capable of, and, because the air is heated when it is pumped in, the power — and hence the trajectory — fluctuates as it cools. Uniform velocity from shot to shot is almost impossible to obtain with a pneumatic. The major drawback with this design, however, is maintenance. Like the CO_2's, pneumatics employ delicate, complex valves which are not easy to repair in the field. One possible exception in this regard is the rather crude, Korean made Yewha "Dynamite" which Robert Beeman, who sells it, says was "designed to be fixed by a Korean peasant on a flat rock." This gun is a

Yewha .25 caliber pneumatic smoothbore which fires round balls, pellets and bird shot. Sturdy but crude, its practical capabilities are overrated by some.

.25 caliber smoothbore which will fire bird shot, .25 caliber round balls and pellets as well as rice or even rocks. Given such versatility, it would appear to be an excellent survival tool and some may like it but I do not. It is almost as loud on firing as a standard velocity .22 long rifle — much noisier than the CCI Long CB Caps mentioned in the last chapter. It requires 160 pump strokes to make it ready for initial firing and its accuracy is marginal at best. It is a poor killer with shot beyond 30 feet and its sights are vestigial. Nevertheless, the Yewha is the most powerful air gun regularly available and with Laetare .25 caliber pellets it will develop a muzzle velocity close to 1000 fps.

Tales are told of hunting pheasants with shot-loaded Yewhas and bringing down deer with pellets or round balls. I suppose it *could* be done if the tooth fairy blessed your endeavor, but it seems somewhat less likely than Golda Meir's receiving the Volkswagen franchise for Kuwait. You might find one of these guns useful under some circumstances, but do not buy one as your sole air gun.

If, for some reason, you want a conventional pneumatic despite the drawbacks of questionable durability and accuracy, I would suggest the Sheridan, the Smith & Wesson or the Benjamin in that order.

The spring piston guns are the design of choice for practical use. They are cocked by a single easy stroke and, since the air is compressed only at the moment of firing, their power is very uniform. They are much more accurate and durable than any other type of air gun and many of them are quite simple to repair because they employ no valves or other very complex parts. They are also quieter and usually more powerful than other designs and they can be made virtually recoilless. All of the best spring piston air guns are presently of German manufacture, although the Spanish "El Gamo" offers a lot of performance for very little money.

Spring piston rifles fall into two categories, match or target guns and sporters. Match rifles are capable of the finest accuracy — .058″ at 25′ — but they tend to be heavy and their velocity level is usually no more than 650 fps. The sporters are much lighter and trimmer with velocities running from just under 700 fps. to more than 800 fps. Some, but by no means all, of the sporters are capable of accuracy approaching match grade.

Without question, the Feinwerkbau Sport Model (known variously as the F-12 or the F-124) is the best air rifle for survival use made anywhere in the world — and by a considerable margin. It is extraordinarily durable, simple to repair, more powerful than any other rifled air arm and it is capable of a very high order of accuracy. Mine has fired several 5 shot groups at 25′ which measure between .095″ and .12″ on centers, and after several months of shooting it now develops a muzzle velocity of 855 fps. In normal use, only three parts can be expected to need replacement: the main spring, the breech seal and the piston seal. Both of these seals are made of durable synthetics which tend to resist both wear and deterioration, and the massive mainspring is unusually sturdy. It is unlikely that any of these components would fail during a single lifetime, given reasonable care and barring abuse, but it would be prudent to stock two spares of each, nevertheless; they are quite inexpensive.

Diana, Weirauch and Wisho all make excellent competi-

The author's choice: Feinwerkbau F-12 with 4x scope, supplied and accurized by Air Rifle Headquarters.

Hy-Score 809, a handsome, good shooting air rifle, but not the best choice for survival use because of leather washers and difficult assembly.

tive guns, but their best models, which approach the accuracy and velocity of the Feinwerkbau — but do not equal it — come within twenty dollars or so of being as expensive as the F-12. Further, some of these models — notably the Diana — employ leather seals which require constant attention and need regular replacement. Almost all of them are quite difficult for the ordinary user to service without special tools and detailed knowledge. If you intend to make serious use of air guns in your survival plans, the Feinwerkbau is your clear first choice. If you would also like to have a much less expensive "knock-around" gun as a backup or for youngsters to use, consider the El Gamo 68 XP which sells for considerably less than $100. It can produce 3/8" to 1/4" groups at 25' with velocities up to 680 or 690 fps. and it is very rugged. The only other quality model which costs enough less than the Feinwerkbau to be considered for a second gun is the Weirauch 30S, which offers about the same velocity as the El Gamo, slightly better accuracy and sells for about $20 more.

Let me urge you not to consider one of these economy models as your only air rifle choice. Even though the difference in performance may not sound like much, it can be critical. Remember that we are talking about very low energy levels with even the most powerful air guns. Perhaps the following information will help to place these elements in a practical perspective.

Approximate Field Accuracy

Projectile	Muzzle Velocity (fps.)	Average Group Size at 50 yards
.22 Long Rifle Std. velocity 40 gr. bullet	1145	1"
.20 cal. Sheridan 16 gr. pellet — 8 pumps (max. recommended)	605	4"+
.177 cal. El Gamo, 8-1/2 gr. pellet	680	2-1/4"
.177 cal. Feinwerkbau Sport Model, 8-1/2 gr. pellet	850	1-1/4"

	Approximate Lethal Area Sizes	Velocity Required at Point of Impact (fps.)
Sparrow, Mouse, Ground Squirrel	1/2"	325
Gray & Fox Squirrel, Pigeon, Rat	3/4—1"	400
Crow, Rabbit, Game Birds	1-3/4—2"	500-550
Opossum, Groundhog-Woodchuck, Jackrabbit	2"	600
Raccoon and Fox	2-1/2"	675+

Approximate Velocity Table
8.5gr. .177 cal. Pellet

Muzzle	35 Yards	50 Yards
450	350	300
630	475	420
705	550	475
780	610	525
850	765	600

As you can see from these tables, the success and variety of your hunting will be strictly limited by the accuracy and velocity of the air rifle you choose, and even small differences in either factor will noticeably affect your results.

These same two elements — velocity and accuracy — should also determine the caliber you select. Most of the better European air rifles are made in both .22 and .177, but the latter is the overwhelming choice of experts. There is so little power involved that the normal criteria of caliber choice does not apply. Air rifle pellets kill strictly by penetration in a vital area, usually the brain (although chest shots are better for crows), so impact area is less important than delivering the pellet to the precise point of aim with enough remaining velocity to achieve penetration. Trajectory (and, hence, your ability to hit at unknown distances), velocity, accuracy and range are all notably better with the .177. Practical shooting with .22 pellets is limited to about 40 yards at the outside; the .177 extends that distance to about 65 yards. Velocity is about 25% greater at the muzzle with the .177 and groups with the smaller pellet can be 40% tighter. In addition, the cost of .177 pellets is approximately 1/3 less than equivalent .22's and they are much more compact.

Thus far, we have omitted pistols from our discussion of air powered arms. Because they are far less powerful and harder to develop fine accuracy with, I believe that their usefulness in survival planning is limited. In the field, I would hesitate to use even the best of them on anything larger than pigeons and I would confine the range to 25 yards or less. For training purposes, however, there are two models which I especially recommend, the Feinwerkbau F-65 and the British Webley Premier.

The F-65 is simply the finest air pistol I have ever seen. It is incredibly precise in all of its adjustments and functions, it is so durable that I doubt that one could be worn out simply through use, and it is accurate enough to hit a pinhead consistently from across an average room. All of the international match records have been fired with the F-65 and it is so trouble free that the factory recommends no maintenance except lubrication every six million rounds. In normal operation, all recoil and vibration are completely dampened, but there is an adjustment which allows for the simulation of recoil, if desired. Velocity (470 fps.) is the highest of any air pistol of which I am aware.

The Webley lies at the other end of the scale from the F-65. It is about the least expensive air pistol which has any practical value, and it is quite crude by comparison with the Feinwerkbau. It is, however, much smaller than any of its competitors and its velocity (450 fps.) is one of the highest. Accuracy is marginal, but it is good enough for birds and rats to perhaps 20 yards, if you do your part. It has a terrible trigger and it kicks at least as much as a .22 pistol using a high velocity long rifle cartridge. But it is in these apparent shortcomings that its chief value lies as a trainer.

One factor concerning recoil and air guns which I have never seen discussed in print derives from the fact that in the spring type arms which have recoil or vibration, the disturbance is a result of the plunger's building up air

Webley Premier: least expensive practical air pistol for field use. A good firearm training substitute.

pressure to expel the pellet. Hence, it occurs *before* the pellet leaves the gun — unlike a firearm in which most of the recoil effect is felt at the moment when the bullet exits the barrel. Now, at first glance, this difference would seem to contraindicate air guns as understudies for firearms, but just the opposite is true. You will soon discover that you can't hit anything with a heavy recoil air pistol, such as the Webley, unless 1) your grip is consistent from shot to shot and 2) you find an effective means to counteract the recoil effect. This latter consideration is the basic "trick" involved in combat shooting, which demands recoil control as a requisite to effective rapid fire.

Shooters of light recoil firearms frequently develop bad habits in this regard, often using a loose hold and allowing the gun to recoil freely, since they can shoot such guns accurately with these techniques. Unless you hold the Webley rigidly with both hands and provide strong opposing force (i.e., pushing with the shooting hand and pulling with the other), you simply cannot develop any useful, consistent accuracy with it. Even the rather poor trigger with which the Webleys seem to be cursed can be an asset to training, since that element too demands that your hold provide an absolutely rigid mounting platform for the gun.

Finally, the considerable cocking effort of the Webley helps to tone the very muscles used in pistol shooting. Warts and all, the Premier is well worth its modest price as a trainer, whatever its practical value in the field.

Ammunition and Accessories

Although the best air powered arms are extremely durable and accurate, there are two errors that a neophyte is likely to make which can greatly reduce their efficiency or render them entirely useless. First, *NEVER*, for any reason, fire a spring type air gun without a pellet seated in the chamber. Such abuse allows the piston to slam into the cylinder unbraked, and doing it even once may render the gun inoperable. Second, exercise care in selecting your pellet supply. Cheap, bargain brand pellets are often irregular and they allow air blow-by, which can have almost the same damaging effect on the mechanism as dry firing. At best, such ammunition will greatly reduce the velocity and accuracy of any arm in which it is used. Even the very best imported pellets are quite inexpensive in comparison to cartridges for firearms, and the difference in performance between them and the poor ones which sell for a few cents less is tremendous, even in modestly priced guns. In fact, you may get better performance using the best pellets in an inexpensive gun than you will using cheap pellets in the finest match rifle. Mt. Star Diablo and National Brand are both good utility pellets, and either will serve for plinking and general familiarization shooting. Nationals are not quite as uniform as the Mt. Star but they are heavier and they retain their velocity better at longer ranges. Either brand will cost about $4.00 per thousand. The most accurate pellet at shorter ranges in almost all pellet guns is the H&N Premium Match. Its blunt head cuts very clean holes for scoring targets and makes it quite effective on small animals within its range. The H&N does not hold velocity well for long distance shooting. Cost is about $6.00 per thousand. The very best pellets for game shooting are the Mount Star Jets or Silver Jets, and they are also the most accurate beyond 30 yards. Both are heavy and employ a series of air sealing rings near the head. The Silver Jet is pointed and the Jet has a round nose. I have not conducted controlled tests between the two, but I think the regular Jet may have a slight edge in killing power; however, any difference is small and either will serve you well for hunting. Price is about $6.00 per thousand.

All of the above pellets are available in .177 caliber, which I recommend. You may occasionally find that size referred to as #1 bore or 4.5mm. Twenty-two pellets are also known as #2 bore or 5.5mm., and .25 caliber is the same as #3 bore or 6 1/3mm. The Sheridan pneumatics are made only in .20 caliber (5mm.) and I believe that their own brand of pellets in a single design is currently the only ammunition available for them, although at one time Air Rifle Headquarters carried AmPells in that size. Many of the better brands are not available in .22 caliber since most experts agree that the .177 is generally superior; however, the Jets and Silver Jets are, and if you choose a .22 air gun, I suggest that you use them.

You may want to make provision, as I have done, for carrying an emergency supply of pellets in the butt of your rifle. Simply remove the butt plate and drill one or more holes longitudinally into the stock, being careful not to go too deep or to weaken the wood structurally. Two 3/4″ holes about 5″ deep will hold more than a thousand pellets. Good insurance.

Except for the match rifles, the sights which are supplied on even the better air rifles do not do justice to the inherent accuracy of the guns themselves. Most companies specializing in air arms can provide you with an excellent Williams aperture sight to fit almost any of the rifles I have mentioned except the El Gamo. Even better, consider mounting a scope. Nothing else will give you the precision of which these guns are capable. For best results, you should buy a scope which has had the parallax especially corrected for air rifle use, and be cautious of the inexpensive variable powered scopes designed for the .22's. They do not seem to hold up well on air rifles; however, either the fixed four power .22 scopes or the better quality 1″ diameter models, either fixed or variable, are excellent.

Two small accessories which you may overlook are the

trigger shoe and the pellet pouch, but nothing else will contribute so much to the efficiency of your air arms kit. The shoes will greatly improve the feel of most air gun triggers and allow you to shoot them with much greater accuracy. The pouches are a necessity, because there is simply no other method of carrying the pellets so that they are both protected from damage or foreign substances and still easily available for use. A cleaning rod is also a good idea, not so much for cleaning — which is almost never necessary — as for removing stuck pellets or other obstructions from the barrel. You will also need a good supply of special chamber lubricants which have a low flash point so that they will not "diesel" when the air is compressed on firing. A carrying sling is also useful as is a bullet trap for practice. Both Beeman's and Air Rifle Headquarters sell special traps for air arms which are silenced with "ballistic putty." The metal ones used with firearms are so noisy that they obviate one of the chief advantages of air guns for indoor practice.

Lest you think, because of my frequent mention of Air Rifle Headquarters and Beeman's Precision Airguns, that I have a financial interest in those companies, let me say that I do not. I have referred to them only because of my strong belief that you will probably be better off buying your air guns from a specialist. For one thing, many of the most useful accessories which I have mentioned are available only through such sources, but more important, the guns you receive will not have been abused and they are guaranteed. More than once I have seen clerks in sporting goods stores dry firing spring piston air rifles when demonstrating them to customers. Further, both of the firms above offer optional "accurization" for the guns which they sell, and I highly recommend it. This special lubrication and "deburring" process significantly increases not only the accuracy but the velocity as well, and it is not expensive. Air Rifle Headquarters will even allow you to order any gun of your choice for a free 10 day home trial with only a 50% deposit, and both firms guarantee their merchandise fully. Beeman's carries a larger number of items and their prices are somewhat lower but Air Rifle Headquarters gives faster service, more complete instruction and service manuals and I like their accuracy work better. If you are interested in air guns, I suggest that you order both of their catalogs; they are, together, a complete crash course in what you need to know about the subject. Clients have reported to me, and my own experience confirms, that both companies will provide virtually unlimited advice by telephone. Ordering by mail can be a painful experience and I am pleased to report that it is not with these two sources.

Combination Guns

Although never very popular or well known in this country, combination guns were the favorite hunting weapons among the aristocracy in Continental Europe before World War II. Even then, when labor was cheap and craftsmanship was not unusual, these multiple barreled guns were expensive because of the highly skilled handwork necessary to cause several shotgun and rifle barrels to shoot to the same point of aim. Three-barreled guns, known as *drillings*, and four-barreled guns, *vierlings*, were the most common, but since these arms were, for the most part, custom-built, the buyer could have almost any combination he desired and a few examples still exist which offer two shotgun gauges and four different rifle calibers, ranging from light varmint to African class — all joined to a single receiver and stock.

A rich variety of game animals and rather generous bag limits contributed to the popularity of combination guns on the Continent. If a fine stag or roebuck wandered into

225

view while you were out gunning for pheasants, a deft press on the selector switched the firing mechanism from the shotgun barrels to the rifle, and you were instantly prepared for almost any target of opportunity.

Living self-sufficiently makes a gun of similar versatility desirable in your working battery. Most hunters know the mild chagrin of flushing a covey of birds while hunting for deer, when armed only with a scope sighted rifle. If food were scarce, such an occasion might lose its humorous aspect.

The primary objections to combination guns as survival weapons are 1) cost — the best models can be *very* expensive, from $1500 to $5000, 2) weight, 3) limited firepower — each barrel is a single-shot. Further, some of them do not balance and swing quite as well as the best examples of either rifles or shotguns and scoping the rifle barrels presents some problems and inconveniences, although it can be done. On the plus side, these arms can offer great versatility in a comparatively small package and, because of their simplicity, they are usually quite durable.

These considerations, taken together, have led me to regard combination guns as special purpose weapons and not as required components of the primary survival battery. They can, however, perform at least three roles extremely well. First, nothing else is quite as good a candidate for the emergency kit. Whenever I travel by automobile or private plane, I always carry one of the little Savage .22/20 gauges taken down in my duffel. Remember, even if you are living under survival conditions in the midst of an emergency, an even more pressing emergency can occur. Contingencies could develop at your retreat which might cause you to leave it and most of your equipment — in a hurry. Whatever your circumstances, a well thought out survival kit is good insurance, and it

226

should include a versatile firearm together with a supply of ammunition.

Another function which combination guns admirably fulfill is that of serving as spares or backup guns. Inexpensive, U.S. made two-barreled designs cost very little more than simple single-shot rifles or shotguns alone, and they are more useful than either, while still providing the security of having more than one arm which can use your primary ammunition supply.

Finally, the combinations can be used for additional calibers and gauges which may not otherwise be represented in your battery. It is good survival strategy, I think, to have the potential of being able to use as many of the most popular ammunition sizes as possible, and the less expensive two-barrel guns offer a comparatively economical means of satisfying that objective.

If you want to use a combination gun as one of your primary hunting weapons or if you simply want the highest possible quality in all of your survival guns, you will have to turn to the import market. A number of European makers, such as Sauer & Sohn or Krieghoff, can produce almost anything you are willing to pay for. Be cautious of some of the fine pre-war guns which you may find on the used shelves, however, because most of them are chambered for the less popular (in the U.S.) 16 gauge shotgun shells and European metric rifle calibers for which you may have difficulty obtaining ammunition. Colt is presently importing a handsome Sauer-made drilling with two barrels chambered for 12 gauge and the other for either .30-'06 Springfield or .243 Winchester. It looks very good, but I have not had an opportunity to test one. Price is about $1700.

Savage offers the broadest selection of combination guns in this country. The top of their line is a very well made over-and-under by Valmet, chambered for either the .308 (7.62 NATO) or the .222 rifle caliber and the 12 gauge shotgun. Selling for $400, this model 2400 is certainly not cheap, but it is a quality product and a very practical hunting weapon indeed. The test gun which I examined and fired threw excellent modified choke patterns and the .308 rifle barrel produced 3", three shot groups at 100 yards with open sights and Remington factory ammunition. Workmanship was very good throughout and while I cannot certify its durability because it is so new, I see no obvious flaws or weak points in the design. I can think of few guns better suited for hunting in dense cover than this one loaded with a .308 in one barrel and a Brenneke slug in the other.

There are four models of the Savage 24 series. The 24V offers a choice of either a .30-30 or a .222 rifle barrel coupled with a 3" 20 ga. Magnum shotgun tube. The 24D and 24 Field Grade are identical to one another except for their stocks, and each is available with either a .22 long rifle or a .22 Magnum barrel over a .410 bore or 3" 20 ga. Magnum. The 24C, or Camper's Model, is a pound lighter and 4" shorter than the other 24's and it is furnished with an extremely useful soft takedown case, allowing the gun to be stored in an area measuring only 5" x 22". The stock is designed with a trap door butt plate which conceals a reserve ammunition storage area. It is available only in .22 long rifle and standard 20 gauge chamberings.

For emergency survival kit use, I have found nothing better than the 24C. It is extremely versatile, and, with a bit of ingenuity, it can be made even more useful. The butt stock is designed to hold 10 long rifle cartridges and two shotgun shells. In mine I can squeeze in six CCI Long CB Caps, four long rifle hollow points, four hi-speed short hollow points, two high base 2 3/4" shotgun shells loaded with #6 shot and a tightly rolled book of paper matches with three fishhooks inside, secured by wrapping with 100 feet of 20 pound test braided nylon fishing line. The self-contained ammunition supply can be increased by six long rifle hollow points, two Brenneke slugs and two more shotgun shells, with the addition of a lace-on leather cheekpiece and ammunition holder such as the one I designed for the "Sandalmaker." The case also has room for a "shell-shrinker" in .45 ACP caliber and another in .30-30 is stored in the shotgun barrel. Ten .30-30 cartridges in one of the plastic Federal cartridge slides also go in the case. Add a heavy folding knife and, perhaps a 6 foot square of plastic folded in your pocket, and you should be able to live off the land for several months with such an outfit.

These Savage over/under combination guns are among the most versatile survival tools. Above: Model 24C Camper's Model with takedown case and author's lace-on ammo carrier. Additional rounds are stored in a trap in the butt. Standard model below.

All of these 24's cost about $100 and none of them is perfect. In addition to the fact that they are a bit rough — as you might expect from the price tag — there are several improvements which need to be made. Every one I have seen badly needs a trigger job and some require a little "deburring" internally. All except the 24C are furnished only with full choke shotgun barrels and the patterns are entirely too tight for anything except long range waterfowl shooting, but a good gunsmith can open them up to improved cylinder inexpensively. I wish that these guns were available in 12 gauge instead of 20, if for no other reason than the fact that 12 gauge slugs are considerably more effective on large game, but the 20 will do for deer out to 50 yards. I also wish my favorite Camper's Model were chambered for 3" shells as the other 24's are and I suppose it could be rechambered, but I haven't tried it. A Williams Dovetail Open Sight with a wide, shallow English "V" blade should be installed to replace the somewhat rudimentary sight furnished. Such an arrangement will not interfere with your shotgun pointing and it will do justice to the superb rifle accuracy of which these guns are capable. Although each model is grooved for scope mounting, I think optical sights on a gun of this type are more trouble than they are worth.

For those who want a combination gun of better quality but more limited caliber choice, the LSA-55 Turkey Gun is worth examining. It mounts a full choke standard 12 gauge shotgun barrel over a .222 and it should be close to ideal for pest control around a farm or retreat. Price is about $330.

I hope my enthusiasm for combination guns as special purpose weapons does not tempt you to choose one of them as a one gun survival battery. Although they are quite versatile and can perform a number of functions in an emergency, your survival potential over the long term will be severely limited if you have nothing else.

Rifles in Pistol Calibers

Another useful special purpose weapon is a rifle chambered for one of the primary handgun calibers in your battery. In addition to the obvious advantage of simplifying your storage problems, there is also the consideration of gaining increased power from compact pistol cartridges. Further, if your ammunition supply proves to be inadequate, you will be able to increase the food gathering potential of each remaining handgun cartridge by using it in an accurate rifle.

Because very few guns of this type are produced in centerfire, your practical caliber choice is limited to .357 Magnum and .44 Magnum. A few custom lever action conversions have been made for the .45 Colt but, because of the small case rim, extraction problems were common. In most cases, however, the .357 rifles will also accept .38 Specials and the .44 Magnums can use .44 Specials.

The improvement in the performance of a .357 when used in a rifle is dramatic. By careful handloading, the velocity of a 158 gr. jacketed soft point bullet can be made to exceed 2000 fps. in an 18″ rifle barrel and that places the .357 comfortably in the deer class. Further, a good rifle will fire that cartridge accurately to a greater range and most people will be able to place their shots with greater certainty. In short, from a rifle, the .357 cartridge *will do* what most people *think* it will do from a pistol. The best .357 Magnum rifle I have ever seen is currently being imported from Italy by Navy Arms. It is a near perfect replica of the 1873 Model Winchester and it is finely made. Three versions are available: a Trapper's Model with a 16 1/2″ barrel, a carbine with a 20″ and a rifle with a heavy 24″ octagon barrel. Either a blued or a handsome color case hardened receiver is available. Ballistically, the 20″ is probably the optimum length, but 16 1/2" is handier and the long, heavy octagon barrel holds more steadily. I have only tested the rifle, and I was impressed by its performance. Factory loaded 140gr. Speer hollow points averaged 7/8" groups at 50 yards and velocity clocked 1985 fps. at the muzzle. This is a fairly expensive gun, but both its appearance and its performance justify the price. It is also available in .22 LR and .44/40.

Both Navy Arms and Garcia import single-shot replicas of the Remington Rolling Block in .357 Magnum. I have been unable to obtain the Garcia Star for testing either from local gun stores or from the importers, but the Navy Arms model is an excellent, practical gun, carrying a reasonable price tag. Considering the uses to which such a gun might be put, I don't consider the single-shot limitation a serious one, and the rolling block action certainly makes for a compact arm. With a 20" octagon barrel the Navy Arms Rolling Block Baby Carbine weighs 4 3/4 lbs. and has an overall length of only 35".

.38 Special or .357 cases with semi-wadcutter Keith type bullets loaded to produce about 1200 fps. in a rifle are close to ideal for small game hunting. Even full power loads are not too destructive when a hard, non-expanding bullet is used, and they are also excellent for the larger varmints

A pair of pistol caliber rifles: Navy Arms superb replica of Winchester's '73 in .357 Magnum, above. Marlin .44 Magnum below.

such as coyote, mountain lion or bobcat, as well as wild pig and similar game. A good, heavily constructed jacketed hollow point or soft point weighing from 150 to 160 gr. and driven to 2000 fps. should work well on deer out to 150 yards or so.

In .44 Magnum, there are two commercial rifles available. Marlin makes a good lever action called the Model 1894 and Ruger an autoloader known as the Model .44 Carbine, which is a look alike for their 10/22 rimfire. Both of the Rugers I have tried gave poor accuracy with all loads tested and I had feeding problems (jams) with them regardless of the ammunition used. It could be that I got two lemons in a row, but I have heard enough similar reports from other writers and clients to cause me not to recommend this model. It seems not to measure up to the usually high Ruger standards.

The lifter latch, which probably should be made of steel, may be part of the problem, although the fact that several of the assembly pins shift on recoil could also be a factor. The firing pin retaining pin is particularly troublesome in this regard and it should be staked or otherwise more firmly fixed. Further, the magazine capacity is limited to four rounds and the barrel leads badly with anything but jacketed bullets. Finally, since it is an autoloader, it will not function unless the power level of its ammunition is held to narrow tolerances, thereby limiting the variety of loads that can be conveniently used in it.

One of the handiest small carbines available — the Marlin .44 Magnum lever action with heavy octagon barrel.

Fortunately, there are no such serious problems with the Marlin. Virtually any bullet design will feed reliably from its 10 shot tubular magazine, and accuracy is excellent from the Micro-groove barrel. Mine produces 2 1/2" groups at 100 yards with 240 gr. jacketed bullets.

For reasons which I do not entirely comprehend, the .44 Magnum — particularly when fired from a rifle — is a much more certain game getter than many cartridges which look better on paper. Within 175 yards or so, it is one of the very best I have ever used for deer and black bear. The trajectory, and hence, the range limitations, are approximately the same as the .30-30, but recoil seems lighter and killing power is noticeably better.

Until very recently, Marlin offered this carbine with either a round or a heavy octagonal barrel, and the latter is my first choice. A few may still be on dealers' shelves, but the somewhat less expensive standard model, which can be bought for just over a hundred dollars, is entirely satisfactory and it is a very good value. You may need a trigger job and an aperture sight, but no other modifications seem necessary.

Some experts argue against the wisdom of rifle-pistol combinations using the same ammunition, pointing out that if you are going to carry a rifle, you might as well have one that shoots something more potent than a pistol cartridge. There is certainly something to be said for that point of view. On the other hand, it is possible that you don't need any more power under some circumstances than that provided by a rifle shooting a .357 or .44 Magnum and the pistol is along just in case the rifle malfunctions or is lost. Few would deny that most people can place their shots more reliably with a rifle, and it does simplify matters if both your primary weapon and your backup can use the same ammunition. A lot of cowboys in the Old West thought highly of the idea and carried rifles and pistols chambered for cartridges like the .44/40. Many explorers in remote areas of South America still follow the practice, but with more modern calibers.

If your budget can absorb a non-essential item or two, I think you will find a handy little carbine chambered for your working pistol caliber to be one of your most useful options.

Thompson Contender

People who have developed some skill with the handgun or who must have the greatest possible firearm versatility in the most compact package will find the T/C Contender an extraordinarily useful tool. It is a break-open single-shot pistol which will accept any of two dozen or so interchangeable barrels ranging from .22 rimfire to .44 Magnum and .30-30, including shot barrels complete with screw-on chokes. The hammer easily adjusts to actuate either the rimfire or centerfire firing pins contained in the receiver, and barrels can be changed in less than 30 seconds simply by pushing out an oversized pin. A kit containing the basic pistol and a rimfire barrel, a scoped varmint barrel, a heavy hunting barrel and shotgun barrel can be as small as 9" x 16" with room left inside for a small ammunition supply. With a standard 10" barrel in place the Contender measures only 13 1/2" in length and weighs just 43 oz.

Accuracy is superb. Minute of angle groups are possible with a scope from a steady rest in some calibers such as the .22 Hornet. Velocity from the long 10" barrels is uniformly excellent and the extremely strong action allows very heavy handloads to be used safely. The .45 Colt, for example, can be loaded to equal .44 Magnum ballistics in this gun. In fact, the Contender provides the maximum in pistol performance and its practical usefulness in a survival situation is limited only by the ability of its user.

With suitable barrels it can handle any game and pest hunting chore from the smallest animals to birds in flight, deer and, possibly, bear, in expert hands.

Extra barrels for the Contender provide a comparatively economical means of being prepared to use virtually any ammunition which you may acquire by trading or other means. In addition to several wildcats, available calibers include: .22 LR, .22 Win. Mag., 5 mm. Rem. Mag., .22 Hornet, .22 Rem. Jet, .218 BEE, .221 Fireball, .222 Rem., .256 Win. Mag., .25/35, 30 M1 Carbine, .30-30 Win., .38 Super Auto, .38 Spl., .357 Mag., 9 mm. Parabellum, .45 ACP, .45 Colt and .44 Mag. I have not tested samples of each, but all I have used were excellent. I have heard reports that the .30-30 barrel occasionally dislodges the wooden fore-end, but that has not been my experience with it. That caliber *does* kick, however, as you might expect in an arm of this weight.

The most useful of all these options may be the 10″ .45 Colt with the detachable choke (#4139). A good gunsmith can deepen the chamber enough to accept a standard 3″ .410 shotgun shell, which is about the same diameter as the .45 Colt. With the choke in place to counteract the spin imparted to the shot charge by the rifled barrel, good patterns can be obtained out to 25 yards or so with #6's and 7 1/2's. The shorter 2 1/2″ .410 shells can also be used with less recoil, although the effective range is reduced by 10 or 12 yards. This modification, when properly done, seems to have no effect whatsoever on the excellent accuracy of the barrel with the .45 Colt, but remember to remove the choke when firing bullets instead of shot. With a supply of shotgun shells and heavy .45 Colt handloads, this one barrel is suitable for short range pest extermination, pot shooting and deer hunting. Add a rimfire barrel and possibly a scoped .222 and you have an ultra compact, mini-survival battery. Such an arrangement is, of course, inadequate for defense because of the single-shot limitation and it requires a high level of skill to produce game regularly, but it certainly could be useful in a pinch. A soft, fleece-lined zipper case, which can be tucked away in a very small space, is available to hold the Contender and three barrels.

Although I do not usually favor scoping pistols, it makes sense to use an optical sight on the Contender varmint barrels because you cannot otherwise take full advantage of their remarkable accuracy and range. Inexpensive pistol scopes, such as the Bushnell Phantom, will do,

A mini-survival battery in a case — for those who have the skill to realize its potential: the T/C Contender with three interchangeable barrels in .222 (with Leupold M8-2x scope in Buhler mounts), .22 Long Rifle and .45 Colt — .410 shotgun (with detachable choke).

and they can be attached by light mounts supplied by the gun manufacturer, since the recoil of such cartridges is very light. I much prefer to use the fine, long eye-relief Leupold M8-2X in Buhler mounts, however. The difference in price is not great, but the difference in performance and durability is.

The .44 Magnum and .357 Magnum barrels are both available with detachable chokes for use with special "Hot Shot" loads offered by Thompson Contender in those calibers; however, neither shot load comes close to the performance of a 3" .410 in the modified .45 Colt barrel, and .410 shotgun shells are much easier to find and far less expensive.

The most convenient way to carry a Contender in the field, particularly if it is scoped, is in a shoulder holster and Thompson offers one, but both Milt Sparks and Lawrence can supply models which I think you will like better.

There are a number of other single-shot pistols on the market, such as the Remington .221 Fireball, but none of them offer the versatility of the Contender and most of them are more nearly playthings than serious survival weapons. The Contender is a practical tool for those who have the skill to use it well.

Auto Mag

Despite the load flexibility and better case handling features of the revolver, some will prefer an autopistol as a field or working handgun and, for them, there is only one serious choice: the Auto Mag. This is a large (one foot long), heavy (57 oz.), stainless steel auto of unique design, which is available with interchangeable barrels in a variety of calibers.

In some circles, the Auto Mag has a bad reputation, not so much for any flaw in the gun itself, but because the original company that designed and produced it went bankrupt, leaving some prospective purchasers holding worthless receipts for undelivered pistols. The present manufacturer, TDE, Inc., has at its helm not only the man responsible for the gun's development, Harry Sanford, but also a corporate finance attorney of considerable sophistication and substance, Graham Sterling. I know these men, and I believe that they are making a sincere effort to produce a quality product. They are certainly succeeding in producing one which has no direct competitor.

The Auto Mag was originally designed around a rimless, and potentially more powerful version of the .44 Magnum. Cases can be made easily by trimming .308 or .30-'06 brass to length. Standard .44 Magnum bullets are used, but loads developing very high pressures can be employed because of the strength of both the thick, cut down rifle case and the short recoil, rotary bolt action. Barrels are now available in wildcat calibers which use the basic case necked to either .357 or .41 caliber and initial velocities claimed with these lighter bullets are substantial. Personally, I prefer the original large diameter heavy bullets even at long ranges, because heavy projectiles re-

The most powerful autopistol in regular production anywhere in the world: the stainless steel .44 Auto Mag.

tain velocity better than light ones, but I will concede that the .357 Auto Mag delivers remarkably flat trajectory.

My own experience and that of everyone I have talked to who has used the Auto Mag extensively is positive. The guns often need a "tune-up" with some judicious polishing and stoning here and there, and at present, you will have to make your own ammunition, or order it from a custom loading service[1], but the design is basically sound, it has the durability of stainless steel and it offers the potential of performance available in no other regularly available repeating handgun.

I understand that plans to make factory ammunition available in the Auto Mag calibers are underway, and until that becomes a reality, the wildcat aspect of this pistol is a handicap; however, at a retreat it could be useful to own a gun which can use your discarded rifle brass. Split necks are the most common case failure in reloading, and empties which for that reason would be unusable in rifles could be reclaimed for the Auto Mag simply by trimming.

Like the Thompson Center Contender and most other oversized handguns, the Auto Mag is carried most conveniently in a shoulder holster such as the Hardy-Cooper made by Milt Sparks. If you prefer a belt holster, Safariland makes a good one especially designed for this gun. The Auto Mag is not a good choice for every battery, but for some uses, there is nothing better.

Derringers

These miserable little gats are extremely popular among

---

[1]The factory informs me that Auto Mag ammunition is now available from the following sources:
R.S. Beal, 170 W. Marshall Rd., Lansdowne, Penn. 19050
L.E. Jurras & Assoc., Box 846, Roswell, NM 88201
Kent Lomont, 4420 S. Wayne, Fort Wayne, Ind. 46807
Pac. Int. Import, 2416 16th, Sacramento, CA 95818
Sandia Die & Cart. Co., Rt. 5, Box 5400, Albuquerque, NM 87123

the uninformed despite the fact that most of them are at least as dangerous to the user as they are to an opponent. Usually, they are two shot affairs with superposed barrels and single action outside hammer designs. When loaded, they must be carried on half-cock and they almost always fire if accidentally dropped. In most cases the two barrels do not group anywhere near one another, they have poor grips and worse sights.

Only one model that I know of is safe to carry fully loaded, the High Standard double action — on which the trigger pull is so heavy and gritty that it is a challenge even to fire deliberately. Despite its ills, there is one valuable use for the High Standard. The .22 Magnum model,

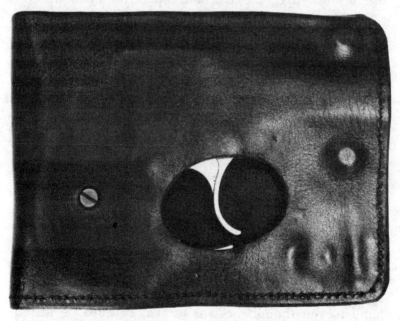

This little stinger could give a mugger an unpleasant surprise — if you can get a permit to carry it. The leather simulated wallet contains a double action, 2 shot, .22 Magnum High Standard Derringer. The leather should be thicker so that the outline of the gun doesn't show.

mounted in a leather simulated wallet, could provide a rather unpleasant surprise for a would-be mugger. Do not overestimate this arrangement, however. Its chief value is that it may catch an assailant off guard. Its sure hitting range cannot be extended much beyond arms length and even then, the .22 Magnum is by no means a certain fight stopper. I would feel very uncomfortable if this were my only weapon when serious trouble started, but it is a worthwhile backup device.

Some gun shops sell a cheap version of the Derringer wallet but I find it unsatisfactory because the exposed brass brads which hold it together are a giveaway, the leather is so thin that it molds to the gun after only a little use, and the trigger access hole is poorly shaped and too small. A better one, made to my specifications, is available from the "Sandalmaker", 133 Westwood Blvd., Los Angeles, CA 90024. If you order one, tell him to make it of thicker leather than he made mine.

Non-Lethal Weapons

The chief drawback in using non-lethal weapons for defending your life is that once force has been initiated, you may receive more of it than is good for your health unless you can deliver enough to end the affair quickly. Still, there are occasions when levels of force below that which is potentially deadly are called for. I strongly suggest, however, that you do not resort to milder devices unless you have ready access to something more certain should they prove inadequate and merely provoke your attacker to more determined aggression. I have a friend who responded to a teen-aged mugger's attack with his bare hands, even though he was armed, because he feared harming the boy. Twenty years after that encounter he eats five small meals a day — largely rice or toast and milk — because he lost 2/3's of his stomach to the concealed knife which that 13 year old wielded.

Never use your bare hands in a fight if you are armed, even though you may fancy yourself a master of Kung-Fu or one of the higher degrees of black belt in Karate. It is all too easy to injure your hands and you may need them both for shooting if things take an unexpected turn.

Since Mace and tear gas projectors are prohibited to honest citizens in most states, and in some, like California, the mere possession of them carries a stiffer penalty than packing a gun, I do not recommend them. Almost anything that comes in a spray can may deter an attack at close range, however. Oven cleaners containing lye are probably the best, but "Bee Bop," insecticides and even hair spray can be effective. Synthetic lubricants such as LPS 1 and WD-40 serve a dual purpose. Read the cannister labels and look for warnings against contact with skin or eyes. Something which squirts a substantial stream instead of a fine spray is best.

Yawara Stick

In most cases, weapons which propel a deterrent are safer to use than those which require your assailant be allowed within reach. Grappling with an opponent is a good way to fall prey to the concealed weapon you didn't know he had. In particular, knives are almost useless for defense to anyone but an expert, and, if it really matters to you, you are more likely to wound your opponent fatally with a knife by accident than with a gun. The most efficient weapon I know for use in close quarters is the Yawara stick. It can be lethal, but only when used deliberately for that end. A very good one is made by Kel-Lite and both it and an instruction book are marketed by Safariland. Ra-Mana Industries of Evanston, Illinois also distributes several different designs. Once you become expert in its use, you will be able to employ any number of substitutes almost as effectively. The most convenient of these ersatz devices and one of the most innocuous is the German made Mont Blanc "Meisterstück" fountain pen. This is not only a devastating weapon, properly used, it is also the best writing instrument I have ever seen. I am seldom without one.

Stun Gun and Prowler Fouler

Two devices which throw cloth containers full of lead shot — much like bean bags — are now on the market, one called a "Stun Gun" and the other a "Prowler Fouler." Both are rather large plastic tube-like affairs and the chief difference between them is that the former is powered by gunpowder and the latter by CO_2 cartridges such as those used in siphon bottles. Both weapons are single-shots and are meant to be used only at very close range. Much is made of the fact that the heavy lexan plastic tubes can be used as clubs, and that is probably a good feature to

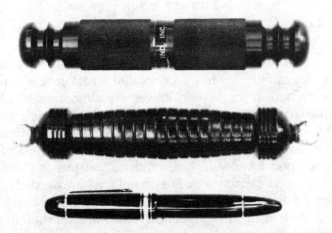

Three devastating inert hand weapons. Top to bottom: Kel-Lite "judo stick," Yawara stick from Ra-mana, Mont Blanc "Meisterstück" fountain pen — originally designed for more sedate purposes.

emphasize, given the limitations of these appliances when used as intended. MBA, which produces both items, also makes .38 Special cartridges which can be used in ordinary revolvers and they toss even smaller bags, if that is of interest.

Taser

The latest gadget designed to protect criminals from harm while attempting to interfere with their plans is the Taser TF-1. This is a $200 plastic rechargeable flashlight which carries beneath its lens two special cartridges. Each fires two tiny barbs attached to 18 foot lengths of thin wire. Assuming that these miniature missiles hit the target, penetrate the clothing and pierce the skin, the operator can send an electrical charge through the wires by pressing a button on the flashlight.

The Taser is a relatively new product and its practicality is still in question; however, there appear to be a number of drawbacks from the standpoint of survival use. For one thing, it must be recharged periodically from a source of electrical current. For another, it offers only two shots. Perhaps most important is its range limitation. Statistically, most defensive shooting situations occur at 7 yards — 21 feet. The Taser wires are only 18 feet long. You might feel rather foolish firing your barbs at some brigand who had a shotgun aimed at your navel, 19 feet away. The fact that the cartridges cost $10 apiece will also matter to some.

I am aware of only two reports of the Taser's use to date — both by criminals. The first was a successful gas station holdup in California. The victim in the second case was brought to his knees by the electrical shock but, seeing the wires, he simply brushed them away with his hand and then chased the would-be assailant from his home.

The Taser seems an ideal weapon for criminal use. Perhaps strict Federal laws prohibiting them should be encouraged in order to insure their widespread availability to lawbreakers. The rest of us can then probably muddle through with handguns.

Cap-Chur Guns

One class of non-lethal devices which might prove very useful under some circumstances consists of the two Cap-Chur rifles and one pistol offered through the NASCO Farm and Ranch Catalog. These guns propel a syringe which usually carries a nicotine alkaloid drug designed to immobilize wild or domestic animals, although it can be used to inject any fluid in quantities ranging from 1cc. to 15cc.

Probably the most useful is the "Extra Long Range Projector — Rifle Type" catalog #C 4240N. It uses .22 blanks for power and has a range of up to 80 yards. The other rifle and the pistol are powered by CO_2 cylinders and are effective to 30 yards or 40 feet, respectively. The #C4240 appears to be a highly modified H&R single-shot action, and you may be able to fit the appropriate H&R shotgun and rifle barrels to it in order to provide greater versatility. I haven't tried it, but I think it will work.

Black Powder Guns

All of the "survival experts" who aren't pushing bows and arrows or .22's seem to think that black powder guns offer the best solution to the problem of survival weaponry. Since percussion arms only eliminate cartridge cases from the ammunition equation I can't buy that argument; you must still store caps which are at least as bulky as primers, powder — or its ingredients — and bullets, or the lead for making them. Further, black powder presents a much greater storage hazard than modern smokeless, and if you plan to make your own from sulphur, potassium nitrate and charcoal, your sanity is in

You will have to decide for yourself whether black powder guns are practical for your battery. If the answer is yes, these are as good as the best. Top to bottom: Thompson Center .45 cal. Seneca, Parker Hale Enfield, .58 cal., Ruger Old Army .44 percussion revolver; percussion caps, capper and powder measure also shown.

question. Black powder making is an EXTREMELY dangerous process. In order to keep the ingredients from separating you must make a paste of them with alcohol or water and then let it dry. Grinding this dried compound into powder, even when it is done in small quantities, results in serious accidents more often than not.

Flintlocks eliminate the need for primers and you can usually improvise sparking material when your supply of flints is exhausted; however, you still need powder and lead, and you are still handicapped by the slow, awkward muzzle loading process. Because of this drastic firepower limitation, these guns cannot be considered for serious defensive use.

I do not deny that shooting black powder weapons is good, messy fun, but I question their practicality over more modern guns in survival planning. You can buy a lot of cartridge cases for the money you will spend on a muzzle loader and its accessories.

If you can afford the cost and space, however, there is certainly no reason not to add some good black powder guns to your battery. The more options you give yourself in a survival situation the better. In this context there are several excellent models on the market that make very satisfactory hunting weapons.

The best modern percussion rifle I have ever seen is the Parker Hale replica of the Enfield imported by Navy Arms. It is available in either rifle or short carbine configuration and both are extremely accurate, even by today's standards. These guns will fire either .58 Caliber (.577) mini or round balls and they are entirely adequate for deer, black bear and even elk at reasonable ranges. They are better made than many cartridge guns and their price tag reflects their quality.

My second choice, by a narrow margin, would be either the Thompson Center Hawken or Seneca. Both have precision double set triggers and are soundly constructed. The Hawken, which is available with either a percussion or a flintlock, can be had in .45 or .50 caliber and the 6 lb., percussion only Seneca in .36 or .45. In the larger calibers, both are practical big game hunting rifles within the limitations of their single-shot capabilities. I would choose .45 caliber in either for all-around use.

All of the black powder revolvers use percussion caps for ignition and the most practical of them is clearly the stainless steel version of the Ruger Old Army model. This is a .44 caliber single action with a 7 1/2" barrel and good, modern adjustable sights. Black powder residue is hydroscopic, and the moisture it attracts will rust ordinary steel quickly after shooting; therefore, the stainless construction of the Ruger is especially valuable.

If you want a flintlock pistol, you will have to go to a single-shot, and several suitable models are offered in the Dixie Gunworks catalog, which is a treasure trove of information for black powder shooters. In it you will find all of the accessories which you will need, such as patch material, bullet molds, capping devices, flints, etc. One other accessory is a must for black powder shooting: protective shooting glasses. The risk from small flying — often burning — debris is great even with the best of the muzzle loaders.

Archery

You may have gathered by now that I do not share the enthusiasm of some for bows and arrows as primary survival weaponry. Contrary to the opinion of many who have never tired it, hunting with a bow is not easy. Just drawing an adequate hunting bow with its 45 to 70 lb. pull weight would require weeks of conditioning for many people, and learning actually to hit a moving target consistently at, say, 50 yards usually involves at least a year or two of instruction and diligent practice. Further, arrows are fragile, easily damaged or lost and fabrication of workable replacements is a job for an expert with extensive specialized tools. Most people can learn to reload empty cartridge cases successfully with no more than an evening's reading and an hour's practice — and those loads are usually better than the factory product. Learning to make a completely straight arrow and fletching it with feathers so that it will fly true is tantamount to learning a trade like welding or auto body repair.

Finally, there is the matter of effectiveness. Even the best commercial broadhead hunting arrow produces no shock and hence no stopping power. Animals shot with arrows die from hemorrhage: they simply bleed to death, and that can be a slow process during which the animal may escape to die a painful and useless death. I have no qualms about killing game for food, but I do object — even under survival conditions — to inflicting *needless* suffering. A good shot with a rifle or a heavy pistol has the potential of taking his quarry instantly and without causing lingering pain; a bowman does not have that option except, perhaps, in the case of very small animals such as rabbits shot at close range with blunt tipped arrows.

As in the case of black powder guns, there is certainly no harm in adding archery equipment to your kit; in fact, it is probably a good idea, so long as you do not regard it as a substitute for more efficient weapons. There could be occasions when the silence of a bow might be useful.

Crossbows

One of the most effective and certainly the easiest archery device to master is the crossbow. Learning to shoot one is as easy as learning to shoot a rifle and, since the archer is relieved of the need of holding the bow at full draw by physical effort, a much more powerful bow can be used. Seventy or eighty pound pull weights are not uncommon and they are no more difficult to handle when mounted on a crossbow frame than lighter bows.

A number of models on the market seem entirely satisfactory, including one of the least expensive — the Powermaster made by Wham-O. It features an 80 lb. pull metal bow, rifle type aperture sights, good accuracy and power. I have owned one for 15 years and have never found reason to fault it, except with regard to one feature which it shares with other models. With few exceptions, crossbows use short, unnocked bolts instead of arrows and the head of the bolt is usually supported in such a way that only flat broadheads can be used instead of some of the better, new designs. The easy marksmanship and high velocity of the crossbow tend to offset the disadvantage, however. Most firms offer special barbed fishing bolts and line holders and these devices can be very useful. There are many times when fish are not biting but they can be seen and shot with arrows.

For those who have the inclination to make their own

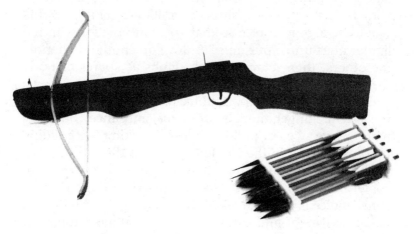

Wham-O crossbow with a dozen hunting broadhead bolts.

crossbows, plans and unfinished kits are available from "The Crossbowman" (P.O. Box 2159, Petaluma, CA 94952) and other sources.

Bows

The American hunting bow is an amalgam of several historical designs and it is superior to any of its forebears. The very best models are usually laminated with fiber glass on the back and belly and hard rock maple in between, but less expensive all fiber glass bows will give good service. You will get a much better pull and greater cast (velocity — trajectory) with a design that employs a full working recurve. At best, the bow is a short range weapon but even at ranges of 50 yards or less you will need all of the power you can get for animals the size of deer. A 35 lb. pull weight should be regarded as an absolute minimum for any bow that is to be used for serious hunting and 45 or 50 lbs. is much better. Buy the heaviest pull weight bow you can learn to handle comfortably.

One solution to the weight problem is to choose a good takedown bow and get extra limbs of different degrees of stiffness with it. One pair each of 40 and 50 lb. weights would be a good choice so that you can practice with the lighter ones until your muscles develop enough to handle the others, then retain the light limbs as spares or trade them for still heavier ones.

Length is also an important factor in selecting a bow. In the brush, longer models are a real nuisance, but they tend to give sweeter pulls with less "stacking" or building up of resistance in the last few inches of the draw.

The most popular fixed bow length is about 66" but some prefer 50 or 52" models for brush hunting. My personal choice is for a 60" takedown made by Bear with a 60 lb. draw weight and extra 50 lb. limbs. Illness, injury or fatigue can lessen your ability with a bow and I think it's a good idea to have a spare, or in the case of a takedown, extra limbs, 10 or 15 lbs. lighter than you normally use — just in case. Most of the well known makes such as Bear, Hoyt, Jennings and Browning offer a wide selection and give good service, but I am partial to Bear, personally. Recently, a new design known as a compound bow has become very popular. These devices employ a system of pulleys to increase cast while lessening draw weight. They work, and for those who cannot otherwise use a bow of sufficient power, they may be the best answer, but I find them too complex and bulky for survival use. Whatever you choose, buy at least a dozen Dacron-polyester fiber bowstrings matched to your bow. Nothing you can improvise in the wilderness will come even close to matching their performance. And while you are at it, install brush buttons to prevent catching twigs between your string and bow and to help silence the "twang" or string noise. One other very useful gadget for your bow is the Bear Hunting Stabilizer, which seems to improve accuracy greatly.

Arrows

Arrows deserve a great deal more attention than they are usually given by the casual archer. Of the three shaft materials available, wood is the least satisfactory because it warps and shatters easily. I prefer aluminum shafts with screw-on interchangeable heads, but many choose fiber glass and it also works well.

For big game hunting you must use razor sharp broadheads and I prefer what is known as a "delta" design with four cutting edges, one of which is a disposable insert. The insert blade is as thin and sharp as a double-edged razor blade and it is intended to cut like one, yet it will fold or break off if bone is struck, allowing greater penetration. You will also need some blunt tips for small game and perhaps a few snare tips for birds. Some "flu flu" shafts equipped with blunt tips are also useful for close range. The length and weight of your arrow shafts must be matched to your own length of pull and the draw weight of your bow. If you buy your equipment at an archery pro shop, they can fit you properly. Otherwise, try to borrow a bow and the longest arrow you can find. At full draw, measure the distance from the string (*not* the end of the arrow) to the front of the bow face.

You will also need a quiver, or some other means of carrying the arrows so that they do not rattle or become blunt from contact with one another. The kind which attaches to your bow is especially convenient. A guard for your left forearm to protect it from the bowstring is an absolute must. If you don't care to take my word on the necessity of this item, just take one shot with a heavy hunting bow and then form your own opinion. Be sure to assemble bandages and adhesive tape before conducting this experiment. A good three fingered archer's glove or a tab to protect your fingers from the string and allow a smooth release will complete the mandatory equipment list, but I also recommend nylon nocking points to position the arrow consistently from shot to shot and a bow sling and string keeper for convenience. Buy enough hunting arrows to allow for losing or destroying one every second shot and at least a dozen more for practice. If you never need any of this gear to provide food for your family, learning how to use it is good for your timing and it is *great* exercise.

Primitive Weapons

In many parts of the world, people have for centuries lived by primitive means, and some still do. It is easy to romanticize these cultures and their methods when considering basic survival needs; however, one cannot afford to overlook the fact that in most societies, the average life span is only 1/3 of that in the United States. Usually, the high death rate results from starvation, diseases caused by poor nutrition and inadequate protection from dangerous animals or neighboring tribes — all of which could be remedied by better weapons. None of the primitive weapons I know has the range, power and certainty of a gun and anyone who is forced by circumstances to rely on them entirely will be severely handicapped in gathering food and protecting himself.

Some of these devices, however, can provide a practical means of stretching a limited ammunition supply or coping with an unanticipated emergency. One of them, the boleadoras of Argentina, is probably the most practical contrivance ever devised for capturing an animal alive. Should you ever find yourself afoot in wild horse country, one of these "bolas" can be an efficient means of providing transportation — assuming that you have the stalking ability necessary to get close enough to a wild horse to use it.

Another factor in assessing the practical usefulness of primitive weapons is the skill required to employ them effectively. One of the reasons why guns are such popular tools is that most people can learn to shoot them quickly and easily. I fire master class scores with both rifle and pistol, but it took years of practice before I could hit a quart milk container regularly at 50 feet with a slingshot and I am still something less than an ace with a boomerang. Consequently, even though most of these items can be fabricated by hand, I suggest that you buy commercial samples of the primitive weapons that interest you instead of planning to improvise them when they are needed, because you will require plenty of practice with them before they will be of any real value to your survival. Also, studying the commercial products will give you a better idea of how to make your own, should the occasion arise.

Blowguns

One of the most efficient primitive weapons and one of the easiest to learn to use effectively is the blowgun. It can be extremely accurate out to 40 yards and it is deadly on small game. Deer-sized animals have often been taken with darts from a blowgun, but for such use they must be tipped with curare, a similar drug, or even a strychnine derivative; however, with the latter, you must take care to cut away all contaminated flesh as soon as the animal is down.

The best blowguns I have used have been made of metal, but a tube of almost any material can be employed. The longer the blowgun the greater range and accuracy it will have — up to a point. Unless you have tremendous lung capacity, you will run out of breath before the dart exits a tube more than 6 or 8 feet in length.

Darts may range in length from a few inches to 2 feet or so and they may be made of metal, wood or almost any substance that will take the stresses involved in firing and penetrating the target. Fairly light projectiles seem to be the most satisfactory; however, some of the very best darts I have ever seen were made of fairly dense wood and measured 22". The shaft of the dart is usually about the diameter of a knitting needle, and, in fact, knitting needles cut about in half serve well, with a proper, snug stopper fitted on the blunt end. Some darts have barbs and others are plain. The most important consideration in making or buying them is that they fit the blowgun correctly. All darts must be "stoppered"; that is, some sort of plug or winding of cotton or thread must be attached near the rear end of the dart, more or less in the same place that feathers are found on arrows. The purpose of this contrivance is to make a seal in the barrel against which the breath can work to propel the dart. It should provide a snug but friction free fit.

Blowguns are capable of shooting these projectiles with amazing force, if they are used skillfully. A single, quick, hard puff which expires just as the dart exits the barrel is the proper technique. Sights are really unnecessary, but some like to mount something similar to a shotgun bead on the front of the tube.

You can make a very effective blowgun from 1/2" metal tubing. Six feet seems a good length. Make sure that the muzzle end of the tube is cut smoothly and square, then chamfer it lightly on the inside. On the other end, you must fit a mouthpiece of some sort for your lips to press against or you cannot build up sufficient pressure for a proper puff. A good one can easily be whittled from wood, plastic or hard rubber, but the very best I have ever had was the brass mouthpiece from an old trumpet, opened up slightly for greater air flow. One sixteenth of an inch diameter drill rod cut in 3 to 5" lengths can be used for blunt, small game darts. I twist cotton secured with glue around them in an area 1/2" wide, 1/2" from the end, and then wind the cotton with thread and cover the wound area with varnish. The cotton alone will do, held in place with tree sap, chewing gum or even, temporarily, saliva.

I believe that some silly law curtailing the sale of blowguns has recently gone into effect, but The Crossbowman still carries a pretty good one in their catalog.

Boomerangs

The boomerang flies farther and hits harder than any other hand launched projectile, and its length — usually about 3 feet — allows a greater margin of aiming error. It is, nevertheless, one of the most primitive of all weapons — only a step removed from throwing rocks. Although booms of various types were popular during the 18th dynasty in Egypt, among the early desert Semites and in India, only the Australian aborigines and the Hopi Indians continue to employ them as primary weapons.

There are two basic types of boomerangs: those sold in toy stores which are shaped like "v's" and return to the thrower when thrown hard enough and at the right angle, and "war" or hunting sticks. The former are essentially playthings, but the latter can be, with enough practice, formidable weapons. Properly thrown, a hunting boomerang can crush a skull at 100 yards.

The weight and shape of the boom account for its range. Customarily, it is slightly curved, with one side planed flat and the other rounded to create an airfoil, much like that of an airplane wing; but some are shaped like the letter "S." The best ones are usually made from hard, dense wood such as hickory or oak; but a variety of materials can be used including metal, bone, plastic and ivory. In order to prevent shattering on impact, those made of wood must be bent to shape as barrel staves are, not sawn, so that the grain follows the curve of the boom. The Hopi's simply search for suitably sized branches which have grown into curves of approximately the right angle, finishing them with knives or sharp edged stones.

If you decide to try using boomerangs for hunting, provide yourself with several. They often fly erratically and success comes with throwing a number of them rapidly at the target, hoping that your quarry may run into one while dodging another. This technique is especially effective when you are throwing into a flock of birds. Try to time your throws so that the booms reach the midst of the flock just as the birds are rising or landing and have little maneuverability.

Boomerangs work. They will kill game, sometimes spectacularly, but they are neither consistent nor certain means.

Slingshots

Almost every boy has had some experience with a sling-shot and when I was growing up, quite a few girls played with them as well. Today's commercial models made of spring steel and surgical rubber tubing are a far cry from the forked sticks slung with strips of old inner tube which we used, but the principal shooting techniques, advantages and limitations remain essentially the same.

The reliable killing range of the most powerful modern slingshots with proper ammunition is about 25 or 30 yards — assuming that you confine your shots to game no larger than rabbits, and that you can learn to hit at that distance.

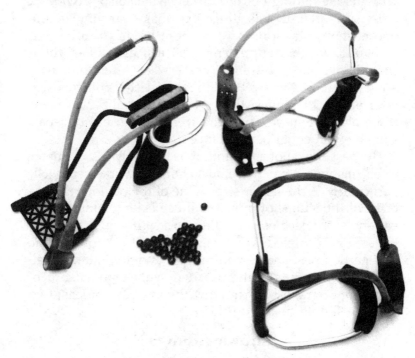

The youngsters' old favorite slingshot in three powerful modern versions. Clockwise from 9 o'clock: Falcon, Pocket Rocket, Wrist Rocket.

259

My own experience is that developing practical hunting accuracy with a slingshot is slightly more difficult than gaining similar skill with a bow; however, practice is so cheap and so much fun that I cannot imagine anyone who is seriously considering the prospect of self-sufficient living denying himself the use of these handy little weapons just because they require some proficiency.

The most powerful model I have found is the Falcon II, made by Saunders Archery, who also manufactures the Wrist Rocket. Both use heavy duty surgical rubber tubing and both offer a wrist brace, but that on the Falcon is far more comfortable. The handiest slingshot I have come across is the folding Pocket Rocket, which also provides a wrist support but it is hinged to make carrying in the pocket more practical. Any of these models can be had with pull weights approaching 50 lbs. and all of them should give long, trouble free service. After long use, however, both the stretch tubing and the pouches will wear out and I suggest that you buy several replacement assemblies when you buy the weapon. No ersatz repair will give you equal performance.

The best slingshot ammunition is probably 1/2" diameter steel balls, but inexpensive buckshot also works very well, particularly in the larger sizes. One of the obvious advantages of the slingshot in survival use is its tolerance for a variety of projectiles including rocks, if that is all you have. With dirt clods or small pebbles, it is probably the best garden pest chaser you can use and it will take small birds at close range when loaded with a pouch full of bird shot or gravel. Considering the low cost, at least two or three should be in your kit.

Throwing Knives

I get a remarkable amount of mail asking about throwing knives for survival use. If you have never tried it or if you watch a lot of TV, it may appear to be a pretty good idea, but in fact knife throwing is a sport and not a very practical means of getting food. The primary problem is that a knife spins end over end in flight and one must know both the rate of these revolutions and the *exact* distance to the target in order to have the blade strike point first. Assuming that you were willing to practice for several years and could also somehow develop a precise ability to judge distances within a few inches, hunting with a throwing knife would still be a very short range proposition.

If, despite these admonitions, you decide to try the sport, at least heed this one warning: never, under any circumstances, throw a knife not specifically designed for that purpose. A good cutting knife is too valuable to your survival to risk its loss or damage by throwing — and it will almost certainly be damaged whether the throw is a good one or not. Neither the handles nor the blade temper of a knife designed for cutting will withstand such abuse. If you must throw a knife, buy one made for the purpose. Randall produces one of the very best and other good ones can be obtained from Corrado Cutlery or Tru-Balance Knife Co. There are two basic types: those designed for handle throwing and those balanced for blade throwing. Either should weigh about 1 oz. for each inch of overall length. Harry McEvoy's little book, *Knife Throwing, A Practical Guide* (Chas. E. Tuttle Co., Publisher) will give you the basics.

An inexpensive and practical substitute for throwing knives can easily be made from one foot lengths of steel rod sharpened on both ends.

Boleadoras

Of all the primitive weapons I have ever used, the one which seems to me the most nearly indispensable for long term self-sufficient living is the Argentine boleadoras or bolas. It can be as simple as three rocks, each tied to a piece of rope, joined at the center, to the elaborate style carried by the Gauchos, which is made from lengths of plaited rawhide and round balls held inside the pouches made from ostrich (rhea) necks. The device is a sort of flying snare which, when properly thrown, wraps itself about the target, enabling the user to capture animals without harming them. By using bolas of suitable size, virtually any animal from birds to horses and cattle can be ensnared. A lariat or lasso can be used for the larger animals, of course, but you must be able to get within 30' or so in order to use one, and since a noose around the neck does little to subdue an animal, you might have something of a struggle on your hands if you do connect. Even a fairly light bola has a range of about 40 yards and it tends to wrap itself about the quarry, often immobilizing it. Gauchos use them for catching wild horses to break for new mounts by throwing at the hind legs, Eskimos have one with eight small balls which is used for birds in flight, and I have had great success with a light weight model for such homely chores as taking chickens for the pot.

There is some risk of harming, or even killing animals with the heavier bolas, either from the impact of the balls or the cutting action of the thongs, so I would suggest that you have several weights and use the lightest one that will do the job you have in mind. Unfortunately, I have not been able to find a source of commercially made bolas in the U.S., but you may be able to purchase one by mail from this address: La Cruz du Sur, Galerias Pacifico, Florida 753 Local F. 17-T.E. 32-0091, Buenos Aires, Argentina. If you have any skill with leather, you can make a set of good bolas easily. You will need a 6 foot length of rawhide (plaited rawhide is better) and a 3 foot length, as well as two balls, or other objects of equal weight and size, and a third, somewhat smaller, preferably egg-shaped. Billiard balls are excellent for a heavy bolas as are 2" diameter lead or 2 1/2" diameter steel balls. Light models for use on birds and rabbits can be made with 1" diameter hardwood balls. Small leather bags filled with bird shot or gravel can also be used. The two equal weights are attached firmly to either end of the 6 foot thong, and the smaller, egg-shaped one is fastened to the 3 foot length — called the mañeque — which is then tied firmly to the exact center of the longer piece. To throw the device, grasp the smaller weight in your throwing hand and whirl the bola horizontally above your head. When you have developed sufficient momentum, take aim and throw the weight you are holding in your hand just as you would a ball. Time your throw so that the two balls of equal weight are behind you at the moment of release. The bola will revolve slowly in the air and the three "legs" will spread. If the device even brushes the target, it will veer toward it and wrap itself around it.

If you decide to try the bola, I think you will be amazed at its efficiency and the variety of chores which it will handle. In my opinion it is one of the most useful of all tools for any ranch, farm or retreat.

I have included this review of primitive weapons here, not to encourage your reliance upon them to the exclusion of more efficient means, but rather to suggest that they may be useful to you in small ways such as occasional silent hunting or stretching your ammunition supply. The more experience you have with such improvised tools, the more confident you will feel about your ability to survive under a variety of conditions — and, I predict, the likelier you will be to lay in an adequate store of firearms and ammunition.

PETERS

P HIGH VELOCITY DU

·75 HOLLAND & HOLLAND MAGN

270 GRAIN SOFT POINT BULLET

20 ·ITER FIR· SMOKELESS CARTRIDGES

Western **X SUPER 308 WIN**
150 GR. POW
20 RIFLE CARTR

Remington.

·57 Magnum
· GR. SEMI-JACKETED H.P.

.C.P.
Short)

380
A.C.P.
(9 mm
Short)

SU

CENTERFIRE CARTRIDGES

LAWMAN AMMUNITION

SPEER

·00 GRAIN

FEDERA
30-30 WI

7 Ammunition

I seldom visit a gun shop or sporting goods store without overhearing at least one customer who wants to buy factory loaded ammunition ask for, "a box of bullets to fit a .30-30," or whatever his gun might be. If you immediately cringe at this statement and recognize at least two blatant errors in connection with it, you may not need to read this chapter. If the customer's request sounds perfectly proper to you, read on.

To begin, let's get some terminology straight. "Bullets" are the projectiles which are fired from a gun at a target and they are only one part of a cartridge or round of ammunition. The other components are the cartridge case, usually made of brass, the powder, or propellant charge, and the primer, which, when suddenly compressed by the gun's firing pin, ignites the propellant and starts the firing cycle. The case, often called an "empty," a "hull" or simply "brass" is the only part of the cartridge which can be reused.

The bullet, since it is what strikes the target, probably

has more to do with the effectiveness of the gun-ammunition equation than any other single factor, yet the casual user of firearms often pays little or no attention to choosing among the vast numbers of bullet shapes and weights available to him as components or loaded in cartridges to fit his gun. In fact, many firearms enthusiasts who spend a great deal of time, thought and money in selecting their guns pay little attention to their ammunition, so long as it is of the correct caliber. No firearm, however, is any more effective than the ammunition fired from it, regardless of what caliber it is or how well made. For this reason, it may be worthwhile to discuss factory ammunition and reloading components suitable for survival use in handguns and rifles, caliber by caliber.

First, however, I think we should consider the strategies involved in accumulating a survival ammunition supply. Although it is somewhat more expensive, I usually recommend to private clients that they purchase a large quantity of factory loaded ammunition as well as bullets, powder and primers for reloading, instead of buying components only. For one thing, commercial factory ammunition will last longer with less deterioration than components will, because the cartridges are sealed against oil and moisture which, along with excessive heat, constitute the chief causes of ammunition breakdown. Good quality factory ammunition will last at least 20 and possibly 30 or more years with no noticeable decrease in performance, provided that it is stored in a reasonably cool, dry place. Further, if you decide to use some of your ammunition for trading goods, the factory product of recognized commercial standards will probably be more valuable than reloads, since the party you are trading with will have only your word for the contents of your home-brewed cartridges, the age of the brass and your skill in putting them together.

You may reasonably ask, "Why bother to reload at all if factory ammunition has so many advantages?" What I have tried to establish is that factory ammunition may last longer than handloads under ordinary storage conditions and that it may be more valuable for barter, but it is not "better" in terms of quality or efficiency. In fact, most people can learn in a few hours to assemble more uniform and more accurate ammunition than the factories generally produce, although some of the commercial loads are

Components of a cartridge, from left to right: primer, case, powder, bullet. The primer is inserted in the primer pocket of the case as shown in the lower (2) photo, the powder is poured into the case mouth and then the bullet is seated. Reloading is as simple as that.

267

very good indeed. Also, by handloading you will be able to produce much that the factories do not offer, including special purpose loads, reduced or more powerful loads. For example, the .44 Magnum, which is more gun than many people can handle with commercial ammunition, may become a very practical, easy to shoot — but still effective — weapon simply by being loaded with cartridges which contain more efficient bullets and slightly reduced powder charges; or the mild mannered .45 Colt can be made to rival the power of a factory loaded .44 Magnum.

Economy is also a factor. The brass cartridge case is the most expensive component in a round of ammunition, making up as much as 5/6 of the total cost, and it can usually be reloaded safely several times — the exact number being determined by the quality and thickness of the brass, the strength of the load used in it, the fit of the chamber it is fired in and the amount of working (sizing and expanding) which it must undergo in the firing-reloading cycle. If a factory loaded round of .44 Magnum ammunition costs $.30 and the components necessary to reload it cost $.06, you can easily see that reloading will effect a considerable saving.

As a rule of thumb, you might get as many as 10 safe reloads from a good case with moderate loads if all of the other variables are in your favor. On the other hand, you might get no more than two or three if the brass is brittle, the load is stiff, your chamber is oversize or if you bell the case mouth excessively and are too vigorous in crimping. I have never had a new factory loaded case crack or become otherwise unusable upon the first firing, so I think you may safely count on one reload as a minimum and, perhaps, 10 as a conservative maximum, in estimating your ammunition requirements.

The saving involved in reloading your own shotshells is

smaller than with rifle and handgun cartridges, particularly in terms of the relative quantities of each which you are likely to need for survival purposes. Further, the loading equipment which you will use for the others is unsuitable for shotshells and you will need, in addition to more equipment, different primers, bulky and heavy bags of shot and, probably, different powders. Since factory shotshells are of excellent quality and reasonably inexpensive, I suggest that you simply buy the amount of loaded shotgun ammunition which you think prudent, unless special considerations in your case require its use in substantial amounts. A possible compromise solution would be to acquire an inexpensive — under $15 — Lee Loader and a few components, just for insurance. Such devices are slow, but they turn out good reloads.

Although I find it somewhat boring, many people enjoy handloading as a hobby and it is incredibly easy to learn. You simply resize the case, squeezing it down to the dimensions it had before it was fired, by running it into a sizing die. You then punch out the spent primer and seat a new one, measure a charge of powder and pour it into the case, slightly expand the case mouth to receive the bullet, which you then seat by running it into the seating die; and, finally, you may or may not slightly crimp the case mouth into the bullet, depending on the cartridge which you are reloading and the gun in which it is to be used. The loading books listed in the bibliography will give you the details as well as a variety of starting loads to work from. If you want to do a bit of experimenting with different powders, bullet weights and designs, you can probably tailor a load that will shoot better in your particular gun than anything you can buy off the dealer's shelves. You can even solve functioning problems in autoloading weapons quite often by altering the bullet shape, the seating depth, or both.

Most of the name brand reloading tools are excellent these days, but buy a heavy duty bench press if you possibly can. The hand tools such as the Lyman 310 and the Lee Loader are very compact and they will turn out first rate ammunition, but they are painfully slow and most of them only neck size the cases. This procedure will give problems with straight walled designs, which include most handgun and some rifle calibers. The very best dies I have ever seen are made by RCBS and I use them exclusively. If you can afford it, buy tungsten carbide lined sizing dies at least for the calibers you expect to reload most frequently. Using them will relieve you of the major nuisance in reloading: lubricating and degreasing the cases.

Making jacketed rifle bullets is a bit ambitious for the average reloader so you will need to lay in a good supply. You can cast your own lead bullets for handguns and light rifle loads but I do not recommend it. Good cast bullets are very cheap and bullet casting is the worst chore in reloading, to my mind. If you decide to do it you will need molds, melting pots, ladles and lead as well as lubricating and sizing equipment. If you want to try, you will find adequate instructions in the loading handbooks. It is simple to do, but it is an evil chore.

If you can't buy all of your ammunition at one time, label each box with the purchase date and use it on a first in, first out basis. When living self-sufficiently, it is also good practice to fire only a small portion of your factory ammunition and then reload those cases repeatedly until they are no longer usable. Personally, I only use once fired cases to put up defense loads, and then I transfer that brass to working gun status only. When hunting, a cracked case or a malfunction may cause you to miss a meal, but in a fight it could be fatal; however, if you inspect your brass carefully after each firing and exercise good sense in reloading, failures of any sort with your home-brewed cartridges should be rare. In 20 years of fairly extensive handloading experience I have had only one round fail to fire perfectly.

For proper storage procedures with both your loaded ammunition and your components, write for free copies of these pamphlets from the Sporting Arms and Ammunition Manufacturers' Institute, Inc., 420 Lexington Ave., New York, NY 10017: *Properties of Sporting Ammunition and Recommendations For Its Storage and Handling, Properties and Storage of Smokeless Powder,* and *Sporting Ammunition Primers: Properties, Handling and Storage For Handloading.* After reading them, any fears you may have about the dangers of storing large quantities of ammunition and components should be erased. These items are considerably safer, even in a fire, than ordinary household cleaners and solvents. Neither loaded ammunition nor smokeless gunpowder will explode by itself. Unless they are closely confined, as they are in the chamber of a gun, they have little force.

Finally, in these general remarks on ammunition, allow me to repeat some comments I have made previously: they are important. In choosing calibers for survival guns, select those in most common use, even though a more exotic caliber may offer a slight edge in performance, because 1) there is a better possibility of resupply if you run short of ammunition and 2) you are more likely to be able to trade your excess for other things which you may need. Buy at least five times as much ammunition for your defense weapons as for your working guns because 1) any attack on your retreat is likely to involve multiple opponents, causing the expenditure of more ammunition in an hour than several years of hunting, 2) on balance, if you must improvise, it is more prudent to attempt hunting for food with a defense weapon than to try defending your life with a hunting gun, and 3) it is unwise to reload cases used for defense loads as many times as those intended for less critical purposes.

Cartridges for Handguns

In general, factory loaded handgun ammunition is less satisfactory than the best factory loaded rifle ammunition, because — in an attempt to cater to uninformed public demand — most high performance pistol cartridges are loaded with hollow point bullets instead of the more reliably efficient semi-wadcutter or Keith design. In the larger calibers — .41 through .45 — this shortcoming poses no particular problem because bullets in these sizes are already large enough to be effective whether they expand or not, and none of the large bore hollow points with which I am familiar is particularly fragile. In the medium bores, except for those rare instances where good semi-wadcutters (SWC) are available, you will have to choose between jacketed soft points (JSP) or jacketed hollow points (JHP) and hope for the best. For small and medium game hunting, which is all that should be attempted with these calibers, the JHP's will do fairly well if the velocity is high enough, but if I were forced to use a 9mm., .38 Special or .357 for defense with factory loads, I would rather have the heaviest available flat pointed JSP than a JHP, because I could then at least be free from concern about whether my bullet would explode on a belt buckle or wallet and fail to penetrate. Solid, round nose designs, whether lead or jacketed, are the most common and the least effective bullet shapes available. In .44 and .45 caliber, however, they have enough diameter so that their inefficient shape is not a critical factor. In the smaller bores, however, they are dangerously ineffective. The standard "police" 158gr. .38 Special, for example, is a very uncertain killer even on cottontail rabbits.

In the following pages, I have outlined my personal choices among currently available factory loaded ammunition and I have included a few of my favorite handloads, but I urge you to do your own experimenting if you can before stocking up. New products are constantly being introduced in the ammunition lines and old ones are being improved, often without much fanfare. Further, one of the advantages of handloading is that you can get what *you* want by that means. **I TAKE NO RESPONSIBILITY FOR THE CONSEQUENCES OF ANYONE'S USE OF THE LOADS LISTED BELOW. THEY HAVE PROVED SAFE IN MY GUNS WHEN ASSEMBLED BY ME, BUT YOUR GUNS WILL UNDOUBTEDLY HAVE SLIGHTLY DIFFERENT DIMENSIONS AND I CAN EXERCISE NO CONTROL OVER THE COMPONENTS YOU USE OR THE MANNER IN WHICH YOU ASSEMBLE THEM. IT IS GOOD HANDLOADING PRACTICE TO APPROACH ANY NEAR MAXIMUM LOAD FROM AT LEAST 15% BELOW THE RECOMMENDED POWDER CHARGE AND WORK UP SLOWLY, LOOKING FOR SIGNS OF EXCESS PRESSURE.**

There are a great variety of powders on the market and I have used most of them, but it seems to me that, in survival planning, whenever one can simplify without significantly reducing quality, it is wise to do so; therefore, I have tried to keep to a minimum the number of different powders necessary to reload a variety of cartridges efficiently.

.380 ACP

This is a pip-squeak round in any safe load, but it may have some value in a hideout, second gun such as the TDE Back Up, so I am including it here. The Super Vel load which advertised an 88gr. JHP at 1065 fps. muzzle velocity (MV) was probably the best factory round ever available for this caliber, but since its recent demise there is not much of a choice. I suppose I would choose the S&W JHP, even though I have not been able to make that bullet expand in any medium from wet pack to concrete construction blocks. You can get the cartridge up off its knees somewhat by handloading the Speer 100gr. JHP over 4.5gr. of Unique for just over 1000 fps. MV. Do *not* crimp this or any other auto cartridge in this list because they all headspace on the mouth of the case. All of the revolver loads, however, require a good, stiff crimp.

9mm. Parabellum

The Speer factory load with the 125gr. JSP is the best I have found for the 9mm. It functions well and it is a good, flat shooting hunting load for game up to 100-125 pounds. The same bullet with 6gr. of Unique is my favorite handload and it chronographs at 1170 fps. MV from my guns. Another excellent hot factory load is the S&W 115gr. jacketed semi-wadcutter. The 100gr. Winchester soft point ("Power Point") functions poorly in every gun I have tested with it. None of the full metal jacket (FMJ) round nose bullets is suitable for anything except target practice.

.38 Special

Any of the name brand .38 Special midrange wadcutters, designed for target use, is excellent for small game to 50 yards and they are pleasant to shoot, even in light guns. In fact, a good 2" snubbie revolver loaded with these cartridges is one of the most convenient pot shooting guns to be found, if you have the skill to use it — despite the fact that many self-serving politicians would have us believe that such guns have no legitimate function except to kill human beings. Even better for all around use in .38 Specials is the excellent Speer 158gr. lead semi-wadcutter. This is not a particularly hot load but it is very accurate and, because of the bullet shape, quite efficient. The sharp shoulders of the SWC design cause them to cut as they penetrate, instead of slipping through tissue without disrupting it as round nose bullets do. In long barreled guns which can take advantage of the increased velocity potential of the new ''+P'' loadings, you might try Remington's 125gr. JHP or 158gr. JSP for pest control or hunting.

I use 4.5-5gr. of Unique with a 148gr. plain base wadcutter, but my favorite all-purpose load in this caliber is the Lyman #358429 bullet designed by Elmer Keith, which weighs 168gr. With 5.0gr. of Unique it gives 900 fps. MV and reasonable pressures. The hottest .38 Special handload I have used is the 140gr. Speer JHP in front of 6gr. of Unique for 1000 fps. MV. An even hotter varmint load, which I have received good reports on but have not personally tried, is the 125gr. Sierra jacketed hollow cavity with 7gr. of Unique for 1150 fps. MV from a 6″ barrel.

.357 Magnum

There is no factory lead bullet load which I like in this caliber because all of them cause severe barrel leading in my guns. This is not true of some handloaded lead bullets, however, if they are cast from hard alloys. Among factory loads, the Speer 140gr. JHP is a fine choice in this caliber for most purposes. It is amazingly accurate and the bullet is well designed for controlled expansion and good penetration in game. The Remington 158gr. JSP is also good for hunting, but it will jar the fillings from your teeth. When they put ''+P'' on the box of this one, they meant it. The same company's 125gr. JHP is outstanding for coyotes and other destructive pests. I do not like the .357 for defense, but if I had to use one with factory loads I would probably use the 158gr. Remington in short guns and the Speer 140gr. in longer ones.

I use the same Lyman #358429 lead semi-wadcutter that I mentioned for the .38 Special in most of my .357 loads. 7.0gr. of Unique is pleasant to shoot and gives about 1100 fps. MV. 13.5gr. of 2400 produces about 1325 fps. MV from a 6″ barrel with 37,500 CUP (copper units of pressure). Many people use a grain or two more powder but such loads are very hard on guns. My favorite is extremely accurate and does all I require from a .357 revolver. If you need more power, you will be better off with a larger caliber. If you want to use jacketed bullets, I like: 140gr. Speer JHP with 16.5 gr. of 2400, Speer 158gr. JSP and 14.7gr. of 2400 or, for varmints, Sierra 125 JHC with 18.5gr. of 2400. That same Sierra bullet performs well in the short Magnums with 10gr. of Unique.

.41 Magnum

As in the .357, all of the lead bullet .41 Magnum loads I have tested lead barrels badly. The Remington JSP is accurate but *very* hot. In handloads, I use Lyman's 220gr. #410459 with 10gr. of Unique or 20gr. of 2400. I also like the 210gr. Hornady JSP with 19gr. of 2400.

.44 Special

There is not much choice here among factory produced cartridges. Remington and Winchester each produce but a single, mild round nose lead bullet load. Either is very accurate, however, and despite being underloaded, they are considerably more potent against man or beast than .38 Specials or 9mm's., the opinion of some "experts" notwithstanding. 7.5gr. of Unique with the excellent Keith designed Lyman #429421 240gr. lead bullet is my favorite .44 Special load. The same bullet with 17.0gr. of 2400 gives about 1150 fps. in heavy framed guns but it is maximum and not intended for pocket revolvers such as the Charter Arms Bulldog. The Keith bullet should work well in that

276

gun, however, with about 7.0gr. of Unique for an estimated 850 fps.

.44 Magnum

The Norma 240gr. JSP is my hands down favorite factory load in this caliber. It is superbly accurate and the mild steel bullet jacket provides the deep penetration necessary for big game. Both the Remington and Speer 240gr. JSP's also perform well, but I do not see the value of any hollow point in this caliber. Expansion is unnecessary in a bullet of .44 caliber and most hollow points lack the integrity necessary for penetrating heavy muscle and bone.

Elmer Keith's Lyman #429421 is my favorite lead bullet for the big Magnum, and Keith's classic load of 22gr. of 2400 leaves little to be desired. It is very accurate, the recoil is manageable and I can't imagine requiring more power from a handgun than this load provides. Dropping the powder charge to 19gr. greatly improves handling for many people, and that is still a more potent load than you are apt to need for anything short of a close cuddle with a grizzly bear. If it will not bring my *machismo* into serious question, I will admit to the frequent use of even a milder load in my 4″ .44: the Keith bullet with 10gr. of Unique. In fact, you will seldom need more power than that load delivers, and it is easy to shoot well. I usually load my working gun with four of these in the first four chambers and place Norma factory or maximum handloads in the last two. In practice, I have never needed the backup rounds.

.45 ACP

For defense, the Winchester, Remington or Federal 230gr. loads will all do the job, despite their FMJ round nose bullets. Fresh U.S. made G.I. ammunition is also satisfactory, although it is somewhat milder. If you must use a .45 ACP as a working gun, try the new Speer 200gr. JHP. It shoots flatter than any other factory load I have tried and it is incredibly accurate. In one of my guns, it has produced several 50 yard 2″ groups. Remington's 185gr. cartridge is also good for field use, but it does not expand well and it is not heavy enough to hold velocity at the longer hunting ranges.

The H&G #61, a smooth feeding lead semi-wadcutter, works well with 7.0 to 7.5gr. of Unique in my guns. I have also had good results with Speer's 200gr. lead SWC but I hesitate to list my powder charge because it is so far away from the one recommended in the Speer handbook. For a hunting handload I like the 200gr. Speer JHP with 7.5gr. of Unique for 1000 fps. MV. I usually load the 230gr. G.I. hardball bullet in front of 7.2gr. of Unique for defense.

For revolvers, where feeding is not a consideration, I use the Keith-Lyman #454424 lead SWC sized .452″ and cast to weigh 240gr. with 7.0gr. of Unique. The 250gr. lead Speer SWC with 6.5gr. of Unique is also excellent. My Model 25 Smith gives superb accuracy with the 225gr. Speer JHP and 7.0gr. of Unique.

.45 Colt

There is really very little difference between the Remington and Winchester factory loads. I prefer the slightly heavier Winchester-Western copper coated "Lubaloy" bullet, but I like the Remington cases somewhat better for reloading.

There is a great deal of confusion about the correct diameter for .45 Colt bullets currently because older guns were often bored .454″ and newer ones, .451″. The best solution to the problem is to drive a soft lead slug through your own barrel with a wooden rod and mallet, then measure it and use bullets .001 over bore size. Factory loads are usually .454", but the lead is soft, the bullets are hollow based so that they can swage down to size and the charges are mild. They have never presented a problem in my .451 bore guns.

For Colt single actions, I load the 250gr. Keith #454424 Lyman or the new Speer 250gr. SWC ahead of 9gr. of Unique. The same load works well in the .45 Colt conversion cylinder of my S&W Model 25. The Rugers and Thompson Contenders will digest much heavier loads but I am reluctant to increase the powder charges substantially, even for these strong guns, because the head area of the .45 Colt case is somewhat weak. Besides, this cartridge is powerful enough for most working gun requirements with the milder loads. 10gr. of Unique or 17.5gr. of 2400 seems safe in my Ruger with either the Keith bullet or the Hornady 250gr. HP, however, and either is more than adequate for deer.

Rifle Cartridges

.222 Remington

In factory ammunition I have had superb results with Remington's "Power-Lokt" 50gr. load and I much prefer Remington cases for reloading. Optimum bullet weight in this caliber seems to be between 50 and 55 gr. and the following combinations have worked well for me:

53gr. Sierra .224 HP	26gr. H335 for 3100+fps. MV
52gr. Speer .224 HP	23gr. 3031 for 3200 fps. MV
55gr. Speer spitzer	23gr. 3031 for 3100+fps. MV.

All of the above loads are good for pest shooting, but they are much too destructive on small game intended for the table. For that purpose try:

55gr. Speer FMJ	18.5gr. 3031 for 2600 fps. MV.

.223 Remington

Here again, I recommend the Remington "Power-Lokt"

factory load, but with a 55gr. bullet. Fresh G.I. surplus is my choice for defense, because the FMJ bullets are less likely to cause feeding problems in light assault rifles. I have had especially good results with the Speer 70gr. bullet ahead of 25.5gr. of 3031 for larger predators and wild pig. Long range varmint shooting at smaller targets can be handled well by either the Sierra 55gr. spitzer and 21.9gr. of IMR 4198 for 3200 fps. MV or the Speer 55gr. spitzer and 25.5gr. of 3031 for 3320.

.243 Winchester

Western's 80gr. Super X is good for varmints and either their 100gr. load or Remington's works fine for deer. My favorite game load is the 100gr. Hornady spire point with 43.3gr. of IMR 4350 for 3100 fps. MV. I like, almost as well, Speer's 105gr. spitzer and 42.0gr. of the same powder. I use Sierra's 85gr. HP boat tail and 42.9gr. of 4350 for 3200 fps. on varmints.

.270

Almost every factory makes a good .270 load with a 130gr. bullet, which is best for most uses, but your rifle may show a preference for one brand over another, so do some experimenting. No one makes a 100 or 110gr. varmint load that I like. Winchester's 150gr. "Power Point" is excellent for really large game such as elk or moose.

Nosler and Bitterroot produce some of the finest game bullets in this caliber that I have ever used. Sierra, Speer and Hornady are also superior. Any of their 130gr. .277 projectiles loaded ahead of 49.5gr. of 4064 should give outstanding results on any but the very largest North American game. I got this load from Jack O'Connor, the spiritual father of the .270, many years ago and I have never found anything better. A good 150gr. bullet and

52.5gr. of 4350 is good medicine for heavier animals and Speer's 170gr. round nose with 51gr. of the same powder is probably the best choice if you must use a .270 for hunting in dense cover. 100 or 110gr. bullets coupled with 49.5 gr. of 4064 is a pleasant, easy-on-the-barrel varmint load.

.30-30

Winchester and Remington both produce good factory loads for the .30-30 but I usually buy Federal because of their handy belt-slide packaging. I can detect no significant difference in performance among the three brands. Only buy the 170gr. loads, however. The 150gr. is not appreciably flatter shooting and it lacks killing power — a characteristic with which the .30-30 is not overly endowed, at best.

My favorite game bullet for handloading this caliber is the Hornady 170gr., but any good bullet of .308 diameter and 170gr. weight will do. Remember to use flat or round nose bullets only, however, if your rifle has a tubular magazine. 30gr. of 3031, 31.8gr. of 4064 or 34.5gr. of 4350 all produce about 2200 fps. MV.

Many farmers use their .30-30's with lighter bullets for pest control and any of the 100-110gr. semi-jacketed bullets such as the Speer Plinkers work well. I like the slightly more expensive 110gr. Speer HP Varminter much better for that purpose, however, because it has a good crimping cannelure and provides better accuracy in my guns. 37gr. of 4064 gives about 2650 fps. with either bullet. Zeroed at 150 yards, it will be only 1 1/2" high at 100 yards and 4" low at 200.

.308 Winchester

Fresh, U.S. made 7.62 NATO ammunition is what I use in my assault rifle for defense. I prefer 180gr. Winchester

Silvertips for heavy game and Remington 150gr. "Core-Lokt" for deer. I don't like any of the light bullet factory loads which are intended for varmint shooting.

One of the best short range deer loads I have ever used in this or any other caliber is 44gr. of 4064 behind the Hornady 170gr. flat point which was designed for the .30-30. It is an instant killer on whitetails, given decent placement. 48.0gr. of 4064 with a 150gr. bullet is a good all-purpose load, or 45gr. with a 165gr. slug. For moose and elk, try 44gr. of the same powder with a 180gr. bullet. The 110gr. Speer Varminter which I recommend for the .30-30 also does well for pests in the .308.

.30-'06

Most experts agree that the optimum bullet weight for the .30-'06 is 165gr., and presently, only Federal produces a factory load with such a bullet. Everybody seems to make a satisfactory 180gr. load, but for heavier game, I prefer the slow opening Winchester Silvertip. Remington's 220gr. load is excellent for elk. All of the factory, light bullet varmint loads seem to be short on accuracy.

The best all-purpose load I have found for the '06 is 52.0gr. of 4350 for 2750 fps. MV with a 165gr. bullet. There are probably more good loads listed in the manuals for the .30-'06 than any other cartridge and I suggest that you do some experimenting to find what you need for the purpose you have in mind.

.375 H&H Magnum

Next to the .30-'06, the .375 H&H is the most flexible cartridge I have ever loaded. It works well with cast lead bullets at 1800 fps. MV or full power loads with the heaviest jacketed slugs available. If you want to take full advantage of this cartridge, you will need far more information than I can provide here. This is not a cartridge for casual use and I do not encourage anyone to buy a rifle in this caliber unless he is willing to do a good deal of practice shooting and experimentation. In factory ammunition I like the Remington 270gr. soft point for everything except grizzly or brown bear, for which I prefer the Western Super X 300gr. Silvertip.

Although the mechanics of reloading are quite simple, ballistic theory, load development, comparisons of loading equipment and detailed instructions in its use go beyond the scope of this book. In this chapter, I have tried simply to introduce a few practical loads which I have come to trust over the years, but I urge you to acquire as many of the books which I have listed on this subject as you can. The better you are at making your own ammunition, the better your survival guns will serve you.

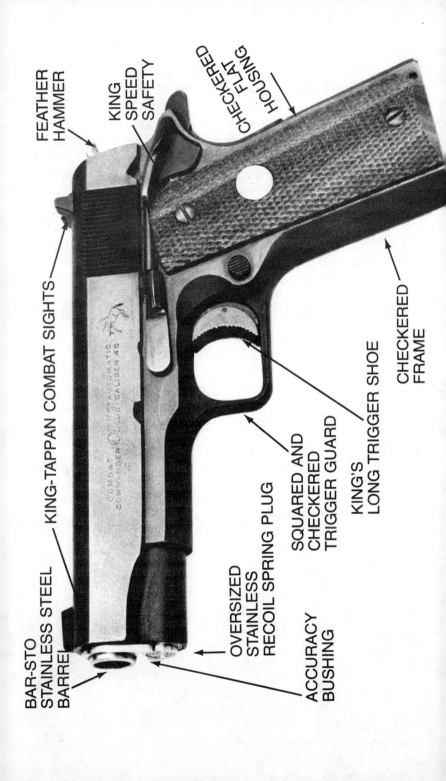

FEATHER HAMMER

KING SPEED SAFETY

CHECKERED FLAT HOUSING

KING-TAPPAN COMBAT SIGHTS

CHECKERED FRAME

BAR-STO STAINLESS STEEL BARREL

OVERSIZED STAINLESS RECOIL SPRING PLUG

SQUARED AND CHECKERED TRIGGER GUARD

KING'S LONG TRIGGER SHOE

ACCURACY BUSHING

8 MODIFICATIONS AND MAINTENANCE

It would be nice if we could simply make our selection of suitable survival guns, pay the inflated prices asked for them, take them from their boxes and use them efficiently just as they come to us from their respective manufacturers. Unfortunately, however, in the majority of instances, we cannot. Most of the guns which you can buy over-the-counter must be gunsmithed to some extent, either to provide the quality of assembly which is lacking, to correct design flaws, or to improve their practical reliability in survival use.

This statement is not meant as an indictment of the gun industry, it is simply a fact of modern life. Very few automobiles, stereos or cameras are mechanically perfect either, and certainly no mass-produced product of complex design will suit every potential use or user exactly. Guns are probably no worse than other manufactured products, but since their functioning under survival conditions may be critical, we must take steps to make them as nearly perfect for our purpose as possible. In some instances, nothing more than adjusting the trigger or installing better sights may be involved; in others, extensive modifications costing as much or more than the gun itself are called for. The Scylla and Charybdis which you must steer between is making unnecessary or even dangerous alterations on the one hand, and failing to make necessary improvements, on the other. No one but you can be the final judge in this matter; however, I will attempt to give you some guidelines based on 30 years of rather extensive experimentation.

The modifications which you will want to consider making on your survival guns fall into three broad categories:

1. those which tend to increase reliability and durability, such as deburring moving parts, polishing feeding ramps, installing recoil buffers, removing magazine safeties, applying long wearing, rustproof finishes both internally and externally;

2. those which tend to increase accuracy, such as rifle tuning and bedding, locking screws tightly in place, installing tight barrel bushings and oversized lugs in autopistols and improving slide fit;

3. those which tend to improve handling qualities, making it easier and faster for you to hit what you aim at, such as efficient sights, custom grips or stocks, installing or remodeling controls such as safeties, adjusting triggers and barrel lengths, installing trigger stops and shoes, roughening gripping surfaces and rounding sharp edges, installing recoil reducing devices, extending or shortening hammer spurs and making various other adjustments which fit the gun to the individual shooter;

4. those which tend to improve the efficiency and flexibility of the gun, such as multi-caliber conversions, extended magazine capacities, variable choke devices on shotguns, etc.

Before you undertake any alterations, however, take your new gun out and shoot it. A disturbing number of our current new guns will not even fire, and since most non-factory modifications will void your warranty, make certain that yours will at least function normally before you begin to improve it. You may also uncover areas which need attention that you would otherwise not discover, or you may find that a trigger which seemed a bit gritty in dry firing suits you fine with live ammunition in the gun.

The second caveat which I would urge you to follow is this: choose your gunsmith with great care. Not everyone who claims to be a gunsmith is competent, and a poor one can ruin your gun. Either follow my recommendations or do some careful investigating before you contract for custom modifications. It is also well to remember that many gunsmiths who have earned fine reputations specializing in one kind of work may be incapable of doing another. For example, a man who specializes in accurizing .45 autopistols for target competition may have no idea of the requirements for combat shooting and although the pistol which he works over for you may be capable of X-ring accuracy, it may be so tightly fitted that it is unreliable.

The third caution which I would suggest to you when considering modifications is: make only those alterations which are necessary. If your trigger pull is adequate as it came from the factory, don't alter it; if the stock on your shotgun fits you, leave it alone. Above all, don't indulge in modifications which are dangerous or questionable, just because they are popular among writers in the gun magazines or because you like the looks of them. The gun shop commandos are fond of many butcheries, such as cutting away the front of revolver trigger guards, installing "fanning hammers" on single actions, or putting giant round levers on .30-30 carbines, after the fashion of "The Rifleman" TV series. Most of these clowns drove cars emblazoned with flames on the hood and slogans such as "try me" or "love me, love my heap" painted on the doors when they were teen-agers. Their gun modifications, like those on their cars, are designed to attract attention and comment, not to improve practical efficiency.

It is impossible to cover in detail all of the useful modifications which might be made on every gun that could be chosen for survival use, but I will outline some of the more essential ones as they apply to some of the guns discussed in previous chapters. The only way that you can be certain of getting exactly the modifications which will suit you individually is by consulting an expert who is willing to take the time to counsel you fully and, perhaps, to confer directly with your gunsmith. If you follow the guidelines in this chapter, however, and temper them with your own common sense, you should make no major blunders.

Handgun Modifications

Handguns are basically reactive weapons; consequently, when they are needed, they must frequently be employed with great speed. They must also be utterly reliable because, since they are normally needed suddenly and at short range, there is no time to remedy a failure. For these reasons — and also because handgun designers do not seem always familiar with the realities of practical handgun use — there are more alterations necessary on revolvers and autopistols to make them as efficient as they can be than is the case with any other class of firearms.

Revolvers

For example, revolver grips appear to be better suited for grasping by the tentacles of an octopus than by the human hand. Almost all double action revolver grips leave a hollow space above the second finger, which must be filled in if a secure hold is to be taken, and many of them do not point well because the angle of the backstrap is wrong. Single actions do not leave the space above the second finger, but most of them are so short that the little finger must be curled under the butt and they shift in the hand with each shot, making even reasonably quick second shots extremely difficult. Fortunately, all of these problems can be alleviated by good custom grips and, occasionally, by inexpensive adapters. Guy Hogue makes some of the very best revolver grips I have ever used and he markets them through King's Gun Works and Martin B. Retting, Inc. Herrett's and Cloyce's also produce excellent grips, and I am particularly fond of the Herrett's Detective series when a design of absolute minimum bulk is called for. Some double action revolvers, particularly Colts, are often made satisfactory by simply adding a small grip adapter such as the Pachmayr or Tyler T-grip. They are easily installed by the user and they are quite inexpensive.

The better revolver actions today are usually acceptable in casual use, particularly the Smith & Wessons, but they can all be improved and they should be if you intend to include them in a survival battery. The double action should be honed completely smooth and require no more than 8 or 9 lbs. of pulling effort throughout its entire cycle. Make absolutely certain that your gunsmith does not intend to produce this effortless pull by weakening your springs, however, or else the ignition may be weak or not uniform. A good single action pull should weigh between 2 and 2 1/2 lbs. and it *must be crisp,* with no creep or roughness. Miniature Machine Co. of Deming, New Mexico can tune double actions as well as I have ever seen it done, and they are one of the few companies who can provide satisfactory caliber alterations and extra cylinders in compatible calibers. One of their specialties is converting heavy framed .357 Magnums to more useful calibers such as .44 Special and .45 Long Colt, and they can fit

.45 ACP revolvers with .45 Colt cylinders. Incidentally, when you are having your action tuned, make sure that the timing is also adjusted carefully.

Sights are at least as important as any other element of a good revolver, but they frequently do not receive the attention which they deserve. All revolvers need rugged, adjustable sights which can be seen easily and aligned precisely. The purpose of adjustable sights is not, as many believe, to allow the shooter to make adjustments for range or wind direction in the field. They provide a means of causing the gun to shoot where the user aims, with a given type of ammunition. Differences in eyesight, hold and ammunition are all factors in determining the bullet's point of impact, so it is impossible for a single sight setting to be correct under all circumstances. Simply changing brands of ammunition can cause you to miss your target by a substantial margin unless you have some means of zeroing the new load. For this reason, all guns except possibly combat pistols which are always used with the same ammunition or very small pocket pistols meant for point-blank range only, should have adjustable sights.

Plain black sights, which are the most common, were

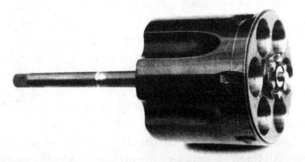

A detailed shot of the .45 Colt cylinder supplied and chambered by Miniature Machine Co. for the author's Model 25 Smith & Wesson. Note the slightly rebated rim to allow clearance on the revolver frame, which was originally designed for the .45 ACP cartridge.

developed for use on black and white targets, and they are less than ideal for most people under the variety of conditions which may be encountered in practical use. I find the S&W sights which are standard on the .41 and .44 Magnums to be very nearly perfect for my eyes. The front

Before and after views of a Colt New Service in .45 Colt caliber. The top photo shows the unaltered revolver and the bottom, with Smith & Wesson adjustable rear sight and custom ramp front installed by King's Gun Works. With some judicious smoothing of the internal working parts and the addition of a Pachmayr Grip Adapter, this now discontinued Colt makes an excellent working revolver.

blade contains an insert of red, orange or yellow plastic and the rear leaf has a white outline around the notch. For me, this arrangement is both quick and precise, but human eyesight varies greatly and you should look at what is available before you buy. Make certain that the sights you choose are of Patridge design, however. "U" shaped notches and gold beads are unreliable in some light. Also be sure that the rear sight is wide enough to allow a good strip of light to be seen on either side of the blade. A few file strokes will solve the problem if it is not. It is also a good idea to have the sharp outer edges of your sights rounded so that they will not catch on holsters and clothing.

This Chiefs Special 2" square butt revolver has been gunsmithed exten-sively. Both the double and single action trigger pulls have been smoothed and lightened and an adjustable S&W Kit Gun rear sight was installed with a matching yellow insert ramp front. A custom, smooth, narrow trigger shoe and a pair of Herrett's Detective series stocks were added. The amount of small game which this little revolver has gath-ered, the number of snakes it has dispatched and the informal target matches it has won give the lie to hysterical claims that small, conceal-able handguns are used only for killing people.

The S&W revolver sights come in three sizes to fit their "J," "K," and "N" frames and they can easily be installed on a variety of other revolvers and autopistols, including many which were designed for fixed sights only. I use them on Colt and S&W pocket revolvers, Colt and Browning autopistols and a variety of other guns. Micro Sight also produces some excellent models, both fixed and adjustable, but they look out of place to me on revolvers and, although they are quite large and rugged looking, I have found them to be no sturdier than the more compact S&W's. Miniature Machine Co., which makes some ingenious sights for autopistols, is rumored to be designing a line for revolvers, but I haven't seen them yet. Their fully adjustable model for the S&W #39 and 59 is a must if you plan to use either of these pistols seriously.

One modification to avoid on handguns for survival use is the installation of ventilated ribs. Their purpose is to provide a flat sighting plane and to break up heat waves caused by continuous firing. Shotguns benefit from such devices but on pistols, they only increase bulk and weight and provide additional areas where rust can begin. The trigger shoe is another gadget which works well on some guns and not on others. They definitely do not belong on double action revolvers. You will find that most expert double action shooters prefer a fairly narrow, smooth trigger for the best control and speed. Hammer spurs as provided by the factories may be either too long or too short for your hand and they should be altered accordingly. Occasionally, they need to be removed entirely, but give some thought to this alteration before you have it done. I can see no reason for removing the spur from a holster gun, but something must be done with small revolvers carried in the pocket, because the spur acts like a fishhook and makes getting them into action quickly somewhat unreliable at best. Colt makes a hammer shroud for its pocket guns which makes them snag free but still allows them to be cocked for deliberate fire. S&W produces two models suitable for pocket carry, the Bodyguard, which has a built-in shroud and the Centennial, which conceals the hammer entirely. All of these solutions increase the bulk of the gun somewhat, so I usually just remove the spur. With practice and extreme caution, these guns can still be cocked for single action fire by starting the hammer back with a gentle pull on the trigger, catching it with the thumb, *removing the trigger finger entirely from the trigger guard*, and then easing the hammer to full cock. If you decide to "de-horn" your gun, try that technique a few

Four approaches to the problem of snagging hammer spurs on pocket revolvers. From left to right, upper row: Smith & Wesson Bodyguard with integral hammer shroud, Smith & Wesson Centennial with completely enclosed hammer; left to right, bottom row: Smith & Wesson Airweight Chief's Special with the hammer spur removed and Colt Agent with factory installed accessory hammer shroud.

thousand times with an empty gun before attempting it with live ammunition.

Barrel length is another matter which might require some attention. Most of the better revolvers offer a choice of lengths, but what the factory provides may not suit you or you may not be able to find the length you want. Remember, long barrels produce the greatest power with a given cartridge and offer the most precise aiming as well. If you want a longer barrel, the only answer is rebarreling, but any good gunsmith can shorten and recrown your existing barrel. Another possibility here is the heavy custom barrel, such as the one made by King's and illustrated in this chapter. These are usually meant for competition use, but if you have a Magnum revolver and need more weight to help control the recoil, this is a possible solution.

Custom heavy barrels for revolvers are usually meant for the target range but they can help the recoil shy to block that kick. This one by King's Gun Works is accurate and tame.

I don't believe in altering barrels, capriciously, but a few changes which I have found useful are:

1. Installing 3" instead of 2" barrels whenever possible on pocket pistols. You will be surprised how much that extra inch will improve performance.

2. Cutting the Ruger .44 Magnum Super Blackhawk even with the ejector rod housing. The long barrel is just too awkward if you intend to carry this big .44 as your everyday working gun.

3. Cutting the S&W Model 25 barrel to 5". This length simply balances better for me on the "N" frame in all calibers than any other.

4. Installing a custom 10" or 12" barrel on the Ruger .44 Magnum for the recoil shy, if the gun is to be used as a substitute rifle.

There are many other possibilities but only your personal needs can determine them.

Finally, finishes for revolvers in the survival battery should be considered. The customary blue wears easily and does not prevent rust. Teflon also wears off rather quickly, but it does retard oxidation. Nickel is a possible answer but it is shiny and, unless expertly applied, can flake off. Industrial hard chrome would be almost ideal if it were dark, and as it is, it may be the best answer. It is harder than a file, rust resistant, and, when applied to moving parts, makes them move with less friction. I have used it on a number of my guns and, except that it is ugly and obtrusive, I have no fault to find with it, although I wish it were somewhat less expensive. If you decide to try it, make certain that your gunsmith understands that you want satin finished, *industrial hard* chrome, not soft, decorative chrome. There is a world of difference.

Stainless steel, particularly if it could be darkened, is the obvious answer for guns which will be subjected to heavy use in an uncertain future, but few models are available

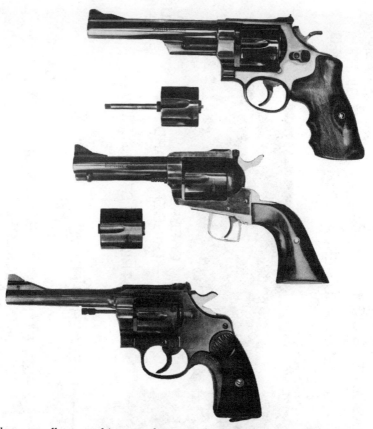

Three excellent working revolvers, each extensively modified. Top, S&W Model 25 with .45 ACP cylinder in place and .45 Colt cylinder below. The front sight has been ramped and a colored insert added. The trigger has been thinned and smoothed, the action polished and lightened by Miniature Machine and Guy Hogue's custom grips added. Middle: Ruger Convertible .45 shown with both .45 ACP and .45 Colt cylinders. King's Gun Works has completely rebuilt this revolver, color case hardening the frame, adding a plated steel grip assembly from the .44 Magnum Dragoon, a steel ejector rod housing from a Colt single action, a custom front sight and ramp, and a steel Micro Sight. All internal parts have been smoothed and polished and the hammer has been jewelled. Bottom: a Colt New Service .45 Colt with Smith & Wesson adjustable rear sight and a custom ramp front by King's Gun Works.

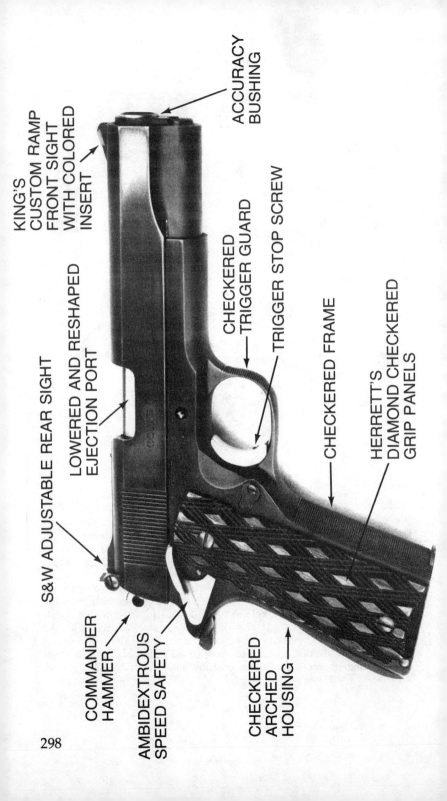

KING'S CUSTOM RAMP FRONT SIGHT WITH COLORED INSERT

ACCURACY BUSHING

S&W ADJUSTABLE REAR SIGHT

LOWERED AND RESHAPED EJECTION PORT

CHECKERED TRIGGER GUARD

TRIGGER STOP SCREW

CHECKERED FRAME

HERRETT'S DIAMOND CHECKERED GRIP PANELS

COMMANDER HAMMER

AMBIDEXTROUS SPEED SAFETY

CHECKERED ARCHED HOUSING

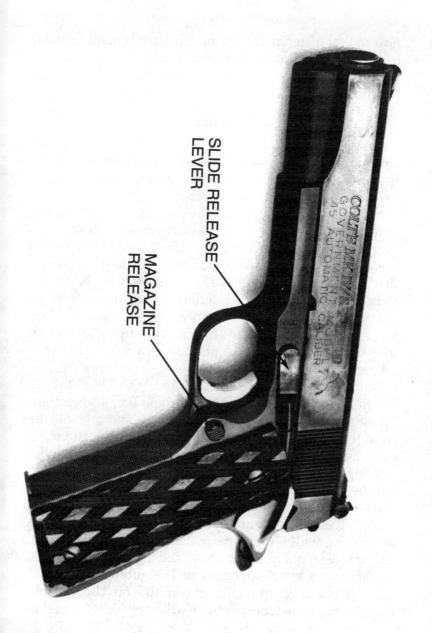

SLIDE RELEASE
LEVER

MAGAZINE
RELEASE

COLT'S MK IV/SERIES 70
GOVERNMENT MODEL
45 AUTOMATIC CALIBER

299

now in that material. If the gun you want is made in stainless, or if your choice is between two similar guns, one of which is stainless, it is certainly the material of choice for survival use.

Autopistols

Since I am recommending autopistols here only for combat purposes, I will confine my remarks on their modification to the only really suitable fighting pistol available, the Colt .45 ACP and its variants.

It is a curious paradox that the one pistol which has the potential of becoming the greatest personal defense handgun in the world is eminently unsuited for that purpose as it is regularly supplied by the factory. Aside from the fact that these guns may not fire, feed or eject as they come from the box, they have inferior sights, they cannot be manipulated quickly or certainly and occasionally their level of accuracy is inadequate for the purpose, although that latter complaint is seldom heard in connection with the new Mark IV.

Not all Colt .45 autos are afflicted with all of the ills which I have enumerated. Most of them fire, a large number of them eject, some feed flawlessly, and a few really good trigger pulls get through, but even if your gun functions well and has a usable trigger, there are still a number of things which should be done so that you will be able to handle it more easily and more effectively.

As I have pointed out before, defending your life is a competitive activity, and if you can increase your chances of winning with nothing more than a bit of gunsmithing, only a fool would hesitate. I have cataloged more than 200 modifications which are more or less routine for the .45 auto, depending upon the gunsmith you choose, and many of them are foolish, others will apply only in special-

LONG TANG

COLT'S COMBAT COMMANDER

An all steel Colt Combat Commander .45 with S&W sights, Bar-Sto barrel and bushing, Pachmayr Signature rubber grips, and a long tang from the Government Model.

ized cases but a few are needed by almost everyone who wants to use the pistol as efficiently as possible under practical circumstances. Without talking to you, I cannot possibly recommend all of the alterations which might be useful to you, but here are some of the more common ones, together with the reasons why they are usually needed.

1. Modifications to increase reliability and durability. To be usable at all in a fight, the pistol must function flawlessly, and one of the chief impediments to that end is

A shooter's eye view of the luminous, easily aligned King-Tappan Combat Sights.

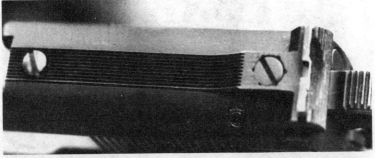

The Smith and Wesson adjustable revolver sight is one of the best for autopistols as well. Few gunsmiths mount it properly, however. The close-up here shows a flawless installation by King's Gun Works.

a poorly radiused and polished feeding ramp. A good gunsmith can eliminate this problem entirely by a process usually called "throating" and your gun will then be able to feed wadcutters as well as round nose jacketed ammunition. If your pistol does not extract properly or if you have "stovepipe" jams, it is almost certainly the fault of the recoil spring or the magazine. Replace them, if necessary.

Installing a recoil buffer may also improve functioning, but its primary purpose is to cushion the peening effect of the slide when the gun fires, making it last longer. Some insist that these devices also reduce recoil somewhat, but I have never noticed that effect.

"Porting" or lowering and reshaping the recoil port sometimes improves ejection, but its most important function is to prevent damage to the empty brass so that it can be reloaded. Note that this procedure is only necessary on Government Models (including Mark IV's); Commanders are supplied with a lowered port.

2. Modifications to increase accuracy. This is the area where most people lose control. You may need to do nothing in this regard, depending upon the performance of your individual pistol. In a handgun to be used for defense, 4" groups at 50 yards are good enough and 6" groups are acceptable. Remember, shooting a 4" group means that you are capable of hitting within 2" of your aiming point. Better accuracy than this is not needed when you are using a powerful defensive pistol such as the .45 ACP, since *any* torso hit will probably disable your opponent. All of the steps which lead to greater accuracy, such as tightening the slide to the frame and installing tightly fitting barrels and bushings, tend to reduce the reliability of your pistol. Autos need clearances to function well and tightening them too much can cause problems. Make absolutely certain that your gunsmith understands

the purpose for which you intend to use your pistol and that you consider flawless functioning an absolute priority, otherwise he may overdo the accurizing, believing he is doing you a favor.

If your pistol will not group within 4" to 6" when fired carefully by a competent shooter, then something will have to be done. One possibility is to install a stainless steel Bar-Sto barrel and bushing, which also offers other advantages. I have noticed lately, however, that the Bar-Stos seem very tightly chambered, apparently in an attempt to provide the best possible accuracy, and they may not function as well as they should. Make sure that your gunsmith is aware of this potential problem and ask him to handpick a barrel with maximum tolerances or to do some extra fitting and polishing.

Another possible solution is to fit a new bushing, tighter than the old one but not as tight as a target bushing. A "combat accuracy" job usually includes this and building up the link at the rear of the barrel.

A really good trigger will make more difference in how well you shoot than any other mechanical factor except good sights. Four pounds is a good weight for most people but a master smith should be able to bring it down to 3 1/2 lbs. Whatever its weight, it must be clean and crisp — like breaking a glass rod — and it must *never* follow even when the slide goes forward violently, so long as a magazine is in place. When the magazine is out of the gun, even some good triggers will follow, but it is a poor practice to allow the slide to slam into battery when the gun is empty. Sooner or later that practice will ruin even the best trigger. For me, backlash or the continued travel of a trigger after it has released the hammer disturbs my shooting considerably. For this reason, I have trigger stops installed in almost all of my guns. Most people find them useful if not absolutely necessary. Stops are one of the things you may not know you need until you try them.

There are two standard trigger lengths for the .45, long and short. Some hands will require one, others, the other; but only the short trigger comes installed in new guns and the long one is very hard to come by. King's Gun Works is now supplying a very well designed shoe which fits over the short trigger and extends its length while at the same time providing a slightly wider, non-slip, checkered surface. I like it very much.

Everything I said about installing good sights on revolvers applies with equal force to autopistols, except that since combat pistols are ordinarily used with only a single type of ammunition, fixed sights may be used when they are properly installed and zeroed.

I will not let modesty prevent my telling you that the very best fixed sights for autopistols that I have ever seen are the "King-Tappan Combat Sights" which I had a very small part in helping to design. (For the record, I have no financial interest whatsoever in either the sights or King's Gun Works and I receive no remuneration of any kind if you buy them. Wish I did.) They can be seen and aligned readily in almost any light and they have a 100 yard index line for long range shooting. Installed, they cost about half the price of good adjustable sights.

The S&W revolver sights are readily adapted to the autopistol and when used with a white outline rear leaf and a colored insert in the front blade, nothing is better. Few gunsmiths install these sights properly on autos, however, and they can be dislodged under recoil when poorly fitted.

"Melted Micros" or low profile Micro Sights with all sharp edges rounded are also popular. They are bulkier than S&W's or the King-Tappan and no more rugged. They are available only in plain black.

Because of requirements of the U.S. Army in 1911, the

Colt autopistol was designed with a grip safety which serves largely to admit dust in the rear of the frame and occasionally to prevent intentional firing of the piece when it is gripped hurriedly. John Browning, the inventor of this pistol, obviously did not care for the gadget because he omitted it in all of his subsequent designs, but there it sits on the 1911 Model, even as manufactured today, about as useful as the sixth finger on a glove. For most people, it should be deactivated, because there is a good chance that it will not be fully depressed when the hand is in firing position, if the thumb rides high on the speed safety as it should. People who do not use this gun for combat shooting, or who do not know how to grip it for maximum control, often have no problem in depressing the grip safety; consequently, even some good gunsmiths who are not combat shooters may tell you that pinning the grip safety is not critical. There is a considerable difference between knowing how to work on a pistol and being able to use it effectively.

Your gunsmith can disconnect it, pin it in or build up the engagement surfaces by welding. You can deactivate it yourself by taping it in with electrician's tape or drilling a small hole and inserting a pin.

The manual safety also needs attention because, in factory form, it can easily be missed by the thumb when the gun is hurriedly drawn. Remember, the proper condition for the autopistol when it is worn on the person is condition one: cocked, with a round in the chamber and the manual or thumb safety on. When the gun is drawn, the thumb of the firing hand should be able to depress the safety reliably, without shifting the grip, and then use it as a thumb rest. In order to make this possible, the safety must be extended out slightly and forward. Most gunsmiths who do much .45 work have developed a speed safety of some sort and both King's and Swenson supply good ones both to individuals and to other 'smiths. I like the feel of King's better than any other I have tried — including one of my own design — but Swenson has a patent on an "ambidextrous model" which can be used with either hand. I find it too narrow to be absolutely reliable, so when I have one installed, I have it widened about 1/16".

Fortunately, the grip on the .45 auto suits most hands, even if it is a trifle large for some, and custom stocks are not required; however, the front strap is slippery, and something must be done to allow for the very tight, non-slip hold which is necessary to control it properly. I think the best solution is to have the front of the frame checkered on steel framed guns, but some prefer stippling or other forms of roughening. The aluminum frame of the Lightweight Commander is too soft to take any of these successfully so I usually put a set of rubber Pachmayr Signature grips on those guns. They wrap around the front of the frame and provide an exceptionally secure grip. For proper speed loading, however, you will have to remove the little rubber lip at the bottom. Sandpaper, cut to shape and secured by the grip panels also works but it needs renewing frequently.

Both the Mark IV and the Commander Models are regularly supplied with an arched mainspring housing; however, a flat housing is available for those who prefer it — and people with very small hands often do. Neither is "better" than the other; it is simply a question of which provides greater control of the pistol in *your* hand.

Most serious .45 shooters find the uncheckered grip panels which are supplied currently unsatisfactory and they usually replace them. I find Herrett's diamond checkered model particularly good but anything you like which offers a secure hold will do. One Spartan chap I know simply coated the factory grips with glue and poured sand on them. True grit.

Many people, including me, find that the standard .45 Government Model hammer occasionally pinches the web of the hand on firing. One solution, if you have this problem, is to install the round hammer from the Commander. It should be fitted by a gunsmith and *before* any trigger work is done, because the hammer notch is a part of the trigger equation and changing hammers will alter the trigger pull. When pinching occurs with a Commander, a portion of the round spur can be cut away, leaving a "feather" hammer or else the long tang from the Government Model can be installed. In severe cases, both may be required or the Tappan "button" hammer may be needed.

I may be shifting out of modifications and into accessories, but this seems an appropriate place to discuss magazines. Buy plenty of them! Without enough loaded spares you lose one of the chief advantages of the autopistol — its ability to be quickly reloaded without being removed from action. Under actual combat conditions or even in realistic practice, your magazines will take a beating. Although they are reasonably rugged, only a small dent or a misalignment of the feeding lips will make them unreliable. Most, if not all, feeding and jamming problems in properly modified autopistols can be traced to faulty magazines. I use only original Colt or U.S. G.I. models and I keep at least a dozen. Anything less than six is sheer folly.

The magazine well in the butt of the pistol requires attention, or so some think. Many people feel that beveling the entrance speeds up the loading process and makes it more certain. I do not find it necessary and I have seen several pistols so altered with frames cracked at that point from being dropped. I realize that pros don't drop pistols, still . . .

Another very common alteration which I dislike half of is squaring and checkering the trigger guard. I have no quarrel with checkering if you use the finger forward hold, but squaring absolutely is not necessary if you know how to grip the pistol; it interferes with proper holstering and it can weaken the frame if improperly done.

You will note that none of the modifications which I have recommended for the .45 auto prevent using un-altered G.I. parts for repair, and I believe that it is well to follow that practice whenever possible in modifying survival guns. If you are tempted to depart from it, consider carefully whether the benefits which you will gain from the proposed modification outweigh the advantages of being able to use standard replacement parts in an emergency.

One final observation on this subject: while it is a waste of money to order unnecessary modifications on a firearm, it is foolish in the extreme not to make every change that will help you succeed in defending your life with it. Nevertheless, I am frequently asked, by people who don't seem to understand the importance of having the most efficient possible pistol with which to protect themselves, "What are the minimum modifications which should be made on the .45 auto?" My stock answer to this question is, "All that *you* need, as determined by someone who thoroughly understands both the gun and modern combat shooting techniques." If they continue to insist, I tell them to install *good sights,* a speed safety, throat it, port it, smooth the trigger, pin the grip safety, install non-slip grips or otherwise insure a secure gripping surface. I am a little sad after I render such advice because I have little confidence in the survival capabilities of such people. Personally, I would rather have a larger mortgage, drive a cheaper car or take an extra job than skimp on my bottom line defense tool.

Rifles

Unless your rifle is poorly stocked, poorly bedded or needs a custom trigger, it probably will not require extensive modifications for survival use; however, it will almost certainly need better sights than it was equipped with at the factory.

Almost any rifle capable of good long range accuracy and trajectory should be fitted with a scope as well as good iron sights for emergency use. There is a tendency today among manufacturers either to use the cheapest iron sights available on high powered sporting rifles or to omit them entirely, since the buyer is almost certain to mount a scope. While I agree that most sporters look cleaner without irons, survival use demands them. I prefer the Lyman #48, with its quick detachable slide and instant return to zero, over anything else; but there are several good aperture sights on the market, including the very functional Williams "Foolproof." I think aperture sights are more accurate and faster than any other non-optical type, but if you insist on open sights either because you like them better or because they are cheaper, I suggest either the Williams Guide or the inexpensive Williams Dovetail Open.

Either of these, when used with the shallow English "V" blade, is adequate. A white line scribed down from the bottom of the "V" improves them. A gold or ivory bead front blade of the proper height on a good ramp is suitable with either the open or aperture rear.

With the possible exception of battle rifles, G.I. .30 M1 Carbines, short range saddle guns such as the .30-30 and a few rimfires, you should plan to mount good scopes on all of your rifles. The most important thing to remember in selecting a scope is that its size and degree of magnification should be suited to the size and ballistic capability of the rifle as well as the primary function which you intend it to fulfill. For example, it would hardly make sense to mount a 24 power target scope on a .30-30 lever action which has a useful range of no more than 175 yards and which is intended for deer-sized animals. Similarly, it would be out of place to use a two power scope on a flat shooting, high velocity .223 sporter with which you intended to eliminate small pests at long range.

The more magnification your scope provides, the harder it will be to locate game in it at close range or to follow moving game. High power scopes are also more difficult to hold steady. As a rule of thumb, you should choose a scope with as little magnification as possible for the job you have in mind. Four power scopes are generally considered to be the best "all-around" power, which is to say that they are a compromise. They are not quite enough for serious long range sniping or pest control and I find them too much for close range shooting in heavy cover. Optical purists tend to denigrate the variable power scopes but I like them, particularly for survival use when you never quite know what you may have to call on your rifle to do. The chief complaint against them seems to be that most people don't really need their versatility. I have had many gun shop clerks tell me that most people crank them to about four power and leave them there. The other objection is that variables do not have as good optics as fixed power scopes. While that may be true so far as performance on an optical bench is concerned, I can find no fault with the best quality variables such as the Leupold. Brightness, contrast, clarity are all superb on these scopes and they give you the flexibility of varying the power if the need arises. The only valid complaint against them in my opinion is that they cost a few dollars more than their fixed power counterparts. To me their versatility is worth the small difference in price.

Variables intended for hunting rifles usually come in three power ranges, 1.5 x 4.5, 2 x 7 and 3 x 9 and the power range you choose should depend on the kind of shooting which you expect to do. For example, on my pet .308 — a rather compact little rifle with a 22" barrel which I use under the broadest possible variety of hunting conditions — I prefer to mount the 1.5 x 4.5. On my 24" barreled .270 plains rifle I have a 3 x 9 and on my .30/'06, a 2 x 7. The family varmint rifle, a .223 Sako, wears a 3 x 9 Leupold with an adjustable objective for maximum resolution of parallax. Both Leupold and Redfield make a full range of variable powered scopes and Bushnell has two specialty items which are of particular interest. Their 1.5 x 4.5 may be had with a "command post" — a very heavy post reticle which superimposes itself over the cross hair when activated. It is particularly useful for shooting in heavy cover or under circumstances when the fastest possible sight alignment is necessary. Bushnell also offers a 3 x 9 variable called the "Lite Site," which projects a small dot of light at the intersection of the cross hairs. So long as there is enough general illumination to see the outline of the target, accurate shot placement is possible with this scope. Even though it may be too dark to see the normal

A close-up of the excellent Jaeger quick detachable scope mount. This one is mounted on a custom-built Newton takedown 30/'06.

reticle, you simply place the dot of light on the target and fire.

If you decide to buy a fixed power scope, don't go above six power except for a long range sniping or pest rifle that will *always* be used from a solid rest. Three or four power seems to be the best compromise for big game rifles and six power for varmint guns. Almost all the name brand makers offer satisfactory fixed power scopes, but Weaver seems to provide especially good value for the money. The optics are excellent and the scope tubes are made of all steel. For rifles that are difficult to scope or which have excessive recoil, requiring long eye relief, you might consider the Leupold M8-2x.

In choosing the correct reticle for your scope you must take into account not only its intended use but also your eyesight. Fine cross hairs probably offer the greatest precision in aiming; however, they are difficult for some people to see except under perfect lighting conditions and they do have a way of disappearing in heavy brush. I find the so-called duplex reticle, which is a combination of fine cross hairs at the center and much broader ones toward the outer rim, the best compromise for most purposes and most people. Whatever you select, avoid the so-called wide field scopes and any sort of cluttered reticle such as one incorporating numbers, dots and comparative indices meant for estimating range. You pay a price in optical quality for the wide field and most of the range finder reticles are simply too difficult to use quickly under most lighting conditions.

Buy a good quality scope. You are better off relying on your iron sights than a cheap, bargain brand. Almost all the better makes today are fog free and filled with inert gas, but it's a good idea to check with the dealer to make sure. Also, be cautious if you decide to buy a used scope. Until very recently, constantly centered reticles were uncommon and even one of the better names a few years old may contain cross hairs which, when the rifle is properly sighted in, will intersect somewhere other than in the center of your field of view. Although workable, such reticles will slow your aiming considerably and they are a nuisance.

It would take an entire chapter to cover thoroughly all of the available devices for mounting scopes on your rifles, so I will confine my remarks to the four which I use and recommend most often. If you want more information, write to the various manufacturers for their catalogs or discuss the matter with your gunsmith. The Sako and Ruger rifles are both designed so that they do not require scope bases, only a set of rings supplied by the rifle manufacturers, and I think owners of those two brands will find the factory arrangement entirely satisfactory. In the great majority of other cases I think you will find that the very inexpensive Weaver rings and bases will do an excellent job. They are simple and unobtrusive and the scope can be removed or replaced simply by tightening or loosening a pair of coin-slotted knurled heads. On rifles of substantial recoil or those which are subjected to extremely rough handling I think the solid Redfield Junior mount provides as much security as any. On my own guns I frequently use the Jaeger quick detachable mounts. By throwing a single lever and pushing a button, the scope can be instantly removed from the rifle either for storage or to allow the unobstructed use of iron sights and it can be replaced as easily without loss of zero. Another approach to the problem of having instant alternate availability of either optical or iron sights is the Pachmayr Lo-Swing mount, which allows the scope to be quickly swung to the side out of view while leaving it firmly attached to the rifle. It too allows the scope to be returned without losing its zero.

This seems as good a place as any to discuss the matter

of zeroing or sighting in a firearm. It is a very simple process and a necessary one, but judging from the mail I get, it mystifies a large number of people. These instructions apply whether you are sighting in a rifle or a handgun and whether you are using metallic or optical sights. Essentially, the purpose of sighting in is simply to cause your aiming point to coincide with the point of impact of your gun at a given distance using a given load. This is a chore which you must do for yourself because no two shooters' eyesight is exactly the same and no two shooters hold a gun in exactly the same way, and both of these factors have an influence on where your bullet will strike in relation to where you aim.

Ideally, you should do your sighting in from a solid shooting bench, although any completely rigid support will serve. Select the distance at which you wish to zero your gun and provide yourself with a supply of the cartridges you intend to use, preferably all from the same box. In the case of centerfire pistols, I think you will find 50 yards to be the most useful sighting in range regardless of the caliber. For rifles, select the distance which will give you the optimal point-blank range from the chart in the rifle chapter. When you buy your gun or have a scope mounted on it, the dealer should boresight it for you with an optical collimator. This device provides a means for aligning the bore of the gun with the sights. Boresighting should insure that your first shots will be on the target paper but it is by no means the same as sighting in. If your gun has not been boresighted or if you don't know whether it has been, you might fire a few shots at approximately 25 yards to insure that your bullets register somewhere on the target paper. You can make rough adjustments to center your group and then move back to your chosen range for the final sighting in.

Arrange yourself comfortably at the shooting bench

and, in the case of a rifle, use sandbags or something similar to help support the gun so that you can reduce human aiming error to a minimum. With a pistol, use both hands and rest your wrists on the sandbags. In either case make certain that no part of your gun is resting on a hard surface. Now fire from three to five carefully aimed shots at the exact center of the target. If properly done, your shots should all be clustered tightly together somewhere on the target paper. If they are not, repeat the process until you get some semblance of a tight group.

At this point there are two ways in which you can proceed. If a vise or some other means of holding your gun rigidly is available, the simplest method is simply to clamp your gun into it so that it cannot move and adjust it so that the sights are bearing on the target in exactly the same way as when you fired your group. You then move the adjustment knobs or screws according to the instruction book for your sights until they bear exactly on the center of the group you have just fired. Your gun should now be sighted in perfectly and in order to determine that it is, remove it from the vise and fire another careful group. This time your shots should be centered exactly at your point of aim.

If you do not have a vise handy, consult the instruction book for your sights to determine how to proceed. Many scopes, for example, move the point of impact 1/4 minute of angle for each index mark: that translates into 1/4" at 100 yards. Let's assume that you intend to zero your rifle at that distance and that your first group was 2" to the left and 1" high from your aiming point. You would simply move the scope adjustment eight clicks to the right and four clicks down.

Atmospheric changes and rough handling frequently misalign your sights so it is a good idea to verify their settings occasionally by the method outlined above.

If your rifle will not produce reasonably tight groups even from a bench rest, it will probably need some attention from your gunsmith. Probably the greatest single cause of inaccuracy in a well designed rifle is poor bedding — the way in which the barrel and action fit in the stock. Occasionally, loose screws are the source of the trouble and simply drawing them tight will solve the problem, but usually the wood of the stock bears on the barrel in such a way that accuracy suffers and rebedding, or at least the judicious removal of some wood, may be necessary. There are as many methods of tuning a rifle as there are good gunsmiths and I wouldn't presume to suggest that I know the best way to perform such a job even most of the time, but if you must try to rebed a rifle yourself either because of cost or because you don't have access to a good gunsmith, I can recommend a technique which has worked for me and which doesn't require a great deal of skill. I simply free float the barrel by removing enough wood from the barrel channel so that the barrel and stock are no longer in contact, and then I glass bed the action with a product called "Acraglass," following the instructions which are packed with it. Brownells, Inc., of Montezuma, Iowa markets Acraglass and $4.00 will buy enough to bed two rifles. Incidentally, Acraglass is also the best thing I have found for repairing broken rifle stocks.

You should examine the safeties on the rifles you have chosen and make sure that they operate easily and noiselessly. It is also a good idea to determine that they work. Many don't. With an empty cocked rifle, engage the safety and try pulling the trigger several times as hard as you can, then bump the butt solidly against a hard surface two or three times and try the trigger again. You should also ascertain that you can operate the safety easily with your scope in place and if you cannot, you may need to install an extension or even a custom safety. Exposed hammer rifles pose a particular problem in this regard but Marlin supplies an offset, extension hammer spur for their guns of this type and a similar device for other makes is offered by Williams Gun Sight Co.

If you want to go into rifle modifications in greater detail, especially if you are interested in converting an inexpensive military surplus bolt action into a sound working rifle, *The NRA Gunsmithing Guide* is a good place to start. You can find information there also on rechambering guns which were designed for obsolete cartridges so that they can fire more popular ammunition, instructions for installing recoil pads, shortening and lengthening stocks, attaching sling swivels, etc.

There is little that can be done for the triggers on your battle rifles, except for some careful adjustment and stoning by a competent gunsmith, but you may want to consider installing a custom trigger on one or more of your bolt action working guns. For long range precision pest shooting, hunting or sniping, even the best factory triggers cannot compare with them. In addition to the standard adjustable models, set triggers are also available for the maximum in precision control. The mechanism is set, usually by pulling an extra, front trigger, or by pushing forward on a lever or the back of the trigger itself. Then, only a few ounces of pressure are necessary to fire the gun. Until you try one of these devices you cannot imagine how much they can improve your shooting. I have had Canjar models installed in most of my working rifles. I think you will find them well worth their reasonable price.

Another modification which you may want to consider for at least one of your working rifles is a takedown conversion. Both King's Gun Works and Pachmayr are well known for such work, and essentially it consists of altering the gun so that it can be separated into two sections for increased portability or ease of storage. This is a job for a master gunsmith only, because accuracy usually suffers if the work is done casually.

I think it is a good idea to make some provision for carrying an emergency supply of ammunition inside the stock of a survival rifle. If you do not use a recoil pad, you can simply unscrew the butt plate and drill a few holes of the appropriate size and depth to hold spare rounds and, perhaps, a few matches as well. Several companies also supply metal traps which can be inletted into the butt for easy access. Some even provide a space for carrying the rear iron sight element when a scope is mounted. Inletting a small compass in the stock, such as the Marbles, is also worth considering.

Rifle magazines do not usually receive as much abuse as pistol magazines, but you should keep a few spares, nevertheless. For battle rifles at least six 20 or 30 round carriers seems about right and probably three or four for each working gun that also uses them. If you must use a semi-automatic sporter for defense, you should have large capacity magazines custom-made for it. Reloading after every four or five rounds during a fight can be somewhat trying.

All of your rifles, both working and defensive, should have slings, at least for convenience in carrying and pre-ferably as an aid to shooting as well. The best way of attaching them is by means of quick detachable swivels so that they can be removed or replaced easily. For carrying, any sort of sling will do, provided that it is wide enough to be comfortable, but I prefer either a Whelen or a military design 1 1/4" wide as a shooting aid. Properly adjusted and employed, either can provide steadiness from a sitting position almost equal to a bench rest, and they are as comfortable and convenient for carrying the rifle as any other. *The Complete Book of Shooting*, edited by Jack O'Connor, gives excellent instructions in their use.

319

Finally, you may want to review those portions of the chapter on rifles concerning barrel lengths and recoil reducing devices. Unless you have a special problem because of a physical condition or the particular circumstances of your retreat area, extensive modifications should not be necessary to adapt your rifles to survival use, if you have chosen them carefully. It would appear that more rifle designers are acquainted with the practical aspects of using their products than pistol designers are with theirs.

Shotgun Modifications

Most of the modifications necessary to adapt shotguns for survival use have already been touched upon in the chapter devoted to those arms: rifle sights for slug barrels, variable chokes, recoil pads, oversized safeties, magazine extensions, lengthening chambers where applicable, general deburring of working parts and trigger jobs where needed. I would like to emphasize here, however, the

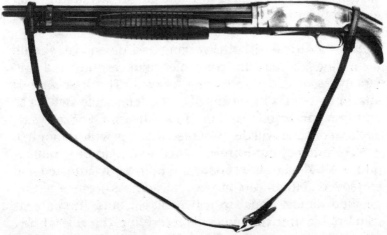

This unusual item is a loop sling for carrying shotguns. It is adaptable to doubles as well as repeaters.

necessity of fitting the individual shotgun to its user. Smoothbores, except when firing slugs, are meant to be used instinctively and they are usually pointed rather than aimed; therefore, unless your gun fits you perfectly, it will not shoot where you look. Obviously, gun fitting is an individual matter and you should consult a competent gunsmith who understands the adjustments necessary and can make them for you. Often no more is needed than shortening or lengthening the stock, but occasionally some judicious bending is required, and perhaps the addition of a cheekpiece or the removal of wood. Remember also that for the kind of shooting required under survival conditions, shorter barrels are no handicap and they are much more convenient. When you are having a variable choke fitted, the barrel can be cut to any length you specify without extra charge.

Maintenance and Repairs

There is a theory abroad among some who write and consult on survival matters that one should acquire at least two identical models of each gun chosen for the survival battery. The rationale for this point of view seems to be that one weapon can always be kept operable by cannibalizing the others for parts. In my opinion, this kind of thinking may have serious consequences for at least two reasons.

Unless you are willing to spend a young fortune, buying duplicates of everything will probably prevent you from having enough different kinds of guns to meet your needs and the "two of a kind" concept may lull you into believing that you have made adequate provision for your maintenance and repair problems when, in fact, you are sadly lacking in that area. Aside from the fact that a whole firearm is a rather expensive spare parts bin, it is also an inadequate one. Many parts almost never need replacement, but those that do, such as firing pins, springs, bushings, screws, sight blades and leaves, may very likely need replacing more than once. Further, many parts which have been fitted to one gun — such as the bolt in a rifle or the cylinder in a revolver — will not fit another "identical" gun, without skillful gunsmithing, except as a fluke.

A far more practical approach to the problem, I think, is to purchase a large but relatively inexpensive kit of spare parts for each gun you own and have any which require substantial gunsmithing fitted to your guns when you buy them.

Each gun in your battery is a law unto itself so far as which parts may need replacement is concerned, but a good gunsmith can give you a list of spares for almost any model with which he has had extensive experience. Make sure he understands that you want all of the parts which might possibly need replacement over an extended period away from civilization, not just a weekend maintenance kit.

I find it useful to package all spares for a specific gun in separate plastic boxes, appropriately labeled, together with a drift punch, screwdriver and any other special tool which might be needed to repair that particular weapon. For example, my .45 autopistol kit, which is packed in two CCI .22 cartridge boxes taped together, contains:

    1 drift punch
    1 screwdriver for grip screws and sights
    2 rear sight leaves
    2 extractors
    2 firing pins
    3 3 leaf trigger springs
    2 sears
    1 trigger with stop
    2 hammers
    2 hammer struts

6 extra stiff recoil springs
1 recoil buffer
2 barrels, bushings, links and pins
2 recoil spring plugs
1 pair extra grips
6 grip screws and bushings

Except for the spare barrels, the entire contents of the kit cost less than $20.00, and it is probably more than twice as extensive as one would really need.

In addition to appropriate spare parts, you should have a few, high quality gunsmithing tools such as a set of screwdrivers made specifically to fit gun screws, a full set of drift punches, a brass hammer, a set of Swiss-pattern needle files, assorted pliers, including needle nose and hardened wire cutters, a vise, an assortment of variously shaped India stones, measuring devices including calipers, a screw cutter and rethreader. The two best sources I have found for gunsmith's supplies are Brownells and Frank Mittermeier. Another excellent supplier of high quality, hard-to-find tools is Brookstone. All of them publish excellent catalogs which you should keep for reference.

You will need a supply of steel wool, fine grit abrasive cloth or paper as well as blueing solutions to keep your blued guns in good condition. Professionals reblue with several heated tanks of hot blueing salts in solution, but that is rather elaborate for retreat use. The very best simple cold blueing I have found is "Formula Super Blue." It requires some skill, however, and you may want to try one of the paste type touch-up compounds which you simply rub on and wipe off. Although oil will do, I prefer to rub in a coat of Simoniz car wax after blueing to insure best results. I often use the same wax on the inside of rifle stocks to seal them against moisture.

Birchwood Casey puts out a very extensive line of products for refinishing and maintaining gunstocks, steel and aluminum parts, and all of them seem to work well. Their aluminum touch-up liquid is the best thing I have ever found for the purpose, and their various wood sealers do a good job of protecting wooden gunstocks from warping and deterioration.

Unless you are an accomplished gunsmith — in which case you certainly need no advice on the subject from me — I suggest that you get every book you can on gunsmithing; there aren't very many. The most indispensable ones include: Bob Brownell's *Gunsmith Kinks*, P.O. Ackley's *Home Gun Care and Repair*, *The NRA Gunsmithing Guide*, Harold MacFarland's *Gunsmithing Simplified*, Roy Dunlap's *Gun Owner's Book of Care, Repair and Improvement*, Bish and Lewis' *Home Gunsmithing Digest*. You will also need good exploded drawings of your guns and assembly-disassembly instructions in detail. The *NRA: Shoulder Arm Assembly*, *NRA: Handgun Assembly* and *The Gun Digest Book of Exploded Firearms Drawings*, should provide all that you will need in this regard.

Cleaning and Lubrication

Your gunsmithing books will give you detailed information on cleaning and lubricating your guns, but a few remarks on the subject seem in order here because misinformation is so easy to come by. Two rival schools of thought are prominent. One holds that modern, non-corrosive ammunition obviates the need for cleaning and the other maintains that guns should be cleaned vigorously immediately after every firing. My own opinion is that while modern ammunition has certainly reduced the urgency for thorough cleaning, metal bullet fouling, leading and powder fouling still must be removed periodically for the most reliable functioning and the longest possible life. Overdoing this routine maintenance, however, can actually be harmful to your guns. More barrels are worn out by improper cleaning and the careless use of cleaning rods than by shooting, and some people use so much oil that stocks become soggy and ruined.

I admit to exercising extra diligence with defensive weapons. In my opinion, they should always be kept scrupulously clean, very lightly lubricated either with a non-flowing substance such as Moly G paste or a dry one such as graphite, and their bores and chambers should be kept bone dry. Leading or metal fouling from jacketed bullets should be promptly removed from any gun because rust can begin, unseen, beneath them and they adversely affect accuracy. Powder fouling should at least be wiped away regularly and all blued guns should be rubbed regularly on the outside surfaces with a silicone treated cloth to prevent rust. Oiling them for this purpose makes them slippery to handle, injures the stock or grips and may cause misfires because of excess oil penetrating the seal of the cartridges and deactivating the powder

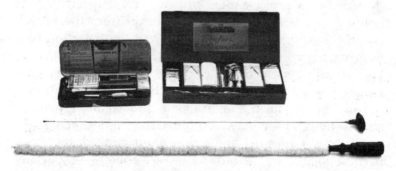

A typical assortment of cleaning gear. On the left above, a Gunslick handgun cleaning kit with rod, assorted tips, patches, powder solvent, oil and lubricating grease. On the right, a fine Parker Hale shotgun cleaning kit with a celluloid covered, jointed rod to protect the bore, a special jag tip and fitted patches. Below: a one-piece .30 caliber brass cleaning rod and a Valet Shotgun Cleaner made of soft pile.

charge. Never under any circumstances spray a loaded gun with penetrating lubricants such as WD-40 or you will almost certainly ruin the cartridges. Also be cautious about using vapor phase rust inhibiting papers or crystals when storing firearms. They often cause wood to deteriorate. Even when you use lubricants sparingly, it is a good idea to stand your freshly cleaned guns up muzzle down for overnight drainage before putting them away. This latter advice is especially applicable to bolt action rifles, since excess oil in the bolt often squirts into your eyes when the trigger is pulled (another good reason to wear shooting glasses whenever you fire any gun).

If you must, you can do a pretty good job of cleaning a gun by placing the muzzle in a bucket of hot water and pumping a tight fitting patch up and down from the breech, but that is a messy technique and it invites rust unless you are scrupulous. Whatever method you follow, however, you will need a good cleaning rod of the proper diameter for your barrel. I like one-piece rods best, but jointed ones store more conveniently. They should be threaded to accept cleaning brushes and a special tip for holding patches. Always insert the rod from the breech end if the design of your gun allows it, in order to avoid wearing the rifling at its most critical point: the muzzle. Use your fingers as a guide to prevent unnecessary rubbing of the rod against the barrel, wherever you insert it.

You will also need a great many cloth cleaning patches and, although they may be improvised from scraps, making them is a nuisance and if they are oversized, they may become lodged in the bore. They are cheap — especially when bought in quantity from surplus stores — and I recommend stocking a large supply. A powder solvent, such as Hoppe's #9, is virtually a necessity, as is a quantity of non-gumming gun oil, molybdenum disulfate (Dri Slide or Moly G grease) and powdered graphite. Personally, I would not want to be without J-B Bore Cleaning Compound. It is the very best thing I have found for removing old fouling and preventing further build-ups, when used regularly. A Lewis Lead Remover is also useful if you own a .357 Magnum revolver. A small flashlight with a flexible tip for inspecting the bore is an almost indispensable item, but a piece of mirror or even white paper held to reflect the light will serve. A few stiff toothbrushes for cleaning hard to reach places will complete your cleaning gear. For shotguns, you may want to consider buying a Valet Shotgun Cleaner. It is the easiest satisfactory method I have found for keeping smoothbores tidy.

However fastidious you choose to be about keeping your guns clean, run a dry patch through the bore to remove any oil before you fire, or else your first shot will probably be off target, and *always* look through the barrel of any gun before you load it to make certain that there are no obstructions there. A forgotten cleaning patch or a nesting spider can cause a burst barrel. Guns which are kept loaded in your ready rack or carried on your person should be inspected daily. As in most things, understanding and common sense are your best guides to gun care.

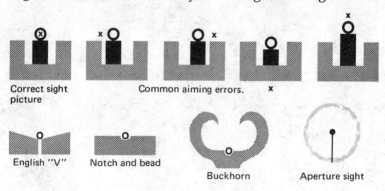

Correct sight picture

Common aiming errors.

English "V"

Notch and bead

Buckhorn

Aperture sight

Typical iron sight patterns.

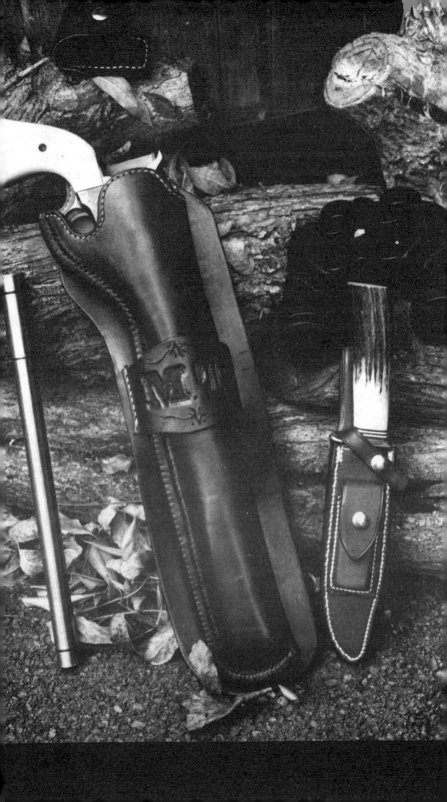

9 ACCESSORIES AND ACCOUTERMENTS

Accessories, like modifications, seem to tempt people to extremes. One tends either to gather up every gadget available or else wants nothing at all to do with them. Once again, the *via media* seems to offer the most practical approach: adding accessories can certainly be overdone, but a few are essential and several others greatly expand the usefulness of the basic battery.

Holsters

Proper holsters are not merely a convenience; they influence to a marked degree the overall efficiency with which handguns may be used. Yet many people consider good holsters unnecessary frills and they buy the cheapest thing available. Aside from the fact that poor holsters are a hindrance to proper gun handling techniques, many of them are also dangerous, and they can cause damage to the guns which ride in them. Most cheap carriers are not fitted to a specific gun. They may accommodate several models of similar size, and when that is the case, they usually accelerate finish wear because of abrasion caused by an inexact fit — and wherever the finish is worn, rust can begin more easily. Further, the leather in these "bargain" brands is usually inferior from the standpoint of both wear and proper curing. I have seen several in which the improperly neutralized tanning compounds caused the guns in them to rust within a few hours. Finally, these designs are usually put together with exposed metal fasteners which abrade and, often, corrode those portions of the guns which they touch. However attractive the price may seem, I can assure you that in one way or another, you will regret buying a cheap holster.

Good holsters are of three general types: 1) those designed for maximum speed and/or concealment, 2) those intended to provide maximum protection to the gun and 3) what might be called utility models, encompassing various styles which offer a compromise between wearing comfort, weapon protection and accessibility. In survival use, you may need all three, possibly even for the same guns. If, for example, you were working in the garden, climbing or hunting during inclement weather, something like a full flap holster offering maximum protection to your gun would be in order, but such a rig could be dangerously slow in a defensive situation.

In fact, holsters for the defensive pistol that are good enough to bet your life on are few indeed. There are, perhaps, a dozen commercial models that almost make it and many people use them. In this critical application, "almost" is not good enough for me; however, I admit to being the kind of chap who checks tire pressures and changes the oil according to the manufacturers recommendations. I also have very firm ideas about the design of a holster which is intended to carry an effective defensive pistol safely, ready for immediate and unanticipated use.

For one thing, such a carrier must require no preparation to make it ready, such as releasing flaps or retaining straps. If you are expecting trouble, you should have a rifle or a shotgun in your hands. The whole point of carrying a fighting pistol is to allow you to defend yourself when you are attacked unexpectedly, and under those circumstances anything which impedes your draw, however briefly, reduces your chances of staying alive. Nevertheless, any holster must retain the gun securely against reasonable physical activity.

Second, a combat pistol holster must allow full hand contact with the gun butt so that a perfect firing grip can be established instantly without having to shift the pistol in your hand once it is clear of the holster.

Finally, such a carrier must be sufficiently comfortable so that it can be worn constantly; it should not restrict your movements or interfere with your daily activities, and it should be concealable under a jacket. Full race competition rigs, such as those made by Milt Sparks, Andy Anderson, Alphonso and Ed Bohlen fulfill most of

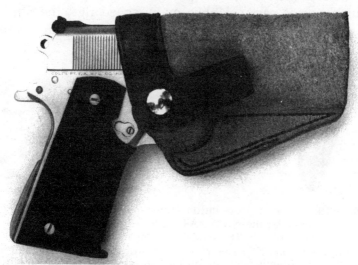

A close-up view of Milt Sparks' excellent Summer Special — a comfortable, concealable, inside-the-pants holster.

these requirements, except concealability, and some may want to consider them for wear at the retreat. They can be very fast, with practice, but I find them bulky and somewhat restrictive for everyday wear — and they are expensive.

For sheer speed, nothing in my experience even approaches a break front design in which the gun is simply pushed forward through the open front of the holster. WHM Enterprises has recently developed a very unusual carrier of this type made of "spring" plastic, and called the "Snick." The material is impact resistant, impervious to water, oil and most solvents, as well as virtually wearproof. Most important, however, it works extremely well. People who have practiced for years with conventional holsters may be able to develop speed from a well designed open top model equivalent to that which can be attained with the Snick, but I know of nothing which will allow beginners to achieve practical combat proficiency as quickly or as easily. Unlike many speed rigs, the Snick also conceals extremely well and it is quite secure, even

The Snick holster line looks unconventional — and it is, but nothing is faster or easier for the novice. All are break front designs fabricated from "spring" plastic. The models shown from left to right hold a Smith & Wesson "K" frame revolver, a Browning P-35 9mm auto, a Colt Combat Commander and a Colt Government Model. Also illustrated is the very comfortable and quick single magazine pouch. Not shown is a style for the S&W Models 39 and 59. Highly recommended.

though it is made — as all combat holsters should be — without retaining or safety straps of any kind. About the only negative comment I could make regarding it is that, like most other really fast holsters, it offers little protection to the gun. For its intended purpose, however, I am aware of nothing better.

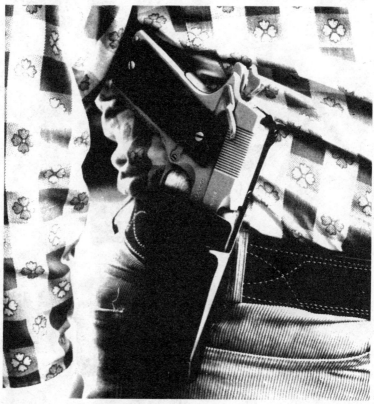

A close-up of the Snick break front speed holster in use. Note that it rides high and holds the butt in close against the body for maximum concealment, yet it exposes enough of the pistol so that a firm shooting grip can be established immediately upon contact. It is held rigidly in place during the draw by bearing against a forward belt loop on the trousers. The style shown here is for the Government Model .45 auto-pistol and it is worn by Michael Harries, a Snick executive.

Perhaps the best combat type holsters of more conventional, open top design are made by Milt Sparks of Idaho City, Idaho. His workmanship is impeccable, and his leathers are the very best obtainable, he understands the design requirements of a really fast, reliable holster and he executes them without compromise.

All of Milt Sparks' fine holsters are made to order. The designs are outstanding and the workmanship impeccable. Shown here are an outstanding shoulder holster, and the Model 200AW revolver holster with hammer protector and adjustable welt above. Below: the Yaqui Slide, an inside-the-pants knife carrier, the Summer Special, the #1 Combat Pouch with adjustable welt and Velcro belt tabs, and an open top twin magazine belt pouch.

His basic speed design for the .45 auto is the #1 Combat Pouch. It rides high and holds the butt close to the body for good concealment. The trigger guard is completely enclosed, as it should be, and Velcro tabs are provided to insure that the holster stays exactly where you want it. This model should be ordered with the adjustable welt which compensates for wear over the years and holds the gun tightly in place without retaining straps.

Sparks also produces the best inside-the-pants concealment holster I have ever used, called the Summer Special, Model 3, as well as a minimum bulk design called the Yaqui Slide. Neither of these has quite the speed potential of either the Combat Pouch or the Snick, but both are very comfortable and concealable.

For carrying and protecting working guns in the field, there are literally dozens of good designs and several good makers. My own preference here is for full flap styles because they offer the best protection to the gun — but it is just that, a personal preference. I suggest that you get catalogs from Lawrence, Safariland, Bianchi and S.D. Myres and choose what you like; however, you might find some of the following comments helpful in choosing something serviceable. I have made a lot of mistakes in buying holsters over the past 30 years and you might as well benefit from my expensive experience.

1) Consider linings. They have no place in a combat holster, but they do protect the finish of a working gun from wear. Chamois, glove kid leather, silicone suede, Orthopedic Elk suede and similar materials all work well.

2) If you don't choose a full flap design because of bulk, try a thumb break model. Most of them shield the hammer and keep it from wearing your clothes and snagging twigs. Also, thumb breaks are more convenient to release than retaining straps and they provide at least as much security.

3) Select a model which is cut to allow your rear sight to be exposed, otherwise the sight leaf will cut the leather and wear itself bright in the process.

4) Make sure that the holster you buy was made to fit your gun exactly and snugly. There is a tendency among some of the larger commercial manufacturers to block a holster so that several similar guns can be used in it. None really fits, however, and that can cause the finish to wear excessively.

5) For carrying large framed, long barreled working guns, particularly in bad weather, consider a shoulder holster. They distribute the weight of the gun well, keep it

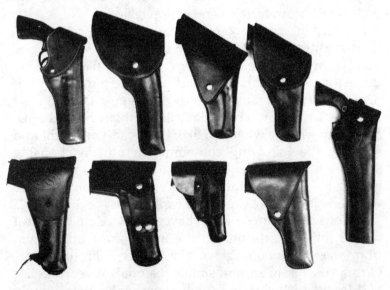

Flap holsters provide maximum protection to the guns they carry and they come in a variety of styles. From left to right: the 1/4 flap by Safariland, a lined Lawrence, a silicone suede lined Bianchi, an unlined Lawrence and a partial flap from Lawrence. Bottom row: a G.I. issue for the .45, Bianchi's new ambidextrous hinged flap model, a European design for small autopistols with a pouch for a spare magazine and Bianchi's #16L, silicone suede lined, for the .45 auto.

out of your way and allow you to protect it from the elements under your coat.

6) Easy on and off features such as belt loops that snap are a great convenience.

7) Crossdraw holsters are very comfortable and offer better access than anything else when you are sitting. If you drive a lot, ride horseback or just like to sit, try one. A proper crossdraw rig *must* tilt the butt *toward* your drawing hand, however, not away from it. Avoid those which have a butt forward speed rake when worn in conventional position and which are advertised as "also suitable for crossdraw." They are not.

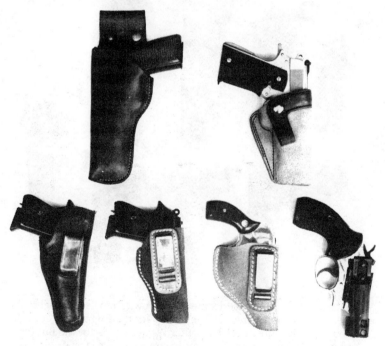

The waistband carry has always been popular and these inside-the-pants holsters will help you to avoid the embarrassment of having your favorite gat slide down your pants leg.

8) There is a curious tendency among many makers to rake their holsters butt forward. Some feel that this angle increases draw speed, although I have not found it so. In any event, there is no excuse for it in a working holster and whenever the option is offered, order yours to hang straight.

9) All leather holsters, except inside-the-pants styles, should be made of stiff, heavy skirting leather and they should remain stiff. *Never* soak them in oil to soften them.

An assortment of Lawrence leather. Top row, from left to right: the #120 for single actions, the #100 semi-flap for the Ruger Dragoon, the Sanchez for a Buntline Special, another Western style for the Buntline, and a lined full flap design. Bottom: Lawrence's own design for a belt pouch to carry Ruger extra cylinders, a .22 auto model with retaining strap, a lined, basket stamped crossdraw model for the Smith & Wesson #41 and a #30 crossdraw for the Colt Commander.

The George Lawrence Co. is one of the best sources of working gun holsters. Their designs are conservative, their materials and workmanship are impeccable and they will give you what you want — which many of the other large manufacturers will not do. You may order raked designs to hang straight and most styles will be cut for crossdraw or left-hand use upon request. Linings, sight protectors and a number of other options are also avail-

Bianchi offers one of the most extensive holster lines in this country. From left to right, #123 spring crossdraw, silicone suede lined #16L, #1 Lawman for single actions with matching cartridge belt, another 16L — this one for long barrel guns, #5BL thumb break. Bottom row: a thumb break design for .25 autos, open and closed spare magazine pouches, a spring crossdraw design for the .45 auto, a full flap for the .45 auto, a minimum bulk style for .22 autopistols and a thumb break for the Smith & Wesson Kit Gun.

able. Incidentally, their #55 O'Connor Rifle Scabbard is one of the finest and most practical rifle carriers to be had. I particularly like their Models 211 and 200 for long barreled guns, their #30 for crossdraw, their #120 for single actions. Model #20 is an excellent full flap design and it is a bargain at their price. Model #100 is a modified flap style which is also fairly fast. Lawrence is still a family business, after more than 100 years, and it shows. These are very good people to deal with.

Bianchi is very well distributed in the gun shops and sporting goods stores so you should have no trouble examining their products first hand. They cater to police buyers and, consequently, they have a large number of uniform-type designs which are of little interest for survival use; however, their line is one of the most extensive and they offer several very good utility holsters. Model #89L is one of the best for .22 autopistols, #1L is excellent for single actions and their spring type crossdraw models 123 and 124 are excellent. Their full flap, silicone suede lined #16L is quite sturdy and it features a snap-on belt loop. For small autos such as the Walther PP or PPK, their 19AH is very good and their #18 is the best thing I have seen for .25's. M66 is a unique ambidextrous hinged flap design for carrying the .45 auto in the field, and if you have need for a compact, secure shoulder holster in which to carry a .38 snubbie, their "upside down" #9R is one of the very best. Model #5BL is a good field holster for almost any revolver. Their catalog is very elaborate.

Safariland also caters to the police and offers a broad line. Some of their two-piece designs are remarkably compact and their adjustable paddle holster is worth noting for those times when you are wearing jeans or beltless slacks. Model #29 is a good thumb break field holster for revolvers and #58B is a modified flap design. Model 8TB is similar to Bianchi's 19AH for PP size autos and #15 is one of the most compact carriers for such guns that I have seen. Model #18TB is excellent for 2″ snub revolvers. Safariland also distributes the excellent Kel-Lite heavy duty police flashlights, judo sticks and other useful items such as belt flashlight holders. Like Bianchi, they put out a large, detailed, well illustrated catalog.

Six popular Safariland holster designs. From left to right: a molded two-piece model for 2 and 3″ barrel guns, a 1/4 flap, next a reverse rake, steel lined speed holster for the Python. Bottom row, left to right: an adjustable paddle holster with thumb break, a minimum bulk two-piece molded design for the Luger and a very compact speed scabbard for the Walther PPK.

S.D. Myres is another established firm whose catalog you may want to examine. They produce a full line and will accept orders for custom modifications.

If none of these commercial lines suits you, contact Milt Sparks. He will make to order virtually any style holster you want and his custom prices are not out of line with those of the better commercial makers. Incidentally, his Cooper-Hardy shoulder holster is the very best I have ever used.

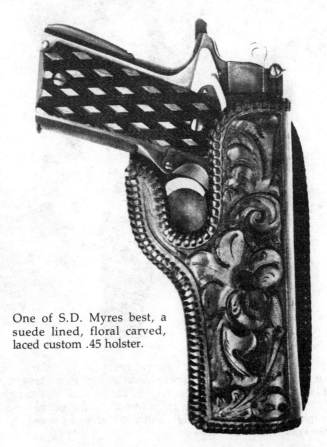

One of S.D. Myres best, a suede lined, floral carved, laced custom .45 holster.

Ammunition Carriers

The old Western gunfighter's dictum, which is still being promulgated by some writers who should know better, holds that any shooting encounter you stand a chance of winning should be settled before your gun is empty. That may be true in a one-on-one duel at 15 paces on a movie set, but such clichés can get you killed in the real world, if you believe them. The truth is that classic gunfights in the best Hollywood tradition are something of a rarity these days, but being assaulted by a gang of hoodlums or terrorists is not. Further, if complete social upheaval is just around the corner, there is every likelihood that such attacks by multiple assailants will increase in frequency and they may occur under a variety of circumstances. Unless you carry spare ammunition on your person, you may find yourself at a social disadvantage.

A pocketful of loose cartridges is hardly the answer to this problem, because you must get them into your gun before they can do you any good and, I might add, the humid, abrasive treatment which they receive in the average pocket does little to enhance the reliability of your spare rounds. Users of the autopistol are graced with an obvious solution. They simply carry a few flat, convenient, loaded magazines which can be fed into their pistols as needed. Although pocket carry for one or two spares is not completely out of the question, a belt mounted carrier of some sort is considerably more efficient. WHM Enterprises, who make the Snick holster, offers the quickest and most comfortable single magazine holder I have used. Made of the same "spring" plastic as their holster, it rides horizontally on the belt, and it is hardly noticeable. Milt Sparks, Bianchi, Safariland and others also make various styles of single carriers and almost every holster maker offers at least one style of double magazine belt pouch, usually with protective flaps and snaps. Milt Sparks' combat style open top design is the fastest of the double carriers I have seen. For those occasions when you are far from your home base or when prudence seems to dictate more than the usual amount of caution, you might want to consider Milt Sparks' "6 Pack" which I helped to design. It is a leather belt pouch with a single snap flap which holds six .45 auto magazines at right angles to the body, each in its separate chamber to prevent rattling. With a full complement of magazines in the "6 Pack," one in your gun and a round in the chamber, you have exactly a full box — 50 rounds — of ammunition conveniently at hand. Even if you prefer to carry only a single or double pouch on your belt, it could be comforting to have a "6 Pack" in your luggage, briefcase, backpack or duffel. (P.S. I have no financial interest in this item either).

For magazine rifle users, Sparks or some other leather craftsman could probably turn out a similar device to fit your magazines or you might shop the surplus stores for something suitable. While you are there, see if you can find some stripper clips for quickly reloading your empty magazines. They are usually quite cheap and they save a lot of time and fumbling.

If you expect to use a shotgun for foraging afield or in a protracted fight, consider a shoulder slung bag, such as a surplus musette bag, or one of the belt pouches of vinyl or leather which skeet and trap shooters carry. Any of these devices will hold about 100 loose shells. Unfortunately, there are no speed loading devices for shotguns of which I am aware.

Second Six

If you intend to rely on a revolver for defense, then you must find a means of reloading it more quickly than stuffing individual rounds into the chamber one at a time.

There are a number of loading devices on the market which are more or less successful in speeding up the process, but only one of all those I have tested seems to possess the virtue of reliability as well as speed: the Second Six (not to be confused with another brand called the "Six Second").

The basic idea of almost all speed loaders is that they line up a cylinder full of cartridges with the chambers so that a single motion introduces a full complement of fresh ammunition into the empty revolver cylinder. Unfortunately, all of these except the Second Six rely on gravity to chamber the rounds and most of them must be deftly twisted or otherwise skillfully manipulated to release the cases. This procedure requires a) that the revolver be pointed down during the reloading process instead of at the target, as it should be and b) an additional step of releasing the cartridges from the loader must be performed after the cartridges have been introduced into the

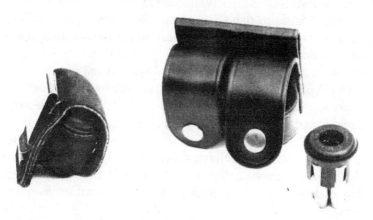

The Second Six speed loader is an accessory which the author highly recommends to revolver users. The small suede pouch at the left holds a single six round loader and the double belt case in the center holds two. Shown at right: the Second Six speed loader filled with six rounds of .357 Magnum ammunition.

cylinder. If the chambers of your revolver are tight, oily, dirty, pitted or even merely fouled from firing, gravity may not provide sufficient force to make the cartridges seat fully, so that still another step — pushing the balky cases into place — may be required.

The Second Six eliminates all of these problems. It positively inserts all cartridges and then falls away as the cylinder is closed. Since it does not rely on gravity, the Second Six functions in any position. You simply locate two rounds above adjacent chambers, slide forward the insertion ring which surrounds the loader and close the cylinder. I have experimented for years with every speed loader I could find, and nothing else I have tried is as positive or as fast as this one. Even the belt cases designed to carry the loading devices are well engineered. The flaps of the double case extend below the bottom so that they can be released easily without fumbling. A single case of soft suede which can be dropped in a pocket or clipped on belt or waistband is also available.

If you decide to use the Second Six, order several; they are inexpensive and while they are not especially fragile, if you should step on one, you will probably crush it. While we are on the subject of ordering, I should tell you that the Second Six is intended for police use only and it is not sold in stores. After much conversation with Bill Griffis, the president of the company which manufactures these little items, he has agreed to honor orders arising from this book, so if you want a Second Six and you are not a police officer or a member of the U.S. Armed Services, direct your order to Mr. Griffis' attention and mention *Survival Guns*.

I realize that all this sounds somewhat peculiar, but I can assure you that I have no interest, financial or otherwise, in the sale of these devices, and if you want to order them through a friendly police officer and never mention a word about where you heard of them, by all means do so.

Next to loose cartridges in your pocket, probably the worst way to carry spare ammo is in cartridge belts. They are not only slow, but they expose their contents to the elements, to bumps and abrasion, and often the leather turns the brass a rather nauseous green. Cases can even become sufficiently corroded in cartridge loops that they will not chamber. For your working guns, MTM Plastics has developed a neat, flat, wallet-like case which I find quite convenient. It is available for various calibers of both rifle and pistol ammunition and it holds the rounds rattle-free in neat, easily accessible rows. The same company makes larger, compartmented, plastic boxes for pistol, rifle and shotgun ammunition and I suggest that you try a few, especially if you plan to reload. The cardboard boxes which most factory cartridges are supplied in are not very

These wallet-like MTM plastic ammunition cases are extremely convenient for carrying extra rounds to feed your working gun. Models are made for both handgun and rifle cartridges.

durable. Under survival conditions, your empty cases are a valuable asset and they should be protected.

Cartridge Converters and Sub-Caliber Devices

One of the most perplexing questions relating to the use of firearms for survival is that of ammunition supply. In addition to the obvious concern of not having enough, there is the problem of having the wrong kind. For example, you lose a gun for which you have stored a large quantity of cartridges, or it becomes inoperative. You need shotgun shells, but the only ones you can trade for are the wrong size. You need a light load for small game, but the only weapon you have immediate access to is a heavy caliber hunting rifle. To some degree, all of these problems can be reduced or, perhaps, even eliminated by careful planning and extensive buying, but one of the simplest and least expensive solutions can be the inclusion in your kit of some cartridge converters and sub-caliber devices.

There are three distinct types available: 1) sub-caliber auxiliary cartridge adapters which allow you to fire other cartridges than your rifle or handgun is chambered for, provided that the bullets match the bore size, 2) shotgun shell converters, which permit firing shells of a smaller gauge or bore than your gun is designed for and 3) "Shell Shrinkers," which make it possible to use rifle and pistol cartridges in a shotgun.

All of these devices are inserts of one type or another, but they differ considerably in detail. The first is essentially a duplicate, externally, of a centerfire rifle cartridge case which is chambered inside for a smaller cartridge. The rimfire adapters allow you to use inexpensive .22's — either shorts, longs, long rifles or .22 Magnums — in rifles or single-shot pistols chambered for .22 centerfires such as .220 Swift, .221 Fireball, .222 Remington, .223 (5.56mm.)

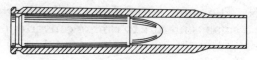

.30 Carbine/.30-06

.30 Carbine/.308 Winchester

.30 Carbine/.30-30 Winchester

.22WMR/.222 Remington

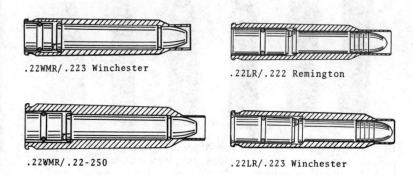

.22WMR/.223 Winchester

.22LR/.222 Remington

.22WMR/.22-250

.22LR/.223 Winchester

Scale, cutaway drawings of the various sub-caliber devices available from Sport Specialties.

or .22/250. The rimfire round is simply inserted in the adapter, a small centerfire to rimfire converter is dropped on top of it and the unit is then chambered, fired and extracted just like an ordinary cartridge. Since the bore sizes of the various .22 centerfires are essentially the same as .22 rimfire bullets, the barrels often direct them with great accuracy.

The centerfire adapters are designed so that .32 ACP and .30 Carbine ammunition may be fired in .30 caliber rifles such as the .30-30, .308, .30/'06 and .300 Winchester Magnum. They function in the same manner as the rimfire models except that no centerfire to rimfire converter is used.

I first began to use auxiliary cartridges of this type years ago when they were produced by the old Marble Arms Co. I found them extremely useful on hunting and camping trips for taking small game for the pot with a big game

These devices made by Sport Specialties of Sunnyvale, CA. allow the use of rimfires, small rifle cartridges and pistol rounds in rifles chambered for centerfire cartridges. The two on the left are for .30 cal. Carbine and .32 ACP in a .30/'06 rifle, the two in the center permit inexpensive .22 long rifle or .22 Magnums to be used in .22/250's and the last pair, on the right, adapt .223 and .222 rifles, respectively, to the .22 long rifle cartridge.

rifle, and for indoor target practice. The Marble units have been off the market for more than a decade now, but Sport Specialties currently offers a very complete line of excellent quality. Harry Owen, who directs that company, is something of a scholar in this field and a collector of antique sub-caliber devices. His encyclopedic knowledge of the subject has led him to produce a very superior product. The .30/'06-.32 ACP adapter which he sent me for testing has produced some remarkable groups from one of

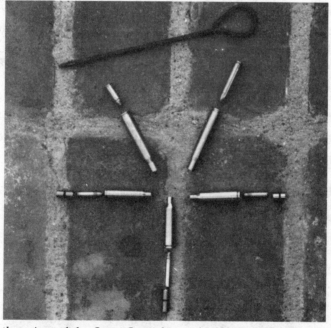

Another view of the Sport Specialties sub-caliber devices. Clockwise from 9, a .223 adapter with a .22 long rifle cartridge and a centerfire to rimfire converter, a .30/'06 adapter with a .32 ACP cartridge, a .30/'06 adapter with a .30 Carbine cartridge, a .22/250 adapter with a .22 long rifle and centerfire to rimfire converter, and at 6 o'clock, a .22/250 adapter with a .22 Magnum and a centerfire to rimfire converter. At the top of the photograph, a combination cleaning rod and empty case remover supplied by Sport Specialties.

351

my rifles, and I have found that the usually anemic .32 ACP cartridge, when fired from a 22" rifle barrel, is an excellent small game getter. For such calibers as these, which are widely distributed but for which few well informed shooters would own guns, the Sport Specialties adapters seem ideal. They are also quite useful for introducing a novice to the feel and functioning of a centerfire rifle without the usual noise and recoil.

I am very enthusiastic about these small devices for survival use and I suggest that you plan to include a few for every caliber in your battery for which they are made. You can order them direct from the manufacturer by mail without registration or red tape.

The shotgun shell converters are similar to the Sport Specialties adapters in that they provide an auxiliary

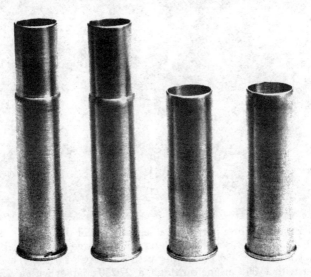

Two sets of custom-made shotgun shell adapters, soon to be available from Survival Vaults in Fillmore, CA. The pair on the left allow 28 ga. shells to be used in a 12 ga. and those on the right adapt 20 ga. shells to 12 ga. guns.

chamber which allows various gauges and bores of shotgun shells to be fired from the same gun. Such contrivances permitting .410 bore shells to be used in 12 gauge guns have been around for some time — the now discontinued Savage "Four-Tenner" being the best known — but only recently have other sizes been developed even on an experimental basis. I have been testing a handmade set for using 16, 20 and 28 ga. shells in a 12 gauge gun and they work remarkably well. By the time you read this, production models should be available from Survival Vaults, P.O. Box 462, Fillmore, CA 93015. They are inexpensive and their advantages should be obvious. They cannot be used conveniently in repeaters, but in the break-open single-shot or double, they are efficient and trouble free. Sport Specialities is occasionally able to locate the Savage .410 converters, and you might drop a line to Harry Owen there if you want a set.

The "Shell Shrinkers" differ from the other devices

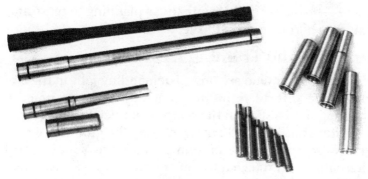

An assortment of sub-caliber devices and cartridge converters. Top left, the Savage "Four-Tenner" and below it, a .45-70 caliber "Shell Shrinker" to fit a 12 ga. shotgun. Next a .45 cal. "Shell Shrinker" for a 20 ga. and a .22 rimfire "Shell Shrinker" for a 12. The six small items in the center which look like empty cartridge cases are, in fact, the excellent rifle sub-caliber devices made by Sport Specialties. At the right, custom shotgun shell converters.

which we have discussed in that they incorporate not only an insert chamber but a rifled barrel as well. The shotguns in which they are used provide only the firing mechanism; they are otherwise self-contained units. Made for 12, 16 and 20 ga. shotguns, they allow the use of a wide variety of pistol and rifle cartridges ranging from .22 rimfire, .38 Special, .44 Special, .45 ACP and .45 Colt to .30-30 and .45-70. You may have almost any barrel length you wish to a maximum of 24". A .30-30 or .45-70 tube of reasonable length turns a shotgun into an effective single-shot deer rifle and a .45 ACP "Shrinker" is a great comfort to those of us who always have a supply of those cartridges on hand. The Sport Specialties adapters can be used in the "Shell Shrinkers" for even greater flexibility. For example, you could fire a .32 ACP or .30 caliber cartridge inside the adapter, chambered in a .30-30 "Shell Shrinker", inserted in your 12 gauge shotgun. The possible combinations are numerous and their practical value in an emergency could be enormous. If you want a "Shell Shrinker" or two, hurry. The owner of the company is planning to retire and liquidate his business in the very near future.

Practice and Training Devices

Those of you who are tied to demanding jobs in the city may have difficulty finding a nearby place to practice shooting, and although there is no completely satisfactory substitute for firing full power loads in the gun with which you wish to become familiar, there are some useful alternatives. In the chapter on special purpose weapons I mentioned the value of air guns in this regard, but there are other approaches as well.

Plastic or wax bullet loads offer good short range practice with handguns. They are simple, inexpensive and they can be used indoors or out with complete safety, so long as a few common sense precautions are observed. A

354

cardboard box with a folded blanket suspended inside is an adequate backstop and the noise involved is about equivalent to that of a cap pistol.

Ordinary empty brass pistol cases are employed with the wax bullet loads. They can remain unaltered for firing in autopistols, but they should be modified if you intend to use them in revolvers because the primers tend to back out in these low pressure loads, tying up the revolver cylinders. Simply drilling a slightly larger flash hole through the primer pocket will remedy the problem, but be certain to mark such altered cases permanently so that they will not later be used inadvertently for normal loads. Excessive pressures and possibly dangerous accidents could result.

Once your cases are prepared and primed, simply press them down, one at a time, into a 1/2" block of paraffin, just

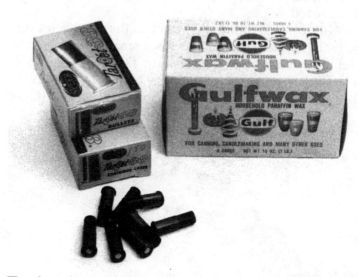

The plastic Speer Target cartridges on the left are propelled by a large pistol primer only and they are reusable. The household paraffin on the right is used for wax bullet loads.

as you would use a cookie cutter. A wadcutter shaped bullet of wax will remain in the case which can then be chambered and fired in the usual manner. The primer alone provides enough power for these light projectiles. A heavy plate glass mirror can be a very useful target for combat practice. When you can beat that image, you've had enough for the day.

If cleaning the wax residue from your barrel after every firing session is too much of a chore, you may prefer to try the excellent plastic bullets and cases made by Speer. Both components are reusable — the cases, almost indefinitely and the bullets, at least half a dozen times. Regardless of caliber, these Speer "Target" cartridges are designed to use large pistol primers only, and with them, velocities run as high as 500 fps. When firing either wax or plastic bullets, reasonable caution and safe gun handling practices should be observed; they are capable of causing injuries if misused.

Another practical training device is the Spot-Shot distributed by Orvis. Essentially, it is a small flashlight contained in a replica of an extra length 12 or 20 gauge shotgun shell. It can be loaded just like a shell in any break-action shotgun of the appropriate gauge. When the trigger

The Spot-Shot flashlight training device partially inserted in one barrel of a 12 ga. shotgun.

is pulled, the gun's firing pin closes the circuit, switching on the light which then shines through the barrel and indicates where a shot charge would have hit. Realistic moving target practice can be simulated by having someone play a flashlight beam on the wall of a semi-darkened room and trying to "hit" it with the light from the Spot-Shot. Floating balloons or hand tossed cardboard disks also work well. AA penlight batteries supply the power and a self-contained lens causes the dispersion of the light beam to equal the average spread of a shot charge from an improved cylinder barrel.

Miscellaneous

A few other accessories which will aid your efforts are detachable bipods for support in precision or long range shooting, an optical range finder which works like the one on your camera to help you estimate distances, and good binoculars to assist you in locating your target. Except for

Useful optical accessories for serious shooters. Top, left to right: Bushnell 7x Custom Compacts, Bausch & Lomb 9 x 35 Featherweights, Bushnell 7 x 35 with insta-focus, Bushnell 7 x 50 night glasses. In the middle, a Rangematic Distance Finder which works like a superimposed image camera range finder to pinpoint distances exactly from 50 to 2000 yards. Below, a 20 x Bushnell spotting scope with provision for tripod mounting.

The Harris bipod shown mounted here on a Browning Safari grade bolt action .30/'06 attaches simply to the front sling swivel.

the binoculars, these items require little discussion for our purposes and I think the accompanying photographs and captions will suffice. Most people like 7x binoculars for general use and a good quality pair of 7 x 35's will serve for most purposes, but 7 x 50's are better for night use and the ultra compact Bushnell 7 x 26's are more convenient to carry. I prefer 9 x 35's when searching for game or locating snipers. A good 20x or 30x spotting scope which can be mounted on a tripod can also be very helpful under some circumstances.

Detachable bipods are useful accessories for long range precision shooting. Shown mounted on the gun, in folded position, the Harris bipod, and below, the Bushnell.

Gun Vaults

Home burglary and armed robbery are increasing at an alarming rate and anyone who is a gun owner has ample reason to be concerned about protecting his battery from theft. The problem of safeguarding valuable weapons is amplified when they are stored at an isolated retreat.

Over the years, I have eagerly examined every new device which has come on the market purporting to offer protection against unauthorized access to firearms. Most of them are simply variations on the theme of sheet metal cabinets or chests, some of which may be bolted to walls or floors; and while they may provide a temporary obstacle to casual tampering, nothing that I have seen, until recently, could prevent theft by a reasonably determined man with a few simple tools.

The Survival Vault Company has added a Gun Vault to their line, however, which solves the problem completely to my satisfaction. It is a steel cylinder which is set in concrete beneath the surface of a floor. Inside it contains a lazy Susan type rotary support for rifles and shotguns as well as hooks for handguns and a shelf for bags of coins, precious metals and other valuables. The circular access hole to the vault is small, and in use, it is filled by a thick, hardened steel removable door containing a combination and a hardened steel tumbler locking mechanism. A metal plate covers the entire device and it may be easily concealed beneath a carpet or rug. Even if it were discovered, no one except a highly trained safe expert would have the slightest chance of getting inside — even with the aid of cutting torches and unlimited time. Other features which I will not discuss for reasons of security make it the most nearly impervious device of its kind available for private use. I recommend it highly and without reservation.

I think a word is in order about the people who make

and sell the Gun Vault because many individuals are concerned about compromising their own security by seeking to purchase such devices. You may safely put all of your apprehensions aside when you deal with the people at Survival Vaults. They are retreat oriented, extremely security minded, and from my long personal acquaintance with the principals, I know them to be completely ethical

Two views of the unique Survival Gun Vaults. On the left, a cutaway demonstration model showing the rotary holder for long guns. When properly installed, they are virtually proof against unauthorized access.

and trustworthy. You may purchase a vault anonymously or have it delivered without the carrier knowing the contents of the shipment. No records of the combinations are kept but instructions are provided so that you may change the combination if you wish. I am very enthusiastic about this product and there is a great deal more which should be said about it, but I suggest that if you have even a casual interest in protecting your guns and other valuables, you would be well advised to contact Survival Vaults directly by telephone or mail. The principals are delightful and knowledgeable people. I think you will enjoy knowing them whether or not you buy one of their excellent vaults.

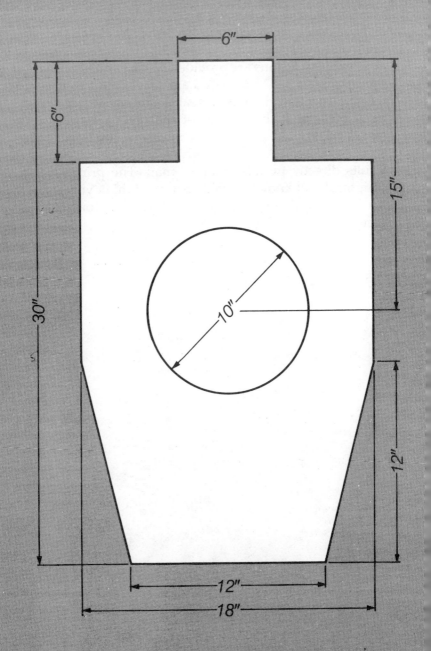

10 Practical Shooting And Tactics

Target shooters are concerned with grouping their shots in tight little clusters, centered in a paper bull's-eye, while observing certain rules and conventions of style. Theirs is a good sport, but it has very little to do with one's ability to gather food or to defend oneself from attack with a firearm. Practical shooting, as I define it, means hitting what you must, within the physical limitations of the weapon you are using, and — especially in the case of defensive shooting — doing it with all deliberate speed.

In a shoot out, the man who starts the fight has the edge, all other factors being equal. The defender must react to aggression already begun, so he undertakes his defense with a time deficit weighing heavily against him. If you want to be prepared to survive such an encounter, therefore, you must take steps to ensure that all other factors are *not* equal. You must overcome your attacker's initial advantage through superior weapons, superior skill and superior mental conditioning.

Weapons

Until now, this entire book has been devoted to selecting the best possible weapons to meet various survival needs. I have gone into great detail — some readers may think excessively — about the most effective calibers, the best guns and the most desirable combat modifications. There is little more that I can do, by means of a book, to help you arm yourself efficiently. If you follow this advice, however, the chances are great that your weapons will be substantially better than your opponent's. Criminals and looters usually steal their guns, so their choices are normally limited to what they can take from others; and those who know enough to own the best seldom have their guns taken from them. Further, although criminal guns are often crudely butchered with hacksaw amputated barrels and the like, they are seldom properly modified to increase their efficiency. Surprisingly few criminals are students of weaponry; in fact, contrary to the propaganda of the anti-gun mongers, most lawbreakers have only a rudimentary knowledge of how guns work or how to use them effectively.

Skill

Just because you have purchased suitable firearms, however, you are not necessarily armed. You must be willing to learn how to use them skillfully. This book is primarily concerned with helping you to select the tools that will best meet your needs, but I do not want to leave you with the impression that any equipment can entirely replace the need for skill. Owning the best may help the beginner to achieve competence more quickly and more easily; it will certainly prevent the expert from being handicapped, but no gun in the world will fulfill its purpose if you don't use it properly.

You *can* learn to shoot well enough to defend your life and to hunt successfully. Many people who know nothing at all about guns believe that they cannot avail themselves of the protection and other benefits which these useful tools provide. That might be true if ignorance were invincible, but fortunately, it is not, with respect to developing shooting skills. Anyone who has the motor ability and intelligence to drive an automobile in city traffic can learn to shoot well enough to pose a serious health threat to potential assailants — if there is sufficient desire and will-ingness to submit to the necessary discipline. And anyone who has learned to shoot well defensively can easily apply that skill to the use of hunting weapons through practice and, perhaps, somewhat greater deliberation.

I find it curious that many of the same people who believe that they could never learn to shoot a gun, frequently spend a great deal of time and money studying judo, karate or some other form of unarmed self-defense. Almost anyone can become a safe gun handler and a rather proficient combat shooter in no more than six to ten hours of instruction with a competent teacher. But it takes years of dedication to learn one of the martial arts well enough for it to be of significant value in a serious fight, and even then, its usefulness is limited. At 7 yards, the statistical average combat encounter range, no karate master in the world is a match for a 16 year old girl with a shotgun and 15 minutes training.

Given enough time and determination, you can learn to shoot on your own, but I urge you to try to find a competent instructor. In some areas, that may be a more difficult task than learning to shoot, because many willing mentors who fancy themselves "gunslingers" are in reality target shooters or "gun shop commandos" who couldn't even qualify in the lowest classification among competitors in the more realistic matches sponsored by organizations such as the South West Pistol League. If you live on the West Coast, you should consider joining and competing in the SWPL. Even if you can't place in the matches, you can learn a lot just by watching the best combat shooters in the world perform. Many of the participants offer shooting instruction, and some of them number among the best.

In the following pages, I am going to outline the basic methods of learning to shoot the pistol in combat, partly because what you learn about grip, sight picture, breath and trigger control in that context can easily be translated without further help to any practical use of firearms. You may also use this information as a check on the quality of your chosen instructor. There are a number of ways to learn combat shooting and I do not pretend to have a patent on the best method, but combat pistolcraft has made rapid strides in just the past few years, and it has come of age through codification of certain basic techniques which are common to all state of the art approaches. If your instructor does not teach eye level aimed fire, the Weaver Stance, using both hands on the pistol, or if he tells you that you must learn to squeeze the trigger in such a manner that you do not know precisely when your gun will fire, if he has you assume a "combat crouch" or insists that you let your gun recoil freely instead of overcoming it by rigid opposition, find yourself another instructor. Overcoming the basic bad habits which you will undoubtedly learn from such a teacher will be infinitely more difficult than learning to shoot from scratch.

One additional caution: unless you participate in a combat shooting club, keep the fact that you are learning to shoot to yourself. With the possible exceptions of religion, politics and medicine, no topic elicits more fluent advice from the uninformed than shooting. Without even trying you will attract veritable throngs of bright-eyed cluricaunes who will gleefully fill your head with tales of recoil so vicious that it mangles digits and reduces strong men to tears, shooting accidents so filled with blood and gore that they bid fair to rival any medical show on TV, and phony statistics designed to convince you that you would be safer to keep a yearling Bengal tiger in your home than a gun. They will tell you that the average person cannot possibly learn a craft so arcane as pistol shooting — even though they will solemnly affirm in the same breath that all of the sociopathic simpletons who may threaten your life or burgle your home are expert gunmen, not to be resisted by an ordinary person such as you. They will say, moreover, that proven combat pistols such as the .45 auto are "unshootable," when what they really mean is that *they* can't shoot them. Twaddle, stuff and nonsense. Such people are like a child who thoughtlessly breaks his own toy and then tries to break the toys of the other children as well. If I can't, then you can't either. This kind of mindless well-poisoning may prevent you from learning a useful and, perhaps, vital skill if you listen to it. Don't.

There is a Latin motto which has been adopted by the South West Pistol League, one of the most prestigious of all combat shooting clubs. It reads, "Diligentia, Vis, Celeritas": Accuracy, Power, Speed, and these three criteria are indeed the ruling considerations in defensive shooting. All three obtain with equal force: speed, because you must stop your adversary before he can harm you; accuracy, because you cannot stop him if you cannot hit him; and power, because even if you hit him he may not stop unless you hit him hard enough. You must work to develop each of these elements equally. If any one of the three is wanting, you are not yet ready to defend yourself with a pistol.

A good bench mark, something like the FDA's recommended daily minimum allowance of vitamins, which guarantees at least minimum health, is what my friend Jeff Cooper calls the "SCT" or standard controllability test. It involves drawing your pistol from wherever you normally carry it — holster, pocket, waistband or handbag — and firing five full power combat rounds within five seconds into a 10" circle at 25 yards. That is certainly not the ultimate test of pistol mastery, but if you can do it six times out of ten, the chances are better than excellent that if an armed assailant ever threatens your life, he has unwittingly committed suicide.

How then does one invoke the seeming magic which arises from this combination of power, speed and accuracy? The first two are simple, though the one requires judgment and the other diligence. Power is achieved by choosing the right combination of gun and cartridge, which for most people will be the .45 ACP fired from an autopistol of modified Browning-Colt design — for reasons set forth at length in the chapter on handguns. Speed comes — after you have learned what to do — by practicing the basic motions again and again until, gradually, quickness arrives almost of its own accord, without specific effort on your part except for the diligent practice which creates neural pathways. Accuracy will take a bit of doing.

First, consider the fact that your initial objective of being able to defend yourself at pistol ranges does not require X-ring accuracy, although it is prudent to continue until you achieve it. The torso of a man, even out to 50 yards, is a substantial target, and, if your pistol is powerful enough, you need not hit it dead center in order to disable your attacker. All combat practice should be done on a simple silhouette target *without scoring rings,* and you should begin at close range — say 10 feet — gradually moving the target farther away as your skill improves. Never rush any element of your practice, and in particular, do not increase the range until you can place every shot from each string of five within a 10″ circle. Do not even begin to think about speed until your technique is as perfect as you can make it and your hitting is completely reliable.

Never fire a single round in practice with any gun without adequate eye and ear protection. Although rare, bits of case or primer metal, burning powder grains, ejected cases or even excess lubricating oil can strike your eyes when you are shooting, if they are unprotected, and the close sound of gunfire will unquestionably damage your ability to hear high frequency sounds, at the very least, unless its intensity is reduced. Further, you are much more likely to develop accuracy robbing flinch from muzzle blast than from recoil. Impact resistant shooting glasses are the answer for your eyes and several manufacturers, such as Bushnell and Mitchell, make good ones in neutral gray or green for bright light use and yellow-amber for night or overcast conditions. Both acoustical ear muffs and ear plugs especially designed for shooters offer good hearing protection. Even wads of cotton will do in an emergency, but you should own something more effective. For casual shooting and even hunting, I am partial to Sonic Ear Valves which have a ball bearing in them that blocks sudden loud noises but permits ordinary sounds to be heard. Ear muffs are the best choice for long sessions on the range.

Keep your first few practice periods fairly short, about an hour to an hour and a half. Shoot no more than 50 to 100 rounds and be very deliberate in making every shot count. While you are learning, at least, shoot only at your silhouette target — no plinking. A paper target may not be as much fun as potting away at targets of opportunity but it has the great advantage of being unforgiving; it records the exact placement of every hit and, by the absence of bullet holes, it reminds you mutely but unremittingly of each miss.

The following regimen can be varied somewhat and other instructors will undoubtedly use a slightly different approach, but I recommend that your first hundred practice shots should all be singles. Draw from a safe condition, aim, fire, make the gun safe and return it to its holster or other carrying place, then repeat the entire cycle. The second hundred can be two shot strings; the third, two shots on each of two silhouettes; then two on each of three silhouettes. By the time that you can draw, place two hits within a 10" circle on each of three silhouettes at 25 yards within 10 seconds you will probably have expended between 500 and 1000 rounds of ammunition if you are working alone, or a bit less if you have a good teacher — and you will be extremely dangerous for *anyone* to tangle with. People do get faster than that, however. A really good man can go through the drill in six seconds, including a speed reload after the second shot, but there are very few such men and the chances of your ever encountering one of them on the wrong side of his pistol is almost non-existent — provided, of course, that you are one of the good guys. Criminals seldom have the self-discipline to learn combat shooting very well; if they did possess that quality, they probably wouldn't be criminals.

Now the three things which you are going to have to learn to do in order to achieve this level of proficiency are: 1) hold the gun properly, 2) achieve a quick, sure sight picture and 3) press the trigger in such a way that no time is wasted and your sight picture is not disturbed or is disturbed only minimally. In less than five minutes you can be shown how to do each of these three things, but it will take a bit of practice — a few hours on the range and a few more of dry firing homework — before you will be able to do them passably well. After that it is simply a matter of more practice to develop speed and your own style. Later, a minimum maintenance program of two hours a month on the range and 20 minutes a day of dry firing will help you to retain the skill you have developed.

The basic idea in holding the pistol is to provide the most rigid mounting platform for it that it is possible for you to devise. Your hold should minimize both random neuromuscular movement, while you are aiming, and re-coil effect when you fire. Obviously, such a hold must be very firm and it can only be accomplished successfully by using both hands on the pistol and employing the principle of opposing force.

Start by placing the pistol in your shooting hand in such a way that the barrel is an extension of your forearm and locked wrist. Close your hand firmly and increase the pressure of your grip until muscle tremor just begins, then extend your arm forward at eye level as far as it is comfortable without locking the elbow. Now bring up your non-shooting hand for support and clasp the fist, holding the gun in it as shown in the accompanying photographs. The first finger of your supporting hand should now be bearing much of the gun's weight via the trigger guard, which should be resting firmly somewhere near the second joint of the first finger of that hand. With your shooting hand, push slightly forward against the resistance of your supporting hand, which should now pull slightly backwards until virtually all muscle tremor ceases and the gun is as motionless as you can make it.

Your trigger finger should be completely free and independent, bearing no portion of the gun's weight, and being in no way involved in gripping the pistol. Practice this a few times.

Now, standing, take a fairly wide step toward the target with the foot opposite to the shooting hand side of your body, i.e., if your shooting hand is your right, take the step with your left foot, so that you stand quartering toward the target. *Slightly* flex your knees and throw the center of your body's gravity *slightly* forward. Do not crouch! Your torso should remain erect; the muscles of your thighs, calves, abdomen and arms should be taut, your trapezius back muscles relaxed. Ideally, you should be exhaling half of a full breath and then stop your breathing glottally, maintaining diaphragm pressure. Some hunch the shoulders slightly and rest the chin on the shoulder of the shooting arm. I do not, but you should try both ways and use the one which you find most comfortable. This tense, solid stance will allow almost anyone, from a 90 pound teen-aged girl to an 80 year old in reasonably good health, literally to shrug off the recoil of any practical defense handgun and, properly assumed, it will rapidly and automatically return the gun to its original alignment with the target. From this position, you can cover a 90° area of fire without strain, by merely pivoting at the waist. By taking a long pivoting step, you can cover a full 180°.

You should practice drawing your empty gun slowly and assuming this stance for 20 minutes twice a day for about a week, or until your muscles become hardened to it. Unless you are in very good shape, this practice will be at least uncomfortable, if not painful, and it will be accompanied with assorted tremors from more muscles than you knew you had.

There are a number of slight variations on this basic posture. Some prefer to stand almost in profile to the target and others face it almost squarely. I think my position in between those two extremes causes less strain and gives better control but I have known good men who disagree.

The placement of one's hands on the pistol is also the subject of some debate. The simple, clasped hands position which I have described works well for me and a number of other passable combat competitors, but just about as many others prefer an alternative method. "Finger forward" is not a new obscene gesture but a well accepted hold in which the first finger of the supporting hand is wrapped around the trigger guard — which is usually checkered or otherwise roughened for the purpose, and occasionally squared. The thumb of that hand

In the ensuing sequence of photographs Michael Harries, a member of
the South West Pistol League, demonstrates both proper and improper
modern technique. Above, although his hands are placed properly, he
is not looking at the target – a fatal mistake.

Notice that full hand contact is made and the final shooting grip is established before the pistol is drawn. The trigger finger remains outside the trigger guard and the left hand is beginning to move away from the body to join the shooting hand in supporting the pistol.

The pistol is thrust forward out of the break front holster. The trigger finger remains outside the trigger guard. In this entire sequence, the shooter's eyes should be on the target — never on his gun.

The left hand has now met the right and, as it encircles the shooting hand and the pistol, the speed safety is depressed. Note that the trigger finger is still outside the trigger guard.

376

This is the proper combat shooting stance. The pistol is aligned and locked onto the target and the shooter's muscles are rigid, his concentration intense.

This is a view of the stance from the left. Notice that the elbow of the supporting arm is slightly flexed.

You never want to see this view of the stance except in pictures. It is prudent to assume that anyone using it with such aplomb knows what he is about.

The speed reloading sequence. The magazine release has been depressed and the empty magazine can be seen, falling, beneath the butt of the pistol. The left hand has already begun to withdraw a spare loaded magazine from the Snick belt carrier. The pistol should remain on target and so should the shooter's eyes.

The shooting hand has resumed its firing grip on the pistol with the right thumb riding high on the speed safety and the spare magazine is being moved toward the pistol.

The fresh magazine is being "looked" into the butt. It will be thrust home with the heel of the left hand; the stance will be resumed and firing continued. It is no longer considered acceptable practice to allow the eyes to stray from the target even during the reloading sequence.

The kneeling position as demonstrated here by Mike Harries is especially steady and quick to assume. It should be used whenever time permits.

The prone position shown here is the best of all for precision long range shooting. It causes much less strain and tremor than the more common PPC prone in which the arms are thrust forward and the body is stretched out directly behind them.

For those rare occasions which may call for one-handed point shooting, the "speed rock" draw is shown here. The beginning position is exactly the same as for the standard combat draw.

"Eyes front!"

The arm is simply rocked forward at the shoulder with the elbow "swapping" places with the gun hand in contact position. Note that the trigger finger remains outside the trigger guard although the speed safety is being depressed at this point.

Line up! Lock on! Fire! The elbow is now exactly where the gun hand was when it first made contact with the holstered pistol, the elbow is rigid and the wrist is locked. The shooter's eyes are fixed on the target and the gun is aligned and fired by "feel." This technique should be limited to very short ranges. With practice, it takes very little longer to bring the gun up to eye level using both hands to support it solidly.

These close-ups show two of the best methods for holding the auto-pistol with both hands. Above, the "finger forward" grip seen from the right.

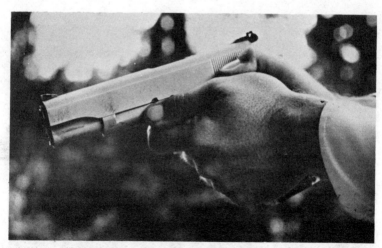

This view of the "finger forward" style shown from the left illustrates the great care that must be used in positioning the left thumb.

The author prefers to use the grip shown above with the trigger guard of the pistol resting on the first finger of the supporting hand and the thumb of that hand overlapping the thumb of the shooting hand. Note that the ball of the finger, not the joint, is used to press the trigger.

The author's grip seen from the right.

The .45 auto pistol shown in full recoil with heavy combat loads. Those who are concerned about recoil should take notice that with a firm two-handed hold the pistol only moves about two inches from firing position.

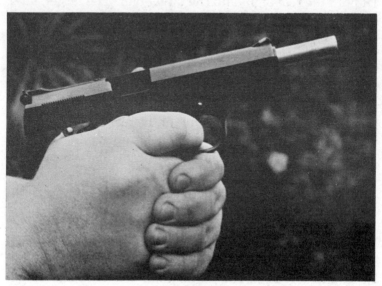

can then usually no longer overlap the thumb of the shooting hand and must be placed, pointing forward, along the frame and below the slide. Curl that thumb up a quarter of an inch too high in that position and you will learn what it feels like to lose a nail. Some do very good shooting with this hold, however, and claim that it provides more positive control. Try both methods if you like, but choose one early in your training and stick to it, otherwise you may never realize your speed potential. All of your training should lead toward automatic actions which require the minimum number of decisions.

As you practice assuming the stance, always working for a smooth draw and firm control of your pistol, align your sights on a silhouette target set up across the room. Now, the first thing you are apt to notice in trying to line up your sights with the target is that your eyes cannot focus on three planes at once. No problem, no one else's eyes can either. Focus sharply on the front sight blade and let both the rear sight and the target blur. The target, after all, is relatively large and all you need to see when you are aiming is its general outline so that you can point at the center of the mass. The rear sight, if the notch is wide enough, actually does its job just as well blurred as sharp. You need only ascertain that strips of light of equal width appear on each side of the blade and that the top of the front blade is level with the top of the rear leaf. When that condition exists, you have the sights properly aligned with one another. You only need move the pistol, taking care to maintain this sight alignment, until the sights bear more or less on the center of the target. Now you have a sight picture and you should practice firing without hesitation at the instant when that sight picture is first achieved. I suspect that more aspiring pistoleros fall short of their goal because they try to improve this initial aim than for any other single reason. For purposes of defensive shooting it does not matter whether the sights bear on the exact center of the silhouette, so long as they are aligned with each other and are well inside the torso area. Alignment of the front and rear sights with each other is far more important than having them directed to an exact spot. For this reason, practice aiming at the silhouette with no visible markings on the target whatsoever. Choose the area where you want your shot to go, align your front and rear sights with each other as well as you can, covering that area, and fire without hesitation.

Firing the gun — or, rather, dropping the hammer, because you should still be practicing with an empty pistol — is accomplished by pressing the trigger carefully, so that you do not appreciably disturb your sight picture, but quickly, nevertheless. I have never been able to describe a proper trigger press exactly with words alone, so I will try to tell you what it is not and hope that, within the confines of what remains, you will be able to discover it for yourself through experimentation. You will know that you have attained it when you can drop the hammer very quickly on command without discernible movement of the pistol or the sight picture.

First, it is neither a pull, a squeeze nor a mash, but it contains elements of all three. It is quick, like a pull, but it does not cause the muzzle to flip as a pull does. It is straight back like a mash except that the finger is kept slightly curled and rigid. Tension is built up smoothly and precisely released as in a squeeze, but much more quickly, and the element of surprise is absent. You should know exactly when the hammer will fall.

It will speed things up considerably if you can find someone to show you how to execute a combat trigger press, but, frankly, very few people really know how and you will doubtless discover it for yourself if you are diligent. In the long run you will be better off to spend the extra time to experiment for yourself than to allow some bezonian to teach you the wrong way. Remember, if you are doing it correctly, your shots will go where you want them to; if not, they won't. It is a very pragmatic technique.

Once you are satisfied that you can assume the stance, acquire a sight picture and press the trigger just as the sights line up, without disturbing them, you are ready to begin firing practice. Assuming that you have found a suitable locale with a safe background which will not endanger either yourself (from ricochet) or others, position your silhouette target 10 feet away and insert a magazine loaded with five rounds into your pistol. Now, pointing the pistol down range, chamber a round, apply the thumb safety and holster your gun. Orient your body toward the target, draw smoothly, releasing the thumb safety as your gun lines up — all the while bringing your support hand up to meet your shooting hand. Assume the stance, stop breathing, lock on a sight picture, fire! Reapply the thumb safety, return your pistol to its holster and smile at the fat round hole that has appeared, as if by magic, in your target. It *will* be there if you have followed all of the steps outlined above.

Once you have become proficient enough consistently to pass the tests outlined earlier in this chapter, you should begin to practice speed reloading. When the slide locks open, your shooting hand thumb presses the magazine release latch and the empty magazine is allowed to fall from the pistol. At the same time your support hand smoothly draws a spare loaded magazine, inserts it in the butt and drives it home securely, at which time the shooting hand releases the slide to chamber a fresh round. During the entire reloading sequence the pistol remains on the target. With very little practice, the time lag between the last shot from one magazine and the first shot from the next should be no more than two seconds. As long as you have loaded magazines, you can maintain a steady cadence of rapid aimed fire, and that is one of the primary advantages of the autopistol. With a revolver, even when using the best speed loaders you will be hard pressed not to move the gun out of battery and take your eyes from the target; and even though you may learn to reload a revolver almost as fast as an auto, you will never do so as certainly.

As soon as your moves have become grooved and automatic and your speed is beginning to surprise you, shift the pistol from your preferred shooting hand to the other and begin again. With a small amount of additional practice, you should be able to do almost as well with your weak hand as you can with your strong hand. If you are ever injured, this ambidexterity may prove quite valuable. Some practice drawing with your weak hand from your holster in its usual position is also helpful. Real life combat situations seldom occur as they are pictured in the movies, so the more practice you get going into action from awkward positions — sitting, lying down, leaning — the better. Try shooting around corners, over and under barriers, while diving for cover and, whenever possible, with both hands.

What you have now learned will serve you for about 90% of the defensive shooting situations which should ever be attempted with a pistol. If you want to cover the other 10%, you will need to learn point shooting. You should be aware, however, that if you do, it may interfere slightly with your best speed when using the technique which you have already learned, because you will then have to make a decision regarding the method to use in any given situation. If you practice enough to become really good, however, any such differential will diminish to the point of imperceptibility.

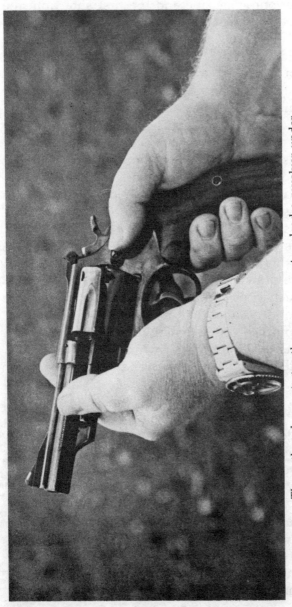

The author demonstrates the proper way to reload a revolver under combat conditions using the Second Six speed reloader which is highly recommended for such applications. The photograph above shows the beginning of the sequence. As the cylinder latch is pressed forward by the thumb of the shooting hand (on a Colt, it would be drawn to the rear), the left hand has moved forward from its supporting position to swing the cylinder out of the frame.

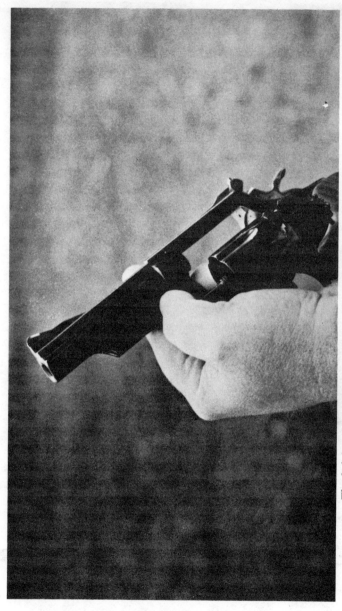

The left hand is now holding the revolver, the second and third fingers are bearing against the cylinder and the thumb depresses the ejector rod to remove the fired cases.

As the thumb, second and third fingers of the left hand hold the cylinder to keep it from turning, the right hand introduces six fresh cartridges into the chambers, held in the Second Six reloader.

The cartridges are seated by thrusting the insertion ring of the speed loader forward with the thumb and index finger of the right hand.

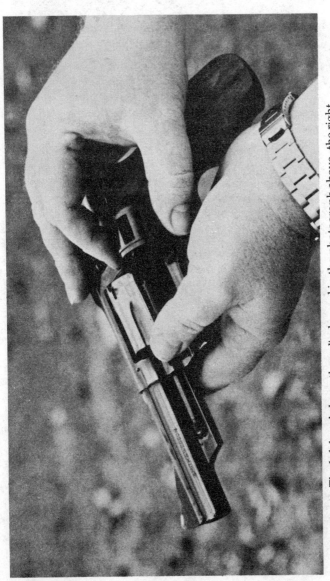

The left hand closes the cylinder and in the photograph above, the right hand is withdrawing the empty Second Six. In practice, the reloading device would simply be allowed to drop to the ground as the cylinder is closed and the right hand would resume its firing position.

Point shooting should only be used when 1) your assailant is at arms length, or just a bit more, and absolute speed is demanded or 2) when it is impossible to use two hands and sights, such as in night shooting when one hand is holding a flashlight, or when one hand is wounded or occupied in maintaining your position or other, similar circumstances. Basically, the technique is accomplished by riveting your eyes on the target, drawing and thrusting the shooting hand toward the target while firing. Point shooting is strictly a close range expedient and even then it is not as reliable as aimed fire, although some become very proficient with it indeed. There seems to be more of a talent involved than is the case with aimed fire. Virtually anyone can learn to shoot rather well with the latter method if he is sufficiently persistent, but some people learn point shooting readily and others don't. It is hard to teach. Suffice it to say that such shooting is more or less directed by muscle memory, much like pointing one's finger.

One of the best discussions of this technique can be found in a book with the grizzly title, *No Second Place Winner*. Its author, Bill Jordan, is one of the greatest gunfighters of the modern era. Although I disagree with his equipment choice — he is, as a former Border Patrol officer, revolver oriented — he is one of the best qualified men in the world to teach point shooting. Keep this technique in perspective, however, if you decide to learn it; it cannot substitute for the versatility, accuracy and recoil control of the basic method outlined in this chapter, and you should not even attempt it until you have mastered two-handed aimed fire. Nevertheless, point shooting could save your life, particularly if you are ever attacked at night and you find yourself blinded by a light in your face.

Mental Conditioning

If reaction time, or the lag between becoming aware of a threat and actually doing something to neutralize it, is the primary cause of the time deficit which gives the advantage to your potential attacker, then alertness — heightened awareness — is certainly one of the prime remedies. There is a hypnotic process, which psychologists call automatization, that is associated with the very routines and mundane experiences of everyday living. If, for example, you are placed in a room which contains a loud, ticking clock, you will automatically become unaware of the sound, after a period of time. EEG, or brain wave studies, confirm this phenomenon and I allude to it here to point up the fact that most of us are far less aware of the details of our environment most of the time than we believe we are. In short, during much of that period when we are supposed to be awake, we are in fact experiencing various levels of hypnotic trance. Almost anyone who drives an automobile has, at one time or another, had the experience of finding himself on the other side of a town he doesn't remember driving through, or at least discovering himself several miles farther down the road than he thought he was. We light another cigarette without noticing that one is still burning in the ashtray, or almost collide with someone on the street because "our minds are a million miles away."

This condition has certain metaphysical implications which need not be dealt with here, but in addition, it renders us less capable of being able to protect ourselves in an emergency. If you are unaware that two rough looking characters are leaning against your car until you reach for the door handle, or that someone is loitering in the dark alley which you are about to enter, you can hardly deal adroitly with the potential dangers which these situations may entail.

400

Arthur J. Deikman and other researchers into the psychology of consciousness have discovered that people who practice certain types of meditation are less susceptible to automatization than the general population and, in fact, I have found one technique in particular to cause deautomatization to occur. Again, EEG studies reveal that repeated stimuli, such as the ticking clock, create undiminished response with people who meditate.

Although I personally practice meditation and have done a great deal of research in the field in connection with writing a book on the subject, I do not intend to urge it upon you or to discuss it here in detail. Some people find the subject highly controversial, and they seem especially threatened by what they regard as the "faith trips" involved in some techniques. Since I am making an honest attempt in this book to help you as much as I can with your survival plans, however, I think the matter should be mentioned here, in the event that you have never investigated it for yourself or thought of it in this connection. Whatever else meditation may involve for you, it will, if you practice it regularly and properly, increase your awareness and level of alertness to a degree which you may not now believe possible, and it can gradually "deautomatize" your perception of your environment.

There are literally thousands of meditation techniques, but generally I would urge you to avoid any which require the use of a mantra — or a repeated sound or phrase. In my opinion, such methods actually lower rather than raise the level of one's conscious awareness, while masking their effect by making you feel exhilarated and "loose."

If you want to look into the subject further, Robert Ornstein's book, *The Psychology of Consciousness,* is one of the most lucid and complete treatments of the subject by a clinical researcher that I know. If you want to learn how to meditate, using a very effective Judeo-Christian technique, write to The Foundation of Human Understanding (P. O. Box 34036, Los Angeles, CA 90034) for their records, which they will send free if you cannot afford to buy them. If you care to investigate meditation, I think you will find it to be the most valuable survival tool of all.

In addition to increasing your awareness, you should also give some thought to practicing the mental conditioning necessary to deal effectively with violent aggression. There is a vast difference between *knowing how* to shoot and *being prepared* to shoot in a life-threatening situation. I know of nothing which will better help you to make the transition from the former condition to the latter than Jeff Cooper's outstanding monograph, *Principles of Personal Defense*, published by Paladin Press. As Jeff states in his introduction, this little booklet is for those who believe that anyone who chooses to attack another human being physically should do so at his own peril. Reading his concise 42 pages should help to ensure that such peril is not inconsequential.

Tactics of Practical Shooting

I intend to write a small book in the near future to be called "The Tactics of Practical Shooting," but with the thought in mind that some of you may have earlier need for some of the information which it will contain, I shall include a few of the more basic admonitions in this chapter.

I am often asked for specific advice on dealing with life-threatening situations, and while there is certainly no formula which is guaranteed to suit all occasions, the following observations may prove useful, assuming that you are armed, reasonably skilled in the use of your weapons and are mentally prepared to do what the situation demands in order to protect your own life or the lives of those whom you care for.

I. Don't bluff. Ever. Bluffing is a kind of specious resistance or opposition which nevertheless elicits an escalation of effort from your opponent. Whenever anyone is threatened, he instinctively looks for a way out of the potential danger and your adversary's way out may be over your dead body. If you simply show signs of resistance without occupying your assailant fully with the reality of your counterattack, you are simply encouraging him to attack more furiously or more quickly than he might have otherwise. Specifically, holding a gun on someone may actually put you at a disadvantage. You are consciously *not* shooting and in order to fire you must not only decide to, but also reverse dozens of neural and muscular "sets." A fairly common stage "gunfighter's" trick which demonstrates this point involves having someone from the audience hold a cocked empty gun while the gunfighter suddenly draws and fires before the startled spectator can drop the hammer. If you really think shooting is called for in a given situation, do it without delay. Don't stand there talking tough and pointing your gun at your opponent; you are simply providing him with the extra shot of adrenalin which he may need to kill you. Remain calm and appear placid, or even a bit languid, until you have reached the decision to act, then move decisively. The less dangerous you seem, the more careless your assailant may be in prosecuting his attack.

II. Don't fire warning shots. This is really just another form of bluffing but I mention it separately because the practice is indulged in so often on TV that some may believe that it is proper technique. Every menacing situation does not call for shooting; you may be able to avoid the attack or use less than deadly force, depending on the circumstances. But if you are ever attacked without provocation in a manner so serious that only shooting appears to offer a reasonable chance of neutralizing the danger, then your attacker does not deserve a warning and you very probably do not have sufficient time to give one. Further, if your assailant is high on emotion or drugs, you may need every cartridge you have to stop him or, when the shooting starts, you may find that he has brought friends to the party. Police officers who must attempt to stop a fleeing felon for arrest may be an exception to this rule, but even they, when directly attacked, would be well advised not to waste ammunition shooting at clouds. A gun wise old Texas Ranger, who taught me a bit about combat shooting when I was a boy, had a pertinent motto engraved on a huge silver concho which he used as a watch fob. It read: "Direct your thoughts always to heaven, confine your gunfire to earth; never the opposite."

III. Never let an adversary get too close. This observation should be apparent to anyone with a shred of sense, but it bears noting. A handgun is one of the easiest things in the world to take away from another person, unless it is being fired effectively in the taker's direction at the time. Yet I have seen supposedly well trained men actually prod opponents with the muzzles of their guns. Such foolishness often carries its own rebuke. I consider 12 feet the absolute minimum distance which should be kept between you and a potentially dangerous opponent, and depending upon the circumstances, I might require a good deal more. For some it may be a difficult decision to shoot someone who has been warned to stop but who continues to advance, particularly if he is showing no weapons. You will have to decide for yourself how much you value your own life in such a situation and whether you think that preserving the life of someone who is menacing your life is more important than preserving your own. I suggest, however that you not ponder the question longer than it takes you to draw.

IV. If you must shoot, shoot for the center of the mass. Second place is not a trophy position in a gunfight. It does not even bring "honorable mention" in most circles; therefore, if you are ever in the unfortunate position of having to shoot another human being in order to prevent your own death or serious injury, aim for the center of the torso where your chances of delivering a disabling hit are the greatest. Never shoot for the arms or legs. Not only are they small targets, but they are usually in motion, and if you miss your mark, you will likely miss your attacker entirely. The head is a poor target for the same reasons and should normally be avoided. If you have the misfortune to be armed only with an inadequate weapon such as a rimfire, a .25, .32, .380, 9mm. or a .38 Special with round nose bullets, which could not ordinarily be relied upon to stop an attacker with a body hit, and if the distance is short enough almost to guarantee success, then a head shot is probably your best option.

Tactics for Women

At the risk of not being regarded as a male chauvinist pig, I must point out that self-defense is certainly an area of equal opportunity — and equal requisites. Armed attackers are no easier to stop just because a woman is shooting at them; consequently, I do not intend to smile condescendingly and list a group of ineffective weapons to be used by women, despite the fact that I am constantly asked to "recommend something for my wife that's small, doesn't kick much and will do the job." If I knew of such a weapon, I would be carrying one myself and recommending it to all of my clients, male and female. Unfortunately, small, light guns, if made to use effective cartridges, would kick too much to be readily controllable by anyone;

and the miniature gats which we do have are simply ineffective, regardless of who uses them.

What then, are women to do about defending themselves? Obviously something effective, considering the fact that one out of every seven women in the United States will be mugged or otherwise assaulted this year — assuming that things get no worse than they are now. And in a retreat situation, anyone who can be taught how to fire a gun should be. Women certainly can be taught to shoot effective weapons, if they are willing to learn. In fact, they are often much better students than men because they are less hampered by their egos. Most men seem to think that they can handle guns well just because they are men. Women, on the other hand, often think that they cannot possibly learn because of their almost reflexive reinforcement of male self-importance through feigning helplessness. Play a role long enough and it becomes no longer a role.

The fact is that any reasonably healthy woman can learn to shoot a .45 auto and similarly effective weapons at least as well as the average man, if she really wants to. Certainly, many women have small hands, but a bit of experimenting with the grip will suffice to make a sound firing stance possible. It is also true that some women's arm and shoulder muscles are less well developed than those of some men, but simple exercises such as squeezing a rubber ball, racking the slide on a .45 several hundred times and holding the pistol at arms length with a weight attached for a few minutes everyday will not only provide all of the muscle development needed for serious defensive shooting, they often have startlingly desirable effects on some of the more noticeable areas of the female form. This is not theory, it is fact. I can't begin to count the number of 90 pound, under 5 feet tall teen-aged girls and women who have become very efficient handlers of the

406

.45. A number of them even compete successfully in the very best combat contests.

Husbands ordinarily do not make the best shooting instructors for their wives — there is often too much resentment and role playing — and husbands who are also gun enthusiasts are the worst of all because they tend to make the subject far more complex and detailed than it needs to be. Women whose only interest in firearms is their potential for self-protection are often easily — and understandably — bored by hubby's lengthy digressions into the finer points of weaponry.

Another area concerning firearms in which women express an especial interest concerns the problems involved in maintaining guns in a ready condition when children are present. There are a number of expedients such as disassembling the weapons, locking them in a closet or keeping them widely separated from their ammunition which I do not endorse but which many will want to consider, nevertheless, in the ordinary home environment. You can't keep weapons readily available, as they must be during an emergency at the retreat, however, and have curious uninformed little people there too. The obvious solution, at least to me, is to remedy the uninformed condition of the little people.

Now, I am quite serious about this. Children who are going to live in households where there are guns, especially under survival conditions, should be taught as much as possible about them at as early an age as possible; in no event later than 5 or 6 years. In fact, many tragic accidents could be averted if the children of gun-hating parents were also taught instead of being endangered by their parents' irrational attitudes. Just because there are no guns in your home does not prevent your children from encountering them when they visit their friends, and their lack of exposure to and familiarity with firearms is apt to make such children even more curious, frequently with fatal results.

Most normal children have sufficient mental maturation and digital skills to learn to operate some firearms between the ages of 3 1/2 and 6. If you are patient with a child, show him graphically what a gun can do by firing it at close range into mud or tightly sealed cans of water, relieve his curiosity by answering all of his questions and even teach him to shoot his own scaled-down .22 or quality air rifle, he will probably be as safe around guns as vacuum cleaners. I had my own gun when I was 6 and I was allowed to keep it and the ammunition for it in my own room. The only restriction was that I was required to call an adult if I wanted to handle it. Any other firearm in the house was also mine to inspect upon request and I was taught, whenever I asked, how each functioned. Such a reasonable attitude by parents calls forth reasonable and responsible behavior on the part of the child. I was never allowed to point toy guns at people and pretend to shoot. Shooting was a real activity which I engaged in with adults, not a game. When children are allowed to indulge in make-believe with toy guns, "shoot" their chums, then see them jump up and run back to play, is it any wonder that they might try the same "game" with a real gun which they have never been allowed to handle, much less fire?

It is a gruesome thought to some no doubt, but it could also be very helpful, should the family retreat ever be attacked, if those children too young to fight were able to load and unload guns for other family members. Older children, 9 to 12, should have their own suitably fitted .22's and the like. Youngsters that age have sharp eyes, keen hearing and are excellent small game hunters as well as patient pest eliminators. You will find that there are many additional benefits which derive from making the children productive, full-fledged members of the survival group, with their own tools, whenever possible.

Tactics

Once the firearms education of the children has been accomplished, you should then consider having a "ready rack" in your retreat. It should be located in the area where the members of your group having primary responsibility for defense spend most of their time. In it you should keep whatever first line defensive rifles and shotguns you have chosen, including at least one scoped hunting rifle, assuming that the latter could conceivably prove useful for sniper defense in your terrain. Pistols should be worn at all times during periods of possible danger and probably at other times as well. Every one of these arms should be clean, regularly inspected and fully loaded, with spare ammunition and loaded magazines nearby. Spares and less frequently used weapons should be kept inside the strong room in locked "Survival Vaults" and/or in well thought out caches on other parts of your property.

The strong room, which is designed to offer maximum resistance to penetration should your retreat be overrun, ought to be designed with a well camouflaged escape exit. No chamber can be constructed that is completely proof against entry if the attackers are determined enough and have sufficient time.

For that matter, any reasonably conventional dwelling is extremely difficult to defend from within. If you have proper escape routes and well chosen, pre-established fire points, a relatively small force can, from the outside, draw fire away from the structure and defend it with greater ease. Incidentally, you can gather some useful information adaptable to the retreat-survival situation by reading some of the accounts of the plight of white farmers in South Africa and Rhodesia whose homes are being attacked on a regular basis. You will build your retreat with fireproof materials, thicker walls and grenade proof shutters, if you do.

Depending upon the sophistication of your potential attackers, you could encounter a virtually infinite variety of attack patterns, some of which no single family unit could possibly repel; however, I will list here four of the most common ones to give you some insight into the tactics involved.

I. Exposed attack. This is by far the most frequently used method by untrained groups and the easiest to cope with. Even if the attacking force is vastly superior, you will have enough warning to escape if your retreat is properly constructed. In its purest form, the entire group of aggressors simply expose themselves and rush their objective noisily, often firing ineffectively because they are running. If the defenders are suitably armed, the retreat well constructed and located, giving practical considerations to fields of fire, and if the ratio of the attacking force is no more than 12 or 15 to 1, the defenders should be able to beat off the attack successfully, causing from 50%-75% casualties among the attacking force during the first assault. Small forces — 3 defenders, 36 attackers — would tend toward the larger percentage figure and large forces, the smaller. Sentries or warning systems should provide advance notice to the defenders of the impending attack.

II. Stealth blitz. This can be one of the most dangerous attacks to the defenders, but it can and should be prevented. Even now, in many of our major cities, this approach is being used by gangs in residential areas. The attack force, often quite small, approaches the target structure by stealth, usually at night, suddenly forces entry at several points simultaneously and overcomes the defenders by surprise. There is no excuse for the success of this method. Sentries, dogs, even ducks or geese and other warning systems should prevent it. If it does occur, only an extraordinarily high level of alertness, mental conditioning and skill on the part of the defenders can neutralize it. Such qualities seldom occur as concomitants with lax warning procedures.

III. Fire blitz. Possibly the most dangerous attack to the defenders and one which normally allows only one viable response: escape from the dwelling by secure, hidden means. A usually superior attacking force surrounds the target structure and simultaneously fire bombs it and hoses it with automatic weapons fire. If the attack is made at night and/or from concealed positions even warning systems cannot prevent a successful attack. Only an area which offers no cover within an effective attack range of the structure and/or strategically placed explosive charges which can be reliably detonated from within the structure by the defenders affords much of a chance of repelling such an attack unless allied forces fron neighboring retreats can outflank the attackers.

IV. Scouting attack. A small advance party is sent ahead of the main body of attackers to reconnoiter and, by exposing themselves at range, draw fire to indicate the strength of the defenders. This is one of the most typical guerilla-type attack strategies. Assuming a reasonably effective defensive force, one of the more viable responses is deliberately ineffective, sporadic fire from rimfire weapons, small caliber pistols or even shotguns loaded with light bird shot in the hope of provoking an exposed attack (Type 1) by the main body.

Some readers will undoubtedly feel that this recital is an unnecessarily gruesome catalog of rather far-fetched eventualities; others may regard it as a somewhat simplistic rendering of the realities which some of us may be forced to encounter in the months ahead. I agree with the latter group of critics while I pray that the former are correct, but I have included this material for those who have never given the matter any serious thought.

Smith & Wesson Colt Ruger Charter Arms
Winchester Remington Browning Savage Weatherl
Sako FN Mossberg Steyr Husqvarna
Ithaca Boss Purdy Westley Richards Perazzi
Speer Sierra Hornady Hodgdon Hercules CCI Fede
RCBS Pacific C&H Forster Lee Saeco Redding
Leupold Redfield Lyman Williams Weaver
Armalite High Standard TDE Thompson-Center Ar
Smith & Wesson Colt Ruger Charter Arms
Winchester Remington Browning Savage Weather
Sako FN Mossberg Steyr Husqvarna
Ithaca Boss Purdy Westley Richards Perazzi
Speer Sierra Hornady Hodgdon Hercules CCI Fede
RCBS Pacific C&H Forster Lee Saeco Redding
Armalite High Standard TDE Thompson-Center Ar
Smith & Wesson Colt Ruger Charter Arms
Winchester Remington Browning Savage Weather
Sako FN Mossberg Steyr Husqvarna
Ithaca Boss Purdy Westley Richards Perazzi
Speer Sierra Hornady Hodgdon Hercules CCI Fede
RCBS Pacific C&H Forster Lee Saeco Redding
Armalite High Standard TDE Thompson-Center Ar

11 CHOOSING YOUR OWN SURVIVAL BATTERY

Most survival literature is concerned with short term emergencies and, consequently, the advice which is given is based on very different assumptions from those with which we are dealing here. For this reason, if you have done much reading on the subject, your head is probably filled with thoughts of minimum equipment, lightweight compact ammunition and a great deal of improvising to see you through the crisis. These are valid considerations if you are lost in the woods for a week or a month, but they are unrealistic guidelines for long term survival. If, for example, in normal times, you become lost while backpacking, you can expect to be rescued within no more than a few days. If you do not panic, if you can avoid hypothermia, if you can find a source of potable water and if you have even a rudimentary knowledge of foraging, you will probably suffer nothing more serious than a few anxious moments, a cold or a few cuts and bruises. Self-defense is probably not a factor unless you encounter a rabid animal or, possibly, an ill humored bear. Under such circumstances a good knife, some matches and a .22 pistol or a .22/20 ga. combination gun, for moral support, should provide admirably for your needs.

But if a social breakdown comes, you may be faced with living under primitive conditions for a year, a decade or even the rest of your life and your basic life support problems will almost certainly be complicated by encounters with desperate, dangerous mobs of people who have made no crisis preparations of their own and who are eager to avail themselves of yours by force. Even if you manage to escape the panic-driven violence of your fellow man, a steady diet of rabbit, dandelion greens and wild hickory nuts is not a pleasant prospect for most of us. I urge you, therefore, to rid yourself of the stereotyped survival thinking which you may have absorbed and approach the selection of your survival battery without romantic illusions — as if it were a stark, pressing matter of life or death. It may be just that.

I want to emphasize that there is no moral virtue in being Spartan when you are selecting equipment on which you may have to rely for food and protection over an extended period of time. If you have a fixed retreat and if you can possibly afford the cost, it is simply unintelligent not to provide yourself with the very best available — and in some depth. The fact that some people might be able to muddle through with nothing but a .22, a .30/'06 rifle and a 12 gauge shotgun does not mean that such arms are enough, any more than driving cross country on a set of bald tires can be regarded as a sound practice even though it may have been done before. No other purchase which you might make in preparation for your survival, with the possible exception of your retreat itself, will have as much to do with whether you stay alive as your survival battery. Unless you are willing to settle for minimum survival odds, do not skimp on your selection of guns.

Let us assume that no one is going to give a prize when the crisis is over for the person who made it through with the fewest and least suitable weapons — or at least that you do not plan to compete for that award. If you can escape the widespread notion that least is best, then what might be called tactical considerations will probably be a major influence on your choice of a battery. If you intend to have a fixed retreat with stored food and tools for building a comfortable life — and if you are committed to defending it, you should plan to include a rather complete array of weapons and a substantial supply of ammunition since weight and space requirements will pose no particular problems. If you do not, all the rest of your careful preparations may be futile.

As a minimum, you should acquire: one battle rifle per person and one spare for each two, one defense pistol each and one spare for each pair, several hunting rifles — the types and calibers determined by the terrain and game in your area — but at least one should be capable of firing the same ammunition as your battle rifles, a combination varmint-sniping rifle, one defense shotgun for each two people, one working handgun each, a hunting shotgun — if your defense model won't serve both purposes — a few rimfires, an air rifle, probably a hideout gun or two and whatever special purpose weapons your situation appears to require. Prudence would seem to dictate secreting a few extra items such as combination guns, Charter Arms AR-7's and the like in hidden caches on various parts of your property together with a small supply of ammunition for emergencies. Even at your retreat it is a good idea to keep a portable kit conveniently at hand containing short term emergency supplies, food and a spare gun and ammunition, just in case you ever need to leave in a hurry. I maintain such a kit in my car at all times now. This list comprises my idea of a no-frills battery for a modest fixed retreat. More would be highly desirable; less, simply inadequate.

If you decide against having a prepared, fixed retreat

home, then you are going to encounter a number of serious additional problems, not the least of which will be paring down your firearms and ammunition stores to minimum bulk and weight. If you choose a boat of reasonable size for your headquarters, however, only a few changes will have to be made to accommodate the basic battery to a sea going environment. You probably will not need a hunting shotgun at all but a defense smoothbore might be critical for repelling boarders and it should be the best you can get. I would suggest at least one for every member of the crew. The working handgun can also probably be eliminated without prejudice and you might even want to consider using a revolver for defense. Autos will fling their empties overboard or else litter the deck with them, causing a serious hazard to quick motion on an already slippery moving surface. Also, shooting encounters at pistol ranges when you are confined to the small space of a boat at sea are likely to be over before the sustained fire superiority of the auto would matter. The varmint rifle should be replaced with a heavier caliber, flat shooting bolt action such as a .270 which could also serve as your hunting rifle ashore. I would suggest that you include at least one very heavy caliber, long range rifle capable of penetrating the hull and disabling the engine of an approaching vessel. Something on the order of a .338 or a .375 H&H Magnum should be ideal. If you think the idea of having to fend off attacking boats during a crisis is preposterous, I suggest that you look into the facts on current incidents of piracy. It is already one of the most serious dangers which blue water pleasure crafts encounter today and it is increasing at an alarming rate. You may want to consider a harpoon gun such as the single-shot model sold by Abercrombie and Fitch, a mechanical spear gun or two if you have diving capabilities, and a flare pistol with both signal and illuminating parachute

416

flares. The remaining items in the fixed retreat battery should serve as well at sea as ashore except that you should have rustproof finishes applied to all exposed steel surfaces that are not stainless. You might even want to compromise somewhat on your handgun choices in order to get all stainless steel models whenever possible. Rimfires and air guns will probably not play a prominent role in your plans except when you go ashore, so they should be in waterproof containers while you are steaming.

If I were going to use a mobile home or a van for retreating, I would not allow space considerations to restrict my firearms options; in fact, the uncertainties involved in a land mobile retreat approach would probably cause me to add several items to the basic fixed retreat battery. For one thing, I would certainly want a .375 Magnum class rifle and probably a pistol caliber carbine and a scope mounted .22 pistol as well. Custom-built racks or cabinets along the walls of the living space should afford convenient storage for an ample arsenal. Because of the confined area, I would want the barrels of all my defense guns as short as possible and I might even consider shortening the stocks on a rifle and a shotgun to make them easier to use from the driver's compartment. Replacing as much of the glass as possible with bullet resistant acrylic might also prove useful.

The alternative of retreating on foot, hiding, taking what comes by way of shelter, carrying everything you own on your back and foraging for food has tremendous emotional appeal and it is great fun for a week or so at a time, but it is hardly a realistic approach to the problem for most people. It requires excellent health and agility as well as a high order of skill and it is so strenuous and nerve wracking that I find it hard to imagine many people being able to do it for an extended period. Obviously, anyone in this category will have to settle for a greatly curtailed and, frankly, inadequate list of weapons. For hunting I would want the best light bolt action rifle I could get in the .30/'06 class. I would probably choose a .308 because of its compact, lightweight ammunition and, ideally I would have it custom-built by King's Gun Works on a Sako short action to weigh no more than 7 lbs. with sling, swivels and a 2 x 7 Leupold scope in Jaeger quick detachable mounts. The Sport Specialties cartridge converters could be used for small game loads. Because of the rifle's limited firepower, I would also carry a combat modified .45 autopistol and a Sparks 6 Pack of spare magazines. Belt and suspender types might also find a small hideout worth its weight, such as a wallet gun or, possibly a PPK Walther .22, which could also be used for small game. Shotguns, battle rifles and all the rest would be out of the question because of their weight and bulk, regardless of how much they might be needed.

One's cast of mind and choice of a retreat mode are not the only factors to be considered in selecting a survival battery; there is also the question of money. Are you willing to spend enough to get what you really need or do you plan simply to buy a gun or two and put the rest of your money into precious metals, play the commodities market until the bell rings, or buy a color TV set to distract you from the realities that may lie ahead? If you are serious about making survival plans, you will find a way to buy what you should have, even if it means borrowing or making sacrifices now. If you are not yet convinced of the need for all-out preparations, you might start accumulating individual guns and ammunition as you are moved to do so and hope that the balance of what you need will still be available at prices you can afford to pay when conditions get bad enough that almost everyone can see the specter of an impending calamity. I might point out that even if we somehow manage to avoid disaster, buying guns is not necessarily throwing money down a rathole. High quality firearms have proved to be a very sound investment in the past. I have never owned a gun that couldn't be sold for more than I paid for it a few years later, despite the fact that I used it — sometimes extensively — in the interim. If trouble does come, of course, the value of sound guns and ammunition could hardly be calculated, either for use or barter.

In spite of these comments, I am sure that some of you will want to move slowly in a manner which you believe to be cautious — however foolish it may appear to someone else. You will want to know priorities and, without a crystal ball, I can only offer an educated guess. Personally, I would buy the hard to get items first and those that may require extensive modifications, which, if they are to be skillfully done, may require a considerable amount of time. Assault rifles and handguns might come first because they are the most likely to be banned first by our far-sighted bureaucrats and legislators. Short shotguns should come next, for the same reason. Whatever you do, buy substantial supplies of ammunition for each gun as you acquire it. Inadequate as it may be for all-purpose use, I would rather have one assault rifle and several thousand rounds of ammunition when the bell rings than a complete battery and no cartridges.

If you must do your buying with one eye on your bank balance, make sure that your economizing will not impair the efficiency of your battery. For example, there are some really good .22 pistols around for very little money, such as the Ruger autos, but there are no good cheap centerfire revolvers or big bore autopistols. Single-shot shotguns are a bargain but inexpensive doubles are not. If you decide to shop for a low priced hunting rifle, don't try to get all of the features of a more expensive model. Be realistic and buy the simplest, most basic design available at your price.

If a cheap gun offers abundant features, they may be there only at the cost of overall quality. Discontinued models from quality makers are often good buys. Sometimes they are being phased out because they are too expensive to manufacture any longer, but make certain that the gun which interests you is not going out of production because of a basic design flaw and be sure to buy the spare parts you will need for your repair kit when you buy the gun.

It might be useful at this point to review some of the actual batteries which I have helped clients to select. They are not, in every instance, exactly as I would have them but they represent an amalgam of my recommendations and the client's personal preferences — which is as it should be. The person who is going to use a weapon — and, perhaps, stake his life on it — should have the last word in its selection.

Battery #1

BACKGROUND: Designed for a couple in their late 30's, both of whom are in excellent physical condition and both of whom have had extensive experience hunting and camping. They will be members of a medium sized group retreat (30-50 people) in a good hunting area with a variety of game. I was asked to recommend a no budget limit battery with every item the best available, but no frills. Spares and overlapping of function would be permitted where I thought prudent.

Defense

Handguns:	3 Colt. 45 autopistols, Mk IV Government Model and 2 Lightweight Commanders, all with custom combat modifications by King's Gun Works.
	18 spare magazines in Sparks 6 Packs
	1 Charter Arms .44 Bulldog

	1 Airweight S&W Chiefs Special
	1 wallet gun .22 Magnum
Rifles:	1 BM-59
	1 Armalite AR-180
	1 Ruger Mini-14
Shotguns:	2 High Standard Model 10B 12 ga. riot guns
	1 Remington 870 riot pump 12 ga. with magazine extension

Working

Handguns:	1 S&W Model 29 .44 Magnum 8 3/8"
	1 S&W Model 29 .44 Magnum 4"
	1 S&W Model 25 .45 ACP
	1 S&W Model 19 .357 6"
	1 Colt Python .357 6"
Rifles:	1 .30/'06 custom bolt action rifle on pre '64 Model '70 action, 2 x 7 scope
	1 .308 Sako bolt action sporter 1.5 x 4.5 scope
	1 .270 Husqvarna bolt action rifle, 3 x 9 scope
	1 .308 Savage 99, 3x scope
	1 .243 Savage 99, 4x scope
	1 .223 Sako bolt action rifle, 3 x 9 AO scope
	1 .30-30 Marlin 336 Carbine cut to 16 1/4"
Shotguns:	1 Perazzi 12 ga. over-and-under Light Game Model with two sets of barrels
	1 Browning 2000 12. ga. auto
	1 Browning 2000 20 ga. auto
	1 Ithaca 200E 20 ga. double
	1 25" barrel only, for Remington 870 defense shotgun with Poly Choke.

Rimfires

Handguns:	1 S&W Kit Gun 4"

1 S&W Model 41 .22 auto
1 Walther PPK .22 auto
1 S&W Kit Gun Magnum 3 1/2"
1 scoped Ruger standard autopistol to be stored regularly in one of two emergency kits.

Rifles:
1 Weatherby Mark XXII, tubular magazine and scope
1 Anschutz Model 54 and scope
1 Anschutz Model 54 Magnum and scope
1 Winchester 9422
1 Winchester 9422M Magnum
2 Charter Arms AR-7's (one to be maintained in an emergency kit and the other in a hidden cache)

Special Purpose Weapons

1 Savage 24C (to be stored in an emergency kit)
1 Marlin .44 Magnum lever action rifle
2 Feinwerkbau F-12 air rifles, one with 4x scope and the other with a Williams receiver sight
1 50 lb. pull Bear Magnum Hunting Bow and a supply of aluminum shaft arrows
1 custom crossbow with bolts
2 Argentine bolas
Assorted slingshots

Several single-shot shotguns and inexpensive .22's were also purchased to be placed in hidden caches for possible use in barter. Appropriate ammunition, reloading tools and components, holsters, accessories and Survival Gun Vaults were also included.

COMMENTS: For people who have the ability to use it, this is very nearly a dream battery. A more stringent budget, a different locale, a wife who would be a less active user of the battery or any number of variables could require changes. Some may feel that it is too elaborate and for some it may be; however, it suits the circumstances of the people for whom it was designed.

Battery #2

BACKGROUND: Designed for a couple in their 20's, who had been saving to buy a second car but decided they needed crisis insurance more. Both are in good health, the husband is of average build and the wife is tiny — under 5' tall and weighs less than 100 lbs. They have a modest fixed retreat in an area with no game larger than deer and very little shooting, hunting or outdoor experience. Budget limitation: the price of a compact car.

Defense

Handguns:	2 .45 autopistols, Colt Mk IV Government Models with custom combat modifications by King's
	12 spare magazines in Sparks 6 Packs and an extensive spare parts kit
Rifles:	1 Armalite AR 180 .223
	1 Ruger Mini 14 .223
Shotguns:	1 Remington 870 with riot barrel

Working

Handguns:	1 Ruger .45 Convertible, 4 5/8″ barrel with modifications
	1 Ruger .357 Convertible, 6 1/2″ barrel
Rifles:	1 Winchester Model 70 .308
	1 H&R Ultra Wildcat bolt action .223
Shotguns:	1 barrel only for the defense shotgun, with Poly Choke

Rimfires

Handguns: 1 Ruger Target Model, barrel cut to 5"
Rifles: 2 Marlin 39M lever actions

Special Purpose Weapons

1 Feinwerkbau F-12 air rifle with 4x scope
1 Charter Arms AR-7 for hidden cache
1 Savage 24C for emergency kit
COMMENTS: I would have liked to include a hideout or pocket pistol of some sort, but with ammunition and reloading supplies, we were already $200 over budget. If time and finances permit, they intend to add several additional items including another .45 — probably a Lightweight Commander — another shotgun, another hunting rifle and perhaps a good bow. Both husband and wife already feel that their money was well spent because of an incident which occurred at their home less than two months after they had bought their guns and started a course in defense shooting. An attempted intrusion by two armed felons — one on parole for murder and the other free on bail from a similar charge — was terminated quite efficiently by these well-armed young householders.

Battery #3

BACKGROUND: Designed for a family of four with some definite ideas of their own. The husband is a machinist in his late 40's, a military rifle target shooter and a fair hand at tinkering with guns. His wife — about the same age — and their two sons, 14 and 16, also enjoy hunting, camping and fishing on a regular basis. They will have a fixed retreat, which they are building themselves, in a good game area which they know well from family vacations. The boys share a pair of Anschutz 164 bolt actions in .22

LR and .22 Magnum and a scoped .243 which their father built from a Springfield barreled action and a Bishop semi-finished stock. We decided to add a pair of .223 Ruger Mini 14's for the boys' use and a revolver for each of them to be chosen from a list I supplied. The younger selected a S&W Model 19 with a 6" barrel and his older brother a 6" Python.

The husband has a pair of accurate, well maintained Garands with which he competes in matches. He knows them thoroughly, shoots them well, has enough spare parts to keep them working indefinitely — and simply prefers them to any other battle rifle. His several thousand rounds of .30/'06 ammunition are all stored in Garand *en bloc* clips. I didn't even try to talk him into a more modern assault rifle. He and his wife share a pair of sporters in .30/'06 and .270 — both built on Springfield '03 actions with a few modifications for added reliability and convenience such as one-piece firing pins and hinged floorplates. After much discussion, we decided to add a Remington 660 carbine in .308 caliber and a good used pre-'64 Winchester .30-30 which the husband will restock and cut down to his own preferences. We decided to keep the G.I. .45 which they own as a spare and add two new Mark IV Government Models with custom combat modifications by King's. The husband's favorite outdoors holster gun — an ancient .45 Colt SA — was retired in favor of a new Ruger Convertible in the same caliber with a spare .45 ACP cylinder, and the wife's venerable K-38 was replaced by a more versatile .357 which almost matches her former gun in feel and appearance — a 6" S&W Model 19. The family already owned a nice pair of Winchester Model 12's in 12 and 20 gauge for hunting and we added an 8 shot Ithaca 37 riot gun in 12 ga., which was purchased on sale at a very attractive price. A Charter Arms AR-7 and a

Savage 24C were added for the two family emergency kits. When the budget allows, an air rifle and a .22 pistol will be purchased. Both boys are learning to fabricate bows and arrows in a Scouting program. Everyone in the family is an experienced reloader.

COMMENTS: Tight budget restrictions prevented anything more than adding a few items to the family's recreational and sporting guns but their defensive capability and flexibility was, nevertheless, considerably upgraded. Although this battery is not at all what I might choose for myself, I consider the family that owns it to be fairly well equipped for most emergencies.

Battery #4

BACKGROUND: This is a very unusual and specialized battery. The young man for whom it was designed has had extensive experience as a professional trapper, guide and woodsman. He is a member of a group retreat, and it will be his job to provide substantially all of the animal food for the group. A great variety of game may be found in the heavily wooded area where his retreat is located, but none of it is abundant. For this reason, my client expects that it will be necessary for him to undertake frequent three to seven day foraging expeditions alone to supply enough food to the other residents on a regular basis. He wanted help in selecting the most versatile, lightest weight equipment possible for taking a mixed bag of large and small game. He already owned several bolt action rifles in calibers ranging from .222 to .30/'06, as well as a pair of 12 gauge over-and-unders, .357 and .44 Magnum revolvers. He is totally opposed to the concept of self-defense and is unwilling even to consider including fighting weapons of any kind.

For his long gun, we chose the new 2400 Savage combination gun chambered for .308 and 12 ga. The shotgun barrel was opened to improved cylinder boring by a gunsmith. This selection appeared to offer the best compromise for versatility, weight, price and quality, although other combination guns might have been selected. We decided that a lightweight, very accurate rimfire would be useful for small game because of the weight problem involved in carrying enough 12 gauge and .308 ammunition. I suggested the S&W .22/32 target, which is nothing more than a light, trim Kit Gun frame with a 6″ barrel installed. It will group almost as well as a rifle out to 50 yards, if a braced shooting position can be assumed, and the 6″ barrel makes precise aiming easier.

For those occasions when a scoped rifle is more suitable than the Savage 2400, my client will leave the .22 revolver behind and carry a Thompson Contender with the modified .410 shotgun barrel, in a shoulder holster.

On shorter trips when only deer is to be taken — and packed out to the retreat — he will take only a Marlin .44 Magnum lever action and a revolver in the same caliber.
COMMENTS: Given the skill of this young man, I have no doubt that he now has the best possible equipment to suit his rather specialized hunting needs. I would not be comfortable with relying on others to provide for my security, but that is a matter of individual conscience.

Battery #5

BACKGROUND: The circumstances here are almost exactly opposite to those in the previous discussion. The battery was designed for an ex-Special Forces officer (Green Beret) who has been hired by a group retreat of 50 people to act as security officer. He will not be expected to provide his own food but it will be his job to be in the forefront of any fighting that needs to be done. He wanted the minimum number of calibers to simplify supply problems.

Handguns:	2 .45 Mk IV Government Model autopistols and 1 .45 Lightweight Commander, all with custom combat modifications by King's Gun Works
(optional)	1 Model 25 S&W .45 ACP revolver, action honed, barrel cut to 5", front sight ramped and hard chrome finish applied
Rifles:	2 SIG AMT .308 assault rifles (client's choice from list of three suggested)
	2 Armalite AR-180 .223 assault rifles — one with 3x scope mounted
	1 custom heavy barrel .308 target rifle on Sako action with Redfield 6 x 18 variable AO scope
	1 Browning BAR .308 semi-auto with Bushnell 3 x 9 variable Lite Sight scope
	1 Sako bolt action .223 with Leupold 3 x 9 AO variable
Shotguns:	2 High Standard Model 10B 12 ga. riot guns with flashlight attachments and custom magazine extension
	1 Remington 870 pump with riot barrel, slug sights and magazine extension

COMMENTS: I also suggested a hideout gun but the client rejected the recommendation because it would add another caliber to his supply list. He will carry a Loveless boot knife instead, which he knows how to use expertly. I hope the occasion which might prove one of us wrong never arises.

Battery #6

BACKGROUND: Designed for a young couple with very little to spend. They will be retreating with the husband's parents who have an extensive battery. They wanted only minimum personal defense weapons for protection now in the city, and possibly, to help them reach their retreat if they should wait too long to leave. Maximum budget $1000, "cannot afford" an assault rifle.

2 .45 Colt Mk IV Government Models with custom combat modifications and three spare magazines each

1 Remington 870 12 ga. pump with 20" riot barrel and magazine extension

1 Savage 99A .308 rifle with 4x Weaver scope in Q.D. mounts

COMMENT: Meets the given criteria, but I am not certain that the criteria are broad enough nor sufficiently realistic.

Battery #7

BACKGROUND: Designed for a couple in good health in their 30's who now reside and expect to retreat in an area which contains large dangerous game. The climate is extremely cold and they have experienced so much difficulty with revolvers at sub-zero temperatures, regardless of the lubrication used, that they refuse to consider them for any purpose. They want a minimum number of calibers and no hunting shotgun. In addition to heavier weapons, they need one light caliber, flat shooting rifle for game no larger than deer.

Defense

Handguns:	2 .45 Mark IV Government Model autos 1 .45 Lightweight Commander, all with custom combat modifications by King's Gun Works
Rifles:	2 SIG AMT .308 assault rifles
Shotgun:	2 Remington 870 12 ga. pump riot guns with magazine extensions

Working

Handguns: 1 .44 Auto Mag pistol
1 Colt Mark IV auto with .38/.45 wildcat conversion

Rifles: 1 pre-'64 Winchester Model 70, cal. .375 H&H Magnum with Weaver 3x scope in Jaeger Q.D. mounts
1 Sako bolt action .308 rifle with Leupold 2 x 7 scope
1 Sako bolt action .243 rifle with Leupold 3 x 9 scope

Rimfires

Handguns: 1 Ruger Target Model, bull barrel
1 Walther PP

Rifles: 2 Ruger 10/22 auto rifles, one with 4x scope
2 Charter Arms AR-7's for emergency kits

Special Purpose Weapons

2 Feinwerkbau F-12 accurized sporters, one with 4x scope and the other with Williams Aperture

COMMENT: I would consider the .375 a necessity for the game in this area. The SIG's were chosen for two reasons: the recoil is light enough so that the rather small wife would be able to handle the same caliber weapon as her husband and also because these guns have excellent folding winter triggers. The .243 was an obvious choice for the light rifle since cases can be formed from .308 brass. The Auto Mag has the same advantage. The .38/.45 conversion on the Colt Government Model provides a flat shooting working pistol, the cases for which can be made simply by necking down empty .45 ACP brass to accept .357 diameter bullets. This is certainly not the ideal all-purpose battery for everyone, but it suits the needs of the people for whom it was designed admirably.

In fact, none of the batteries listed above could be called "typical" because they were all designed to meet specific needs of different people in diverse situations. There is no "correct" combination of weapons in the abstract, nor are there any hard and fast rules which can be applied in selecting them. Choosing an optimal survival battery is not like ordering a meal from a Chinese menu; you cannot simply pick two items from column A, two from column B and one from column C with any reasonable expectation of having a prime *table d'hôte*.

If you are serious about making survival preparations, however, the choices must be made; and if you cannot seek the personal guidance of someone who is qualified to analyze your particular requirements, then, perhaps, a close study of widely varied examples can best serve to stimulate your own thinking. With this purpose in mind, I asked some friends and acquaintances — well known experts in survival, guns or both — to set down the guns and related equipment which they would select personally to see themselves and their families through an extended crisis. In letters to each of them I requested that they observe the following, uniform criteria:

> *The guns you list would not necessarily be recommendations to others, but would reflect your own personal choices for a survival battery, given the following set of circumstances:*
>
> - *no arbitrary limitation of the number of weapons and calibers (except common sense)*
> - *assume a permanent wilderness residence (i.e., portability and storage no particular problem)*
> - *assume no access to gunsmith services or ammunition resupply*
> - *assume a reasonable abundance of both large and small game*
> - *assume the possibility of having to defend your retreat against bands of rioters and looters escaping the collapse*

431

> *of the cities (sustained fire against superior numbers)*
> * *assume the presence of feral animals.*

Please bear in mind, as you read the following material, based on their responses, that their choices are intensely personal, reflecting not only their preferences and taste but their own considerable skills. A Springfield sniping rifle at the shoulder of Burt Miller or a .45 autopistol in the hands of Jeff Cooper are capable of performing tasks which others might need half a dozen weapons to duplicate or even attempt, and I am sure that no one but a Brad Angier could expect to make do with as modest an outfit as Brad's.

Brad Angier's Battery

BACKGROUND: Years ago Brad Angier and his wife, Vena, left their respective careers in journalism and ballet to make a different kind of life for themselves in the wilderness. In their tiny cabin on the Peace River, far north in Hudson Hope, B.C., they began to learn and practice the outdoor skills which became the basis for literally hundreds of magazine articles by Brad and more than 20 books, including *Survival with Style, Feasting Free on Wild Edibles, Living Off the Country,* and *How to Live in the Woods on Pennies a Day.*

Although Brad now spends a portion of his time in the mild climate of Cambria, California living comfortably with all of the amenities of a successful author, his concept of a retreat remains the isolated Far North where big game is still plentiful and the concerns of an agrarian retreater — such as pest control — are non-existent, and the probability of encountering well organized groups of looters from nearby cities is minimal.

His life style in the wilderness has been highly active and mobile; he has often cruised and foraged for extended periods with only the supplies which he could carry conveniently over difficult, often frozen, terrain. Based on his skills and personal experience, Brad responded to my letter, in part:

I follow the Stefansson-proved ounce of cartridge per ounce of meat theory which rules out shotguns, although if the retreater has plenty of room and primary carrying power, a good little .22 is great if only for practice.

But essentially I recommend a light, hard hitting, scope-sighted rifle such as the Winchester Model 70 which, when a heavy enough bullet is placed accurately in the chest cavity will get any North American game and with a shoulder-crippling shot will anchor it. If there is a party, each member should carry the same weapon so that, if for no other reason, one will always be operative and because there is nothing better. A .30/'06 is sufficient.

With this the retreater should bring a reloading outfit with plenty of supplies. I recommend Lyman-Sierra. For small game, I subscribe to the late Colonel Townsend Whelen's light loads practice.

In a subsequent telephone conversation, Brad observed that a short shotgun would be handy for defense and that he liked to keep a handgun around, but he commented that the latter were illegal in Canada to non-Canadian citizens and closely restricted. He also observed that he would prefer to be "so far North no one could find me" and even to remain on the move to avoid encounters with superior forces of armed looters.

COMMENT: Brad knows the North Country as few men do, and if anyone could avoid potential attackers there, I am sure he could. With his skills and knowledge of his chosen environment, such a Spartan battery as he has chosen might work — for him. If you decide to emulate his equipment choice, I hope that you also have his experience and expertise.

433

Colonel Burton T. Miller's Battery

BACKGROUND: Burt Miller is an expert both in survival and weaponry. He was born in Oklahoma and spent his early years working on ranches throughout the West. During his military career he served as a small arms training officer, later in Ordnance Maintenance and, finally, after transferring from the Army to the USAF, he worked on research and development related to survival gear, taught evasion and escape and designed the Air Force's M4 survival rifle.

He has had extensive hunting experience all over the world and he presently serves as a Vice-President of Armalite, Inc., the distinguished arms design and manufacturing firm in California. Burt is also a prolific writer for numerous outdoor magazines including *Petersen's Hunting* and *Guns and Ammo*, which carries his monthly column as well as frequent feature articles. His selections include items which would also be used by his vivacious wife, Alice, an experienced hunter in her own right, and they are based on a retreat area in the northwest United States which offers a reasonable abundance and variety of game animals.

Defense

Handguns:	2 .45 autos with 6 magazines each and 1000 rounds in sealed containers
	2 hideout .380 Walther PP's (100 rounds)
Rifles:	Armalite AR-180 5.56 with scope
	12 magazines: 6 20 round, 6 30 round, 1000 rounds military ammo
Special Purpose:	Mace (or similar)

Working

Rifles:	Springfield .30/'06 with 3 x 9 scope (1903 A4

sniper rifle, sporterized, 200 rounds)

Shotguns: 1 12 ga. Browning over-and-under
1 12 ga. Browning 2000 auto
1 20 ga. Browning 2000 auto
1000 rounds (2 cases) ammo each

Special Purpose Weapons

Bow and 40 arrows. Also a covert weapon if situation demands. Good for feral animals (wild dogs). Can make arrows for replacement.

Rimfires

Rifles: .22 LR Model 9422 Winchester
.22 LR Model 72 Ithaca

Handguns: .22 LR Supermatic (High Standard) auto, 4"
Target Model with holster

COMMENT: Burt makes the following observations, "Ammo loaded will last 20 years — and more. Time and space permitting, I would take loading press and components that I always have on hand. Loaded ammo would provide reloadable cases for 10 years or better."

"The basic premise is to select dependable arms and plan protective needs. The plan should include the evacuation situation where you would have the most suited *one* arm if you had to leave on foot and abandon your arms left in a cache."

Burt also observed that, in order to be as realistic as possible, his list was based on items on hand and remarked that "space available, I'd take many more." With these weapons, the Millers' skill and resourcefulness, I have no doubt that their retreat would be secure and comfortable. I regard this as a bare bones battery, however, and one which might prove inadequate for individuals who lack the broad experience and prodigious ability of the Millers.

Jeff Cooper's Battery

BACKGROUND: Jeff Cooper is the foremost authority in the world today on handguns and their practical use. A retired Lieutenant Colonel of the Marines, he is a veteran of both World War II and the Korean conflict. Jeff is also a legal consultant in court matters relating to small arms and a scholar, holding a Master's degree in History from the University of California. He is a Master Class combat shooter in the South West Pistol League, which he founded, and he has written an avalanche of magazine articles as well as five books on firearms, including: *Fighting Handguns*, *The Complete Book of Modern Handgunning* and *Cooper on Handguns*. He writes a monthly column for *Guns and Ammo* and contributes regularly to *Soldier of Fortune*. His choices below include items for the use of his wife Janelle ("the Memsahib"), one of the most charming and efficient retreat partners one could ask for.

Defense

Handguns:	2 .45 autos with .22 conversion 10 magazines
Rifles:	BM-59 (.308), or SIG 542 (.308), or M1A (.308) or M1 (.30/'06) In effect, any good .30 cal. *sturmgewehr*. 4 mags (20's) Ruger Mini-14 for the Memsahib, 3 20 round mags.
Shotguns:	Remington 1100 "Deer Gun," #4 buck and rifled slugs, 50-50

Special Purpose Weapons

Anything that will fire the 30 Russian Short (7.62 x 39)

Working

Handguns:	Walther PP .22 auto
Rifles:	Remington 660 .308 Leupold 2x forward

mount

Williams receiver aperture for backup

H&R (Sako) .223 Ultra Wildcat, for the Memsahib

Shotguns: Savage #24 3" 20 ga. and .22 LR

COMMENTS: Jeff wrote the following note at the bottom of his list: "All above rustproofed (Armaloy, Teflon, etc.) insofar as possible. Complete spare parts supply, plus shop manuals and/or exploded drawings. Tool kit.

"*Vital* that ammunition be G.I. (.308, .223, .30RS, etc.) or universal (.22 LR, 12 or 20 gauge). I'd get the Savage #24 in 12 ga. if I could."

The weapons suit the man: unpretentious, strong and effective. Whether there are enough of them depends on a number of circumstances, including the question of whether you have the prowess with arms that Jeff has.

Safeguarding Your Guns

Whether or not you agree with the premise of this book that it is prudent to provide yourself with a suitable array of guns against the possibility of an extended crisis period, surely you can see the wisdom of keeping one or two for home protection. The present danger from the mounting crime rate and threats of future massive violence from terrorists and others of their ilk are clearly more than any reasonable amount of law enforcement can handle. With a ratio of one policeman for every 20,000 citizens or so, only a fool would be content to rely solely on this thinly spread blue line for the protection of himself and his family. It is apparent that we must be able to protect ourselves as well as we can from whatever lies ahead in an uncertain future. For most of us, that means owning guns.

Yet despite the fact that an overwhelming majority of the citizens of this country apparently agree with this point of view and more Americans are arming themselves now than ever before, an increasingly vocal, well-financed minority would have us believe that there is something wrong with merely owning an efficient means of self-defense. These propagandists have been so successful in their schemes that we presently have more than 20,000 laws on the books which control our possession and use of firearms. More than 100 additional gun control bills are presently before Congress, and the law abiding gun owners of this country have become so intimidated by the unrelenting pressure from this howling lobby of control-minded bullies that their action, if any, has become purely defensive. They are thinking in terms of appeasement, hoping to prevent more stringent controls by compromising on less clearly threatening issues such as retroactive registration and the so-called "Saturday Night Special."

If we are to keep our guns legally, the last minute has come for reasonable men to assume the offensive. Not only must we refuse absolutely and uncompromisingly to accept any further gun control legislation, we must demand that all unreasonably burdensome existing laws, such as the ill-conceived and patently unworkable 1968 Gun Control Act, be repealed.

The facts are these. Banning guns does not prevent crime. The only effective means of reducing crime is taking the criminals off the streets — a course of action which many of our jurists seem reluctant to follow. According to U.S. Congressman Steve Symms, "There are perhaps 200 million privately owned firearms in the U.S. today, of which only one-sixth of one percent are used in the commission of crimes annually, including less than one percent of all handguns." Does it seem reasonable to attack crime by disarming the owners of 99 5/6% of all the guns in this country in order to reach the 1/6 of 1% who misuse their guns?

Accidents then. Perhaps we should allow the government to protect us from ourselves by disarming us to prevent accidents. Again, Representative Symms offers an interesting statistic. "Firearms and shooting sports are ranked 15th on the list of sports most likely to cause accidents. There are 20 times more accidental deaths with cars, eight times more through falls and three times more through drowning." My almanac even lists choking on food as a more frequent cause of death than firearms accidents.

The fact is that none of the specious arguments put forth by these proponents of a disarmed American public stands up against this basic truth: every human being is born with the undeniable right to protect his own life — presumably by the most efficient means available, and with our present technology, that means firearms.

I suggest to you that we must urgently make our wishes known to our representatives in government and if they remain unresponsive, then we must elect better men — if there is still time. Talking about our dwindling freedoms among ourselves and cursing our fate will not change the course of this nation from its present headlong rush toward collectivism, one world government and the loss of individual self-determination. When we have allowed the government to assume enough power to protect us from ourselves, we will not be able to protect ourselves from our government. Our elected representatives are telling us clearly, with their unremitting attempts to impose further gun control, that they do not trust us; perhaps we should not trust them.

Unarmed men are subject to violence and all manner of coercion by others. Armed men are not — unless they freely choose to be. Free men bear arms; slaves do not.

Access to Information and Sources

BOOKS

The Coming Crisis
Background

The following list of books, taken together, offers some compelling reasons why any reasonable person who is concerned about the safety of himself and his family should consider making serious survival preparations.

BROWNE, HARRY. *You Can Profit from a Monetary Crisis.* New York: Macmillan Publishing Co., Inc., 1974.

——————————. *How You Can Profit From The Coming Devaluation.* New York: Avon Books, 1971.

CANBY, THOMAS Y. AND STEVE RAYMER. "Can the World Feed its People?" *National Geographic,* Vol. 148, No. I (July, 1975), 2-31.

EHRLICH, PAUL R. AND ANNE H. *The End of Affluence.* New York: Ballantine Books, 1974.

TOFFLER, ALVIN. *The Eco-Spasm Report.* New York: Bantam Books, 1975.

VACCA, ROBERTO. *The Coming Dark Age.* Translated by Dr. J.S. Whale. Garden City: Doubleday & Company, Inc. 1973.

Mental Preparation

The single most important factor in being able to cope with any crisis is mental preparation, and heightened awareness is the key to controlling panic. The Ornstein and Tart books provide a good introduction to meditation and other consciousness expanding techniques. There is a tremendous amount of useful literature in this field, most of which is quite recent and the bibliographies in these volumes will lead you to much of it.

ORNSTEIN, ROBERT E. *The Psychology of Consciousness,* New York: The Viking Press, 1972.

TART, CHARLES T. (ed.). *Altered States of Consciousness.* New York: Anchor Books/Doubleday & Company, Inc., 1972.

One of the best ways to gain some grasp of what life may be like during and after the crisis is to read some of the better speculative fiction on the subject. None of the following "post-holocaust" novels is based on an economic collapse, but the aftermath will probably be much the same whatever the cause of the upheaval. The literary quality of these offerings is not uniformly excellent, but each of them provides some valuable insights into the kind of world which we may be facing very soon.

BUDRYS, ALGIS. *Some Will Not Die.* London: Mayflower-Dell Paperbacks, 1964.

CHRISTOPHER, JOHN. *No Blade of Grass.* New York: Avon Books, 1975.

MERLE, ROBERT. *Malevil.* New York: Warner Books, Inc., 1975.

MILLS, JAMES. *One Just Man.* New York: Simon and Schuster, 1974.

FRANK, PAT. *Alas, Babylon.* New York: Bantam Books, Inc., 1974.

RAND, AYN. *Atlas Shrugged.* New York: Signet Books (New American Library of World Literature, Inc.), 1959.

Overcoming fear in a life threatening situation can be a function of knowing what to do. Fright is largely a matter of uncertainty and indecision. Jeff Cooper's little book, *Principles of Personal Defense* offers a "game plan" for behavior in such circumstances.

442

COOPER, JEFF. *Principles of Personal Defense*. Boulder: Paladin Press, 1972.

These two items will give you some idea of the opposition's thinking. I sincerely hope that the terrorists' knowledge of weaponry is no more sophisticated than that represented in *The Anarchist Cookbook*.

POWELL, WILLIAM. *The Anarchist Cookbook*. Secaucus; Lyle Stuart, Inc., 1975.

Prairie Fire: The Political Statement of the Weather Underground. Communications Co., 1974.

Retreat Preparations

Nothing comprehensive has been done in this area yet, but there are a number of useful items from which you can piece together much of the information which you will need.

The *Goode's Atlas* and Don Stephens' Retreaters Maps are helpful in choosing likely retreat areas. Don's little booklets, *Personal Protection, Here and Now* and *Retreating on a Shoestring* contain some useful checklists and general information. *The Retreater's Bibliography* is quite an extensive book list and the only thing of its kind, so far as I know. Volume II contains the most recent listings and I would buy it first.

ESPENSHADE, EDWARD B. Jr. (ed.). *Goode's World Atlas*, Fourteenth Edition. Chicago: Rand McNally & Company, 1974.

LAPPÉ, FRANCES MOORE. *Diet for a Small Planet*, New York: Ballantine Books, Inc., 1971.

STEPHENS, DON AND BARBIE. *The Retreater's Bibliography I and II*. $10 and $12 respectively, postpaid.

STEPHENS, DON. *Personal Protection, Here and Now*. $3 postpaid.

_____. *Retreating on a Shoestring*. $1.50 postpaid.

Retreater's Maps #1 – Estimated Minimum Safe Distance from Major U.S. Metropolitan Areas c 1975

#2– Hazardous Population Density Areas c 1975

#3 – Nuclear Power Plants and Fallout Patterns c 1975

#4 – Short Growing Seasons and Low Rainfall Areas c 1975

One dollar each, any three for two dollars, postpaid. To obtain copies of Don's publications, write to Survival, Inc., 24206 Crenshaw Blvd., Torrance, CA. 90505.

Guns and Shooting
General Reference

AMBER, JOHN T. (ed). *Gun Digest 30th Anniversary 1976 Deluxe Edition.* Northfield: DBI Books, Inc., 1975.

A comprehensive listing with illustrations of virtually all guns and ammunition available in the U.S., together with general interest firearms articles. Annual.

HATCHER, JULIAN S. *Hatcher's Notebook.* Harrisburg: The Stackpole Company, 1962.

Hatcher is one of the great scholars in the firearms field and his *Notebook* contains formulas for almost everything you might want to calculate from recoil to bullet flight.

MURTZ, HAROLD A. AND THE EDITORS OF GUN DIGEST (ed.). *Guns Illustrated 1975.* Northfield: Digest Books, Inc. 1975.

Similar to *Gun Digest* and *Shooter's Bible* in content. Annual.

NONTE, GEORGE C., JR. *Firearms Encyclopedia.* New York: Outdoor Life/Harper & Row, 1973.

A very good general reference work with superb illustrations. If you want to know what "trajectory" means or what a hinged floor plate looks like, this is the place to look.

NRA Firearms & Ammuniton Fact Book. Washington D.C.: The National Rifle Association of America, 1970.

A must.

444

O'CONNOR, JACK WITH ROY DUNLAP, ALEX KERR AND JEFF COOPER. *Complete Book of Shooting.* New York: Outdoor Life/Harper & Row, 1973.

One of the very best general introductory works available. Highly recommended.

RICE, F. PHILIP. *Outdoor Life Gun Data Book.* New York: Outdoor Life/Harper & Row, 1975.

An excellent, conveniently sized general reference book covering almost everything from technical data to aiming areas on various types of game.

Shooter's Bible No. 67. South Hackensack: Stoeger Publishing Company, 1975.

Similar to *Gun Digest*, but with less text, more and frequently larger illustrations. You should examine both of these books before you draw up your "want list." Annual.

SMITH, W. H. B. AND JOSEPH E. *Small Arms of the World.* Harrisburg: The Stackpole Company, 1973.

The standard reference.

Handguns

COOPER, JEFF. *Cooper on Handguns.* Los Angeles; Petersen Publishing Company, 1975.

If, as Cooper says, *Hatcher's Textbook of Pistols and Revolvers* is the Old Testament of handgunning, then this is certainly the Gospel. Comprehensive and up-to-date. I find very little to disagree with here and much to admire. A must.

COOPER, JEFF AND THE EDITORS OF *Guns and Ammo* Magazine. *The Complete Book of Modern Handgunning.* Englewood Cliffs: Prentice-Hall, Inc., 1961.

Very comprehensive. Not a substitute for *Cooper on Handguns*, but a useful companion.

GRENNELL, DEAN AND MASON WILLIAMS. *Law Enforcement Handgun Digest.* Northfield: Digest Books, Inc., 1972.

Very uneven, but contains some useful information which you will not find elsewhere.

HATCHER, MAJOR JULIAN S. *Pistols and Revolvers.*
Marshallton: Small-Arms Technical Publishing
Company, 1927.

A forerunner to the more useful *Textbook of Pistols and Revolvers.* Contains some information not in the later work.

HATCHER, MAJOR JULIAN S. *Textbook of Pistols and Revolvers.*
Plantersville: Small-Arms Technical Publishing
Company, 1935.

If you have a serious interest in handguns, this is where you begin. A seminal work of great importance.

JORDAN, WILLIAM H. "BILL." *No Second Place Winner.*
Shreveport: W.H. Jordan, 1965.

KEITH, ELMER. *Sixguns.* New York: Bonanza Books, 1961.
Originally published in the '50's and now badly in need of revision, but still useful in some areas and highly entertaining. Keith's well known bias in favor of the revolver is evident throughout.

MCGIVERN, ED. *Fast and Fancy Revolver Shooting.* Chicago:
Wilcox & Follett Co., 1957.

Somewhat dated and devoted primarily to the exhibition shooting of revolvers but still useful. McGivern was a magician with a wheel gun.

SMITH, W. H. B. *Book of Pistols and Revolvers,* ed. Joseph E.
Smith. Harrisburg: Stackpole Books, 1968.

A standard reference which gives detailed specifications for most handguns.

TM 9-1005-211-12 Department of the Army Technical Manual,
Caliber .45.

A must for users of the .45 auto. Complete assembly, disassembly, maintenance and operation details.

Rifles

DE HAAS, FRANK. *Bolt Action Rifles,* ed. John T. Amber.
Northfield: Digest Books, Incorporated, 1971.

A very detailed examination of the technical aspects of rifle construction. Detailed critiques of various actions and commercial sporting rifles.

Guns Annual Book of Rifles. Skokie: Publisher's
Development Corp., 1975. Annual.

KEITH, ELMER. *Big Game Rifles.* South Carolina: Thomas G.
Samworth Small-Arms Technical Publishing
Company, 1936.
Highly useful.

O'CONNOR, JACK. *Complete Book of Rifles and Shotguns.* New
York: Outdoor Life/Harper & Row, 1961.
Outstanding.

O'CONNOR, JACK. *The Hunting Rifle.* New York:
Winchester Press, 1975.
Brilliant and indispensable.

Shotguns

KEITH, ELMER. *Shotguns.* Harrisburg: The Stackpole
Company, 1961.
One of Keith's best.

O'CONNOR, JACK. *Complete Book of Rifles and Shotguns. New
York: Outdoor Life/Harper & Row, 1961.*
Required reading.

SELL, FRANCIS E. *The American Shotgunner.* Harrisburg: The
Stackpole Company, 1962.
A very thorough and detailed study of smoothbores.
Excellent.

Ammunition and Reloading

You should have all of the data books on specific load recommendations by the component manufacturers if at all possible.

Hornady Handbook of Cartridge Reloading, Rifle-Pistol, Vol. II.
Grand Island, Nebraska: Hornady Manufacturing
Company, Inc. 1973.
Data book. Available at sporting goods stores.

Lyman Cast Bullet Handbook. Order from Lyman Products
for Shooters ($4.95), Route 147, Middlefield, Conn.
06455 or buy at local sporting goods store.
Data book.

Lyman Reloading Handbook, 45th Ed. Order from address above ($4.95).

Data book.

Sierra Bullets Reloading Manual. Santa Fe Springs: Sierra Bullets, 1971.

Data book. Available at sporting goods stores.

Speer Reloading Manual Number Nine. Lewiston: Speer, Inc., 1974.

Data book. Available at sporting goods stores.

ACKLEY, P.O. *Handbook for Shooters & Reloaders*, Vol. I & II. Salt Lake City: Publishers Press, 1965.

A classic, contains information to be found nowhere else.

AMBER, JOHN T. (ed.). *Handloader's Digest, Sixth Edition.* Northfield: Digest Books, Inc., 1972.

Very good survey of reloading equipment available.

BARNES, FRANK C. *Cartridges of the World.* John T. Amber (ed.). Northfield: Digest Books, Inc., 1972.

A standard reference on metallic cartridges.

NARAMORE, EARL. *Principles and Practice of Loading Ammunition.* Georgetown: Small Arms Technical Publishing Company, A Samworth Book, 1954.

Comprehensive but somewhat dated. Worth having.

The NRA Handloader's Guide, Washington, D.C.: The National Rifle Association of America, 1969.

A must.

SHARPE, PHILIP B. *Complete Guide to Handloading.* New York: Funk & Wagnalls Company, 1953.

A standard reference but, because of its date, does not contain information on some of the newest cartridges.

Gunsmithing, Maintenance and Repairs

ACKLEY, P. O. *Home Gun Care & Repair. Harrisburg: Stackpole Books, 1969.*

Very easy for the layman to understand and completely sound, but not as comprehensive as some. Required reading, nevertheless.

BISH, TOMMY L. *Home Gunsmithing Digest*, ed. Jack
Lewis. Northfield: Gun Digest Publishing
Company, 1970.
Well illustrated and useful.

BROWNELL, F. R. "BOB". *Gunsmith Kinks*, ed. Frank
Brownell. Montezuma, Iowa: F. Brownell & Son, 1969.
This is one of the most useful gunsmithing books ever
written. I would not be without it.

CHAPEL, CHARLES EDWARD. *The Complete Guide to
Gunsmithing*. New York: A.S. Barnes and Co., 1972.
An old standby.

DUNLAP, ROY. *Gun Owner's Book of Care, Repair and
Improvement*. New York: Outdoor Life/Harper &
Row, 1974.
One of the best illustrated and most useful.

Firearms Assembly I. Washington, D.C.: The National Rifle
Association of America, 1972.
A must.

Firearms Assembly II. Washington, D.C.: The National Rifle
Association of America, 1972.
A must.

MACFARLAND, HAROLD E. *Gunsmithing Simplified*. South
Brunswick and New York: A.S. Barnes and
Company, 1971.

MURTZ, HAROLD A. (ed.). *The Gun Digest Book of Exploded
Firearms Drawings*. Northfield: Digest Books, Inc., 1974.
Very useful for assembly and disassembly.

The NRA Gunsmithing Guide. Washington, D.C.: The
National Rifle Association of America, 1971.
A must.

Miscellaneous

Guns & Ammo Complete Guide to Blackpowder, Los Angeles:
Petersen Publishing Co., 1974.

LACHUK, JOHN AND THE EDITORS OF *Guns and Ammo.*
Wonderful World of the .22. Los Angeles: Petersen
Publishing Company, 1972.
A very useful volume on rimfires, even if it is occasionally
somewhat overenthusiastic about the effectiveness of these little
rounds.

MANNIX, DANIEL. *A Sporting Chance.* New York:
E.P. Dutton & Co., Inc. 1967.
One of the few readily available sources of information on
primitive weapons. Anecdotal.

McEVOY, HARRY. *Knife Throwing, A Practical Guide.*
Rutland: Charles E. Tuttle Co., 1973.
A standard beginners guide.

Some Useful Periodicals
Background

Personal Survival Letter ● *Box 598* ● *Rogue River, OR 97537*
Mother Earth News

Guns and Shooting

Guns
Guns & Ammo
Gun Week
Gun World
Shooting Times
Shotgun News
The American Rifleman

Sources
Air Guns

The ARH catalog is free and the Beeman's costs $1.50. You
should see both before you order.

Air Rifle Headquarters, Inc.
247 Court Street
Box 327
Grantsville, West Virginia 26147

Beeman's
P.O. Box 278
San Anselmo, CA 94960

Accessories
Holster Makers

Bianchi
100 Calle Cortez
Temecula, CA 92390

The George Lawrence Co.
306 S.W. 1st Avenue
Portland, Oregon 97204

S.D. Myres Saddle Co., Inc.
5030 Alameda
P.O. Box 9776
El Paso, Texas 79988

Safariland
1941 South Walker Avenue
Monrovia, CA 91016

Milt Sparks
Box 7
Idaho City, Idaho 83631

WHM Enterprises
Snick Products
6535 Wilshire Blvd.
Los Angeles, CA 90048

Custom Handgun Grips

Herrett's and Cloyce both issue well illustrated free catalogs. Hogue no longer sells direct, but you may order his superb designs through either of the sources listed below. Pachmayr offers both inexpensive grip adapters and a complete line of rubber grips for autos and revolvers.

Auto Grip Enterprises
P.O. Box 7078
Burbank, CA 91505

Cloyce's Gun Stocks
P.O. Box 1133
Twin Falls, Idaho 83301

Herrett's Stocks, Inc.
Box 741
Twin Falls, Idaho 83301

Guy Hogue Grips available from:
King's Gun Works
1837 West Glenoaks Blvd.
Glendale, CA 91201

or

Martin B. Retting, Inc.
11029 Washington Blvd.
Culver City, CA

Pachmayr Gun Works, Inc.
1220 S. Grand
Los Angeles, CA 90015

Gun Vaults

If you are going to have more than one gun which you will carry at all times, you should look into this item. There is nothing else even nearly as good. Excellent for safekeeping other valuables, too.

Survival Vaults
P.O. Box 462
Fillmore, CA 93015

Cartridge Converters and Sub-caliber Devices

"Shell Shrinkers"
S. S. Manufacturing Co.
P.O. Box 6143
Lubbock, Texas 79413

Sport Specialties
Box 774
Sunnyvale, CA 94088

Survival Vaults
P.O. Box 462
Fillmore, CA 93015

Speed Loaders

William T. Griffis
Second Six
P.O. Box 215
South Laguna, CA 92677

Practice and Training Devices

Orvis distributes the Spot-Shot for shotgun practice. Their catalog of general outdoor gear, including some of the finest fly rods in the world, is well worth having. Speer makes excellent plastic bullets and cases.

Speer Products, Inc.
Box 896
Lewiston, Idaho 83501

The Orvis Company, Inc.
Manchester, Vermont 05254

Blackpowder, Primitive and Martial Arts Weapons

Corrado Cutlery, Inc.
26 N. Clark St.
Chicago, Illinois 60602
Throwing knives.

Dixie Gun Works, Inc.
Gun Powder Lane
Union City, Tennessee 38261
Black powder guns and accessories. Catalog $2.00.

Ra-Mana Industries
P.O. Box 1109
Evanston, Illinois 60204
Yawara sticks, batons and various other martial arts devices and instruction books.

Randall Knives
Box 1988
Orlando, Florida 32802
  Custom throwing and cutting knives. Catalog $.50.

La Cruz du Sur
Galerias Pacifico
Florida 753 Local F. 17-T.E. 32-0091
Buenos Aires, Argentina
  Bolas

The Crossbowman
P.O. Box 2159
Petaluma, CA 94952
  Crossbows and blowguns.

Firearms and Survival Booksellers

I have dealt with each of the firms listed here and they all gave excellent service. It is worthwhile to write for all of their catalogs because each has a slightly different list and emphasis. Riling and French are excellent sources for out-of-print items in the field.

Adobe Hacienda
Route 3
Box 517
Glendale, Arizona 85301

Howard and Janet French
Fine Sporting Books
284 Redwood Drive
Pasadena, California

Loompanics Unlimited
Box 264
Mason, Michigan 48854

Hillcrest Publications
P.O. Box 395
McDonald, Ohio 44437

Normount Technical Publications
P.O. Drawer N-2
Wickenburg, Arizona 85358

Paladin Press
P.O. Box 1307
Boulder, Colorado 80302

Ray Riling Arms Books Company
6844 Gorsten St.
Philadelphia, PA 19119

Survival, Inc.
16809 Central Ave.
Carson, CA 90746

Gunsmiths

King's .45 auto combat modifications and custom rifles are second to none and the firm is reasonably fast as gunsmiths go — six to eight weeks for a full-house job on the .45 as compared with two years from some firms. Their repairs and general gunsmithing are also a cut above the ordinary. They even do color case hardening and apply rustproof finishes such as hard chrome and teflon. I have good reports from people who have dealt with them by mail.

MMC, who manufactures excellent adjustable sights for autopistols, also does some of the finest work I have ever seen on revolver actions. They specialize in such work as well as in converting certain heavy framed .357 revolvers to more useful calibers such as .44 Special and .45 Colt.

Pachmayr is an excellent source of rifle and shotgun stock blanks. They build fine custom rifles and do first class repair work on both rifles and shotguns.

Brownell, Ackley and Biesen, along with King's, produce the very finest in custom rifles and stocks.

Swenson specializes in accuracy work on the .45 and similar autos. A *long* waiting period is involved.

P.O. Ackley
2235 Arbor Lane
Salt Lake City, Utah 84117

Al Biesen
West 2039 Sinto Ave.
Spokane, Washington 99201

Lenard M. Brownell
Box 25
Wyarno, Wyoming 82845

Arnold "Al" Capone
King's Gun Works
1837 Glenoaks Blvd.
Glendale, CA 91201

Pachmayr Gun Works, Inc.
1220 S. Grand Ave.
Los Angeles, CA 90015

Bob Sconce
Miniature Machine Co.
212 E. Spruce
Deming, New Mexico 88030

A.D. Swenson's .45 Shop
P.O. Box 606
Fallbrook, CA 92028

Gunsmithing Tools and Supplies

All of these firms put out good catalogs which you should have but Brownell's, at $2, is a must.

Brownells, Inc.
Route 2, Box 1
Montezuma, Iowa 50171

Brookstone Company
121 Vose Farm Road
Peterborough, New Hampshire 23458

These people make one of the best knife sharpening devices in the world, as well as a very useful small stone for touching up triggers and deburring parts.

Louis N. Graves Company
Box 308
Anoka, Minnesota 55303

Frank Mittermeier, Inc.
3577 E. Tremont Ave.
P.O. Box 2
Bronx, N.Y. 10465

Williams Guide Line Products
Williams Gun Sight Company
7389 Lapeer Road
Davison, Michigan 48423

Shooting Instruction

Reliable instruction in the latest techniques of combat shooting is *very* hard to come by. Jeff Cooper offers courses from time to time at his ranch in Arizona and it would be well worth the trip to learn from such a master pistolero. If he can't take you, drop me a line and I will try to put you in touch with someone. Letters to either Jeff or me will require some time for a reply and *please* enclose a self-addressed stamped envelope.

Jeff Cooper
GUNSITE
Box 401
Paulden, Arizona 86334

Mel Tappan
Box 598
Rogue River, OR 97537

Miscellaneous Serendipity Catalogs

Nasco carries the Cap-chur guns discussed in Chapter 6 and a great deal more. No one interested in self-sufficient living should be without this catalog. Gander Mountain has very good prices and is an especially good source for reloading equipment. The Vermont Country Store is unique and although it doesn't carry gun related items, anyone interested in this book will find their catalog invaluable. These are excellent people to deal with by mail. Catalog $.25.

Eddie Bauer
1737 Airport Way South
Seattle, Washington 98134

L.L. Bean, Inc.
Freeport, Maine 04032

Gander Mountain, Inc.
P.O. Box 248
Wilmot, Wisconsin 53192

Nasco Farm and Ranch Catalog
Catalog #132
1524 Princeton Ave.
Modesto, CA 95352
    or
901 Janesville Ave.
Fort Atkinson, Wisconsin 53538

Vermont Country Store, Inc.
Weston, Vermont 05161